...ct in most of the known langua-

...owever it is the thirteenth, & in the

...ally the first letter, because it

...ound naturally formed by the

...ed naturally uttered by with

...t constraint, & without any effort

...figuration of the lips. Hence this

...is uttered by infants. which words

...iefs infants are first concerned;

... Hebrew ☐✗ am, is mother,)

...e abba is father; in Arabic aba;

...alese, bappa; in Welsh. tad, whence

...atta; in Irish, aithair; in Cantabrian

..., abba; in Amharic, aba; in Phil-

...ba; & the papa, which is found in

...uma, the breast, which is, in popular

...uma, is a nurse. This list might

...rove it to be the first natural vocal

...nalets. The Hebrew name of this

...e long or slender, as in place, fair

The Forgotten
Founding Father

A is the first letter of the Al-
ges of the earth; in the Ethi-
~~alphabets~~
Munic the _tenth_. It [is] ye
ts
represents the first ~~vocal~~ vocal
uman organs; being the
mo
~~mere~~ opening of the ~~m~~
alter the natural position
..ter is found in many we
the names of the objects w
the breath, & the parents.
ab, is father. In Chaldee
Ethiopie, _abi_; in Malayen
retain _dady_; in Old Greeks &
ita; in Lapponie, _atne_; in Al
..e & Melindane, African dia
any nations. Hence the Latin
c, the name of _mother_; in has
neatly extended; but there exce
und, I entitled to the first place
..ix, _aleph_, signifies, a _leader_.

The Forgotten Founding Father

Noah Webster's Obsession and the
Creation of an American Culture

JOSHUA KENDALL

G. P. PUTNAM'S SONS
New York

PUTNAM

G. P. PUTNAM'S SONS
Publishers Since 1838
Published by the Penguin Group
Penguin Group (USA) Inc., 375 Hudson Street, New York, New York
10014, USA • Penguin Group (Canada), 90 Eglinton Avenue East, Suite
700, Toronto, Ontario M4P 2Y3, Canada (a division of Pearson Penguin
Canada Inc.) • Penguin Books Ltd, 80 Strand, London WC2R 0RL,
England • Penguin Ireland, 25 St Stephen's Green, Dublin 2, Ireland
(a division of Penguin Books Ltd) • Penguin Group (Australia),
250 Camberwell Road, Camberwell, Victoria 3124, Australia
(a division of Pearson Australia Group Pty Ltd) • Penguin Books
India Pvt Ltd, 11 Community Centre, Panchsheel Park,
New Delhi–110 017, India • Penguin Group (NZ), 67 Apollo Drive,
Rosedale, North Shore 0632, New Zealand (a division of Pearson
New Zealand Ltd) • Penguin Books (South Africa) (Pty) Ltd,
24 Sturdee Avenue, Rosebank, Johannesburg 2196, South Africa

Penguin Books Ltd, Registered Offices:
80 Strand, London WC2R 0RL, England

Frontispiece and endpapers: First page of Dictionary, in Webster's hand.
Courtesy The Whitney Library of the New Haven Museum.

Page 346 constitutes an extension of this copyright page.

Library of Congress Cataloging-in-Publication Data
Kendall, Joshua C., date.
The forgotten founding father : Noah Webster's obsession and the creation of an
American culture / Joshua Kendall.
p.   cm.
Includes index.
ISBN 978-0-399-15699-1
1. Webster, Noah, 1758–1843.   2. Lexicographers—United States—Biography.
3. English language—United States—Lexicography.   4. Social reformers—
United States—Biography.   Title.
PE64.W5K46   2010   2010015254
423.092—dc22
[B]

Printed in the United States of America
1   3   5   7   9   10   8   6   4   2

BOOK DESIGN BY AMANDA DEWEY

For word lovers everywhere

"Words have a longer life than deeds."
—Pindar

"If any material good is ever to proceed from my attempts to correct certain disorders and errors in our language, it must be from the influence of my writing on the rising generations."

—*Noah Webster, December 14, 1837,*
letter to his son-in-law William Fowler

Contents

Prologue

George Washington's Cultural Attaché: The Definer of American Identity

AMERICAN, n. A native of America; originally applied to the aboriginals, or copper-colored races, found here by the Europeans; but now applied to the descendants of Europeans born in America. The name *American* must always exalt the pride of patriotism. *Washington.*

The morning of Friday, May 20, 1785, was bright and sunny, though there was a slight chill in the air. In the early afternoon, just as the mercury hit 68 degrees, the brisk southerly wind began to calm down. But not so Noah Webster, Jr. He kept beating his horse with a cane as he traipsed across the rocky roads just south of Alexandria. A young man in a hurry, the gangly six-footer with the flaming red hair, square jaw and gray eyes was dashing off to keep an important appointment. The world-famous General, the man considered by most of America's three million denizens to be "the greatest on earth," had invited *him*—the son of a poor Hartford farmer—to the elegant four-thousand-acre estate known as Mount Vernon. Webster's latest work, *Sketches of American Policy,* offered a series of proposals for the country's malaise, and George Washington, who, upon retirement from the military at the end of the American Revolution, had become America's "first farmer," was eagerly awaiting his arrival.

The twenty-six-year-old writer with the remarkably erect bearing, who had burst onto the national stage two years earlier with the publication of his instant best seller, a spelling text for schoolchildren, had crossed Washington's path once before. In June 1775, as a freshman member of the Yale militia, he had escorted the General out of New Haven as he was about to take up command of the Continental army in Cambridge. But this was to be the first time they would meet man to man. And it was a dinner Webster would never forget. Nearly sixty years later, Webster would record the details in a letter written in "a sturdy, awkward hand very fit for a lexicographer" (according to novelist Nathaniel Hawthorne, who later acquired the document for his personal collection of Colonial memorabilia).

After passing the white picket fence some three hundred yards to the back of Washington's house, Webster dismounted. Washington's secretary, Mr. Shaw, then ushered the visitor into the elegant central passage where Washington greeted Webster. Dressed in a white waistcoat and white silk stockings, the six-foot-two General had to look down ever so slightly to meet Webster's gaze. Washington motioned toward the wood-paneled west parlor, where the two men soon sat down on mahogany chairs near the card table. Designed a generation earlier, the cozy room that Washington called "the best place in my house" still evinced a distinctly British sensibility. The carved overmantel was patterned after a plate in Abraham Swan's *British Architect* and the Palladian detailing on the door frames was lifted from another popular British manual, *Ancient Masonry* by Batty Langley.

Washington was a stickler for routine—he liked to eat dinner promptly at three and go to bed at nine—and before long, it was time to eat. The table was set for four. Dining that afternoon were also the General's wife, Martha, and another houseguest, Richard Boulton, a building contractor from Charles County, Maryland, recently hired to make additions to the mansion.

Sipping a glass of Madeira, Webster got a chance to explain the crucial fourth and final sketch of his pamphlet. The Articles of Confederation, passed in haste by the Second Continental Congress in the summer of 1777, had, according to Webster, failed to unite the thirteen colonies sufficiently. In this political tract, as in his speller, the first schoolbook to substitute the names of America's cities and towns for their British counterparts, Webster urged Americans to celebrate their new national identity. Summarizing his main concern, he told Washington that since each state retained the power to defeat the will of the other twelve states, "our union is but a name and our confederation a cobweb." Webster argued that it was time for the citizens of the new nation to redefine themselves: "We ought not to consider ourselves as inhabitants of a particular state only, but as *Americans,* as the common subjects of a great empire. We cannot and ought not wholly to divest ourselves of provincial views and attachments, but we should subordinate them to the general interests of the continent." A stronger federal government, Webster emphasized, could improve the advantages of the American states, as *provincial interest* would become inseparable from *national interest*. Washington nodded his assent, promising Webster that he would ask his friend the Virginia legislator James Madison to read the entire work as soon as possible.

Over dessert, the conversation turned to less pressing matters, enabling Washington and Webster to cement their emerging bond. As the pancakes were passed around, Webster refused molasses, complaining that as a New Englander, he tended to eat more than his fair share. The typically dour Washington startled his dinner companions by emitting an uncharacteristically loud laugh, stating, "I didn't know about your eating molasses in New England." Then looking over at Boulton, the guest from Charles County, the General proceeded to tell the following anecdote: "During the Revolution, a hogshead of molasses was stove in at the town of Westchester by the oversetting of a wagon, and a body of Maryland troops being near, the soldiers ran hastily and saved all they could by filling their hats and cups with molasses." After dinner, the Connecticut visitor and George and Martha Washington, whom Webster would later describe as "very social," settled down to a game of

whist. Summing up that overnight stay with the Washingtons, he gleefully recorded in his diary: "treated with great attention."

About six months later, Webster, who spent the summer of 1785
running a singing school in Baltimore, traveled back down to Mount
Vernon before heading on to Richmond to discuss his *Sketches* with
Madison. On the evening of November 5, he once again gave the General a civics lesson. At dinner, Washington happened to mention that he
was looking to hire a young man to tutor his two step-grandchildren—
Nelly and Wash Custis, then living at Mount Vernon. He told Webster
that he had asked a colleague in Scotland to offer recommendations. A
stunned Webster shot back, "What would European nations think of this
country if, after the exhibition of great talents and achievements in the
war for independence, we should send to Europe for men to teach the
first rudiments of learning?" Immediately grasping Webster's point, a
humbled Washington asked, "What shall I do?" But even before he had
finished his question, the General himself knew the answer. Out of respect for the emerging new nation, he would restrict his job search to
Americans. Washington initially considered Webster for the post, but
Webster soon took himself out of the running. On December 18, 1785,
Webster wrote that his desire to marry and start a family precluded his
moving to Mount Vernon. In that same letter, Webster also confided to
the man, who was quickly evolving into a surrogate father, his true aspirations: "I wish to enjoy life, but books and business will ever be my
principal pleasure. I must write; it is a happiness I cannot sacrifice."

Together, Noah Webster, Jr., the man of words, and George Washington, the man of action, would continue to work to unify America.
Recognizing Webster's remarkable knack for getting Americans to think
of themselves as Americans, Washington relied time and time again on
his trusted policy advisor. In May 1787, right after he was appointed the
head of the Constitutional Convention in Philadelphia, Washington
would knock at the door of Webster's hotel room. Though bedridden
with a headache, Webster—derived from the Anglo-Saxon word for "female weaver," the family name is a synonym for "uniter"—was honored

to offer strategic assistance. And in the fall of 1793, Washington, who during his first term as president had found the time to exchange missives with Webster about such mundane concerns as "the theory of vegetable manure," would once again turn to this savvy wordsmith to combat divisions among the American people. At Washington's behest, Webster would assume the helm of *American Minerva,* New York City's first daily newspaper. For the next several years, his incisive editorials would help quiet the furor of those Republicans eager to join the French in their rapidly expanding war against England. Washington's heroic stewardship of the young nation would, in turn, have a lasting impact on Webster, whose dictionary would be replete with references to America's first president. To illustrate the meaning of "surpass," Webster would note, "Perhaps no man has ever *surpassed* Washington in genuine patriotism and integrity of life."

Shortly after Washington's death in December 1799, Webster petitioned for access to the family papers so that he could become America's first presidential biographer. Only when he failed to land this plum assignment did the freelance writer begin work on what would eventually become his most illustrious monument to our national identity—his *American Dictionary of the English Language.* Beginning in the spring of 1800, Webster would throw caution to the wind and immerse himself in this massive undertaking, which would turn out to be nearly twice the heft of Samuel Johnson's 1755 *Dictionary of the English Language.* With his 1828 masterpiece, Webster, whom James Murray, the first editor of the *Oxford English Dictionary,* would later describe as a "born definer of words," would succeed in forever unifying the world's most ethnically diverse nation with a common language. Webster's insistence that his work, published at a time when America's population totaled about 13 million, would "furnish a standard of our vernacular tongue . . . to the three hundred millions of people, who are destined . . . to adorn the vast territory within our jurisdiction" has proved remarkably prescient.

But Webster's vast legacy extends far beyond lexicography. As the eminent American historian and former Yale president Howard Lamar recently put it at a 250th birthday celebration, "He was far more than the distinguished writer of the first dictionary of the American language. . . . [Webster was] a multiple American founding father." This polymath wrote extensive treatises on epidemiology, which helped usher in both America's first medical journal and the field of public health. The man whose nervous tic compelled him to conduct his own personal tally of all the houses in America's major cities in the 1780s also helped give rise to America's first census in 1790. A mover and shaker in the publishing world, Webster invented the modern book tour and drafted America's first copyright laws. A progressive pedagogue who championed both female education and public schools, he helped found Amherst College. A political activist who served numerous terms in the state legislatures of both Connecticut and Massachusetts, Webster was an early champion of workman's compensation and unemployment insurance. In short, Webster shaped American culture (or "civilization," to use the term of his era) as a whole. When Americans were groping for a way to carve out their own identity vis-à-vis Great Britain, Webster proved an able guide. "America must be as independent in *literature*," he observed at the beginning of his literary career, "as she is in *politics*—as famous for *arts* as for *arms*."

Webster's reputation was at its height in the decades immediately following his death in 1843. In 1878, renowned historian Charles Lester maintained that Webster stood side by side with Columbus and Washington himself in America's "Trinity of Fame." However, as his speller, which would sell a staggering hundred million copies by the end of the nineteenth century, fell out of favor, this pure-bred New Englander, whom his distant cousin, the eloquent Massachusetts senator Daniel Webster, once called the *vera effigies* [true likeness] of the Webster clan, suddenly lost his prominent place in the history books. When remembered at all, Noah Webster was often ridiculed. In the early twentieth century, he made a cameo in Ambrose Bierce's *The Devil's Dictionary*; the satirist stuck the phlegmatic lexicographer under the definition for "hell," which was presumed to be his eternal resting place. H. L. Mencken was one notable exception. "[Webster's] *American Dictionary*," the sage of Baltimore raved in his 1919 classic, *The American Language*, "was not only thoroughly American: it was superior to any of the current dictionaries of the English, so much so that for a good many years it remained 'a sort of mine for British lexicography to exploit.'" Still, by 1942, when *Saturday Review* dubbed this Connecticut Yankee "the United States' least-known, best-known man," most Americans were convinced that his cousin Daniel had written the dictionary.

America's amnesia about Noah Webster can be traced back to doubts about his character rather than his achievement. His arrogance was hard to miss. After hearing him lecture, one contemporary remarked, "The capital defect is the sheer unbounded vanity of the man . . . which is so great as to excite ridicule." His political opponents went further, with one rival newspaper editor calling him "an incurable lunatic" and another "a spiteful viper." We might prefer not to have among our Founding Fathers such a self-aggrandizing man who was prone to lash out—not only at ideological adversaries, but also at friends and family. In a profile written a generation ago, award-winning biographer Joseph Ellis described Webster as "an irascible and stubborn fellow," who is "not the stuff of American mythology." Likewise, in a recent discussion of Webster's obnoxious personality, *New Yorker* contributor Jill Lepore launched into an extended aside about a murderous dictator before catching herself: "Noah Webster is, of course, no Joseph Stalin. He was an unlikable man, not a dangerous one." Only a handful of full-length biographies exist, and most whitewash Webster's glaring faults, painting him as a selfless patriot. But by skipping over his essence, such hagiography turns him into a lifeless statue.

A full appreciation of what Aristotle might have labeled Webster's "tragic flaw" actually makes him a more sympathetic figure. A close examination of the diaries and letters, including those long suppressed by the family, reveals that his willfulness was not something over which he ever exercised any control. Like his predecessor, Samuel Johnson, who, it is now widely believed, suffered from Tourette's syndrome, the lexicographer battled an intractable form of mental illness. Webster's was what contemporary psychiatrists call obsessive-compulsive personality disorder. Saddled with nearly crippling interpersonal anxiety from child-hood, he had difficulty connecting with other people. "I suspect," he wrote to Rebecca Greenleaf, then his fiancée, in 1788, "I am not formed for society; and I wait only to be convinced that people wish to get rid of my company, and I would instantly leave them for better companions: the reflections of my own mind." While Webster and Greenleaf would stay married for more than half a century and raise seven children, words would always be his best friends. For this order lover, who came close to a complete breakdown on several occasions, defining became his ruling obsession. The thirty-year quest to complete the dictionary was inextri-cably linked to the fight to maintain his own sanity. If the personal stakes hadn't been so high, he would surely have given up. Thus, in contrast to Achilles, whose hubris resulted in his downfall, Webster's pathology was instrumental to his success.

Remarkably, the man who did so much to help America establish its cultural identity lacked a stable sense of self. As an old man, Webster heartily agreed with the sentiment that the eighty-year-old Benjamin Franklin, upon whom he modeled his career, once expressed to him: "I have been all my life changing my opinions." The tempestuous polemi-cist was often at war with himself. Webster's body housed a host of contradictory identities: revolutionary, reactionary, fighter, peacemaker, intellectual, commonsense philosopher, ladies' man, prig, slick networker, and loner. In the attempt to give voice to all these distinct selves, this fragmented man felt compelled to write and to keep on writing. In the end, he would publish more words than any other member of the found-ing generation. While Webster was never quite able to render himself whole, nearly two centuries after his death his words still unite the nation that he loved.

PART ONE

From Farmboy to Best-Selling Author

SUCCESS, n. The favorable or prosperous termination of any thing attempted; a termination which answers the purpose intended; properly in a good sense, but often in a bad sense. . . . Be not discouraged in a laudable undertaking at the ill *success* of the first attempt. *Anon.*

1

Hartford Childhood and Yale Manhood

EDUCATION, n. The bringing up, as of a child; instruction; formation of manners. Education comprehends all that series of instruction and discipline which is intended to enlighten the understanding, correct the temper and form the manners and habits of youth, and fit them for usefulness in their future stations. To give children a good *education* in manners, arts and science, is important; to give them a religious *education* is indispensable.

T he farming community with the fertile soil three miles west of Hartford that Noah Webster would always be proud to call his birthplace owes its strong identity to the fervent Congregationalism of its early inhabitants.

Religious expression was the raison d'être for the incorporation of the West Division of Hartford in the early eighteenth century. Without a church of its own, the settlement's hundred and fifty souls, who had begun migrating over from Hartford in the 1680s, were feeling uneasy. On October 12, 1710, its twenty-eight families sent a petition to the General Assembly in New Haven, requesting a minister. Frustrated that a "good part of God's time [was] spent traveling backward and forwards" to the three churches in Hartford, the petitioners were concerned lest their "children [might not] be present at the public worship of God."

Though Hartford protested—a new independent community would mean the loss of tax revenue—in 1711, the General Assembly of the Colony of Connecticut set up the new parish. And two years later, the Fourth Church of Christ in Hartford was up and running. Located in the epicenter of the West Division, the barnlike meetinghouse with the steep roof, situated on the west side of the town's major north-south artery, would, as one of its longtime ministers later observed, ensure that its residents remain a "united people."

On a ninety-acre farm bordering that same north-south thoroughfare—later named Main Street—the future lexicographer would spend his entire childhood. The farm, which Noah's father, Noah Webster, Sr., acquired soon after his marriage to Mercy Steele in 1749, featured sloping fields of corn, wheat, oats and tobacco. A long fence hemmed in the animals—cows, sheep and chickens—as well as the family horse, which the Websters would use to ride into town. Next to the white clapboard house stood the weaving shed where Noah Sr. could often be found when he wasn't tending the crops.

Noah Webster, Jr., was born on October 16, 1758, in the "best room" of the four-room farmhouse. This sparsely furnished parlor, which doubled as the master bedroom, contained little more than a few straight-backed chairs, a four-poster bed and a writing desk, upon which sat a black Bible. On the other side of the stone chimney, which sliced the pine-walled house in two, was the kitchen with its huge brick oven. The fourth of five children, Noah would share the more rustic of the two upstairs bedrooms with his brothers, Abraham and Charles, born in 1751 and 1762, respectively. His older sisters, Mercy, born in 1749, and Jerusha, born in 1756, were stationed across the hall. The children all slept on straw mattresses, which they would have to tighten from time to time with a large bed key.

Both of Noah's parents came from pure Yankee stock. The first Webster to come to the New World was John Webster, a native of Warwickshire, England. In 1636, as one of the hundred members of Thomas Hooker's Puritan congregation, John Webster traveled from Boston to

Webster House, in West Hartford.

Webster's boyhood home drawn in 1849, a century after the newlyweds Noah
Webster, Sr., and Mercy Steele moved in. After Webster left for Yale, three
additional rooms were added. He made his last visit there in 1789.

Hartford where he helped found Connecticut. Twenty years later, he was
selected as the new colony's governor. John's eldest son, Robert, inher-
ited the vast majority of his father's property and settled in Middletown,
where his eldest son, John Webster II, was born. The youngest son of
this John Webster was Noah's grandfather, Daniel Webster, born in the
West Division in 1693. A captain in the Connecticut army, Daniel Webster fathered seven children, including Noah's father, his second son,
who was born in 1722. Daniel Webster died in 1765, and as a boy of
seven, Noah would attend the funeral, an event he would never forget.
Eager to preserve the history of the Websters, in 1836, at the age of
seventy-eight, Noah would print a family genealogy, one of the first ever
by an American.

Noah also had a direct tie to the founders of another New England
colony. His mother, Mercy Steele, was the great-great-granddaughter of
William Bradford, a native of a small village in Yorkshire, who sailed over
on the *Mayflower* in 1620 and became the second governor of Plymouth

Colony. Noah, who later also showed a keen interest in early Massachusetts history—in 1790, he would edit the journal of the Bay State's first
governor, John Winthrop—was particularly proud of Bradford, who or-
chestrated the first Thanksgiving in 1621 and late in life mastered Latin,
Greek and Hebrew. (As a writer, Noah would take after Bradford; the
governor's prose, one nineteenth-century historian has noted, was far
superior to his "inelegant" verses.) Bradford's granddaughter Meletiah
married Samuel Steele of Hartford, and their seventh son, Eliphalet,
born in the West Division in 1700, went on to marry Catharine Marshfield. Noah's mother, Mercy, born in 1727, was the fourth of this couple's
eleven children. Upon Eliphalet Steele's death in 1773, Noah's grandmother Catharine would move into the farmhouse. Possessing a delicate
constitution, "Mother Steele," as she was known in Noah's family, would
lapse into psychosis in the last few years of her life.

Though he did not attend college—which for Connecticut residents
of the mid-eighteenth century was synonymous with Yale, then the colony's only institution of higher learning—Noah Webster, Sr., turned out
to be both intellectually curious and a highly respected member of the
community. A few years before Noah's birth, he had helped to establish the West Division's first Book Society, the precursor to its public
library. A longtime deacon at the nearby Fourth Church of Christ, Noah
Sr. would read from the King James Bible every evening, stressing to
his children the values of hard work, personal responsibility and piety.
During the Revolution, he became known as Captain Webster for his
service in the town's militia. After independence from Britain, Noah Sr.
would also serve for many years as a justice of the peace in Hartford—
then a civic official appointed by the state legislature and charged with
making such administrative decisions as whether to send criminals to
the stocks.

Mercy Webster, too, possessed a keen mind. She would spend long
hours instructing the children in spelling, mathematics and music. From
his mother, Noah would pick up a love of the flute, which, along with
books, would forever be a source of solace. In the diary that he began

keeping in his mid-twenties, he described his delight that "a little hollow tube of wood should dispel in a few moments, or at least alleviate, the heaviest cares of life!" The boy could never find, however, such comfort in other people, as both his mother and father were emotionally distant. But rather than lamenting this lack of nurturing, Noah would end up idealizing both parents as all-knowing authority figures. In turn, he, too, would become wedded to authoritarian principles. "All government," Webster would later write in an essay on pedagogy, "originates in families, and if neglected there, it will hardly exist in society. . . . The government both of families and schools should be absolute."

Noah Sr. and Mercy burdened their children with a strong sense of obligation. In a letter addressed simply "Dutiful Son," written to the twenty-four-year-old Noah, they expressed their expectation that he would "do good in the world and be useful and . . . so behave as to gain the esteem of all virtuous people that are acquainted with you and . . . especially that you may so live as to obtain the favor of Almighty God and his grace in this world." Self-esteem in the Webster family was de-rived not from feeling comfortable in one's own skin, but from adhering to the moral injunctions of others. Noah never developed a sense of his own intrinsic self-worth. Acutely self-critical, he didn't even like the sound of his own name. As an adult, he would sign his letters "N. Web-ster" (and forbid his children from naming any male heirs "Noah"). He would forever define himself solely by his achievements. Though the intense desire for fame and recognition would lead to excessive vanity, it would also fuel his literary immortality. Without his trademark gran-diosity, Noah Webster, Jr., would never have even thought of attempting such a mammoth project as the *American Dictionary*.

AT THE AGE OF SIX, Noah began attending the South Middle School, one of the five primary schools built by the West Division's Ecclesiastical Society that dotted Main Street at the end of the Colonial era. Con-necticut was then one of just two colonies—the other was neighboring

Massachusetts—with compulsory schooling, and the community put a premium on education. Under the code of laws established by Edward Hopkins, the seventeenth-century governor of Connecticut whose term preceded John Webster's, every town of fifty householders had to appoint a teacher. Even so, the colony's schools were in a dilapidated state. The students sat on rows of benches in the often frigid and rickety one-room schoolhouses. Blackboards were rare. Only the teacher had a desk and a chair. Much of the school day was spent in chopping up wood for the stove, around which the children—up to seventy in a classroom—huddled.

Worse still was the caliber of the teachers, whom Webster would later describe as the "dregs" of humanity. Men ("masters") ran the schools during the six-month winter term, and women ("dames") conducted classes during the three-month summer term. Regardless of gender, their manners tended to be rough; what's more, they could be vicious. Webster had learned how to read at home, and he found their instruction both pointless and terrifying. So, too, did Oliver Wolcott, Jr., a native of nearby Litchfield, who would later attend Yale with Webster. In a memoir, Wolcott recalled his first day of school at the age of six: "[My master] . . . a stout man, probably a foreigner . . . tried me in the Alphabet; and . . . I remained silent. . . . He actually struck me, supposing me to be obstinately mute; my sobs nearly broke my heart, and I was ordered to my seat." While Webster never recalled being whipped, he did later express his annoyance that five of the six hours in the school day had been "spent in idleness, in cutting tables and benches in pieces, in carrying on pin lotteries, or perhaps in some roguish tricks." Before the American Revolution, teachers had few books on hand besides a couple of religious texts and *A New Guide to the English Tongue,* a simplified spelling book by the British author Thomas Dilworth. Subjects such as geography, history and literature remained outside the curriculum. Deep frustration with his own early education, which consisted mostly of "the nurture and admonition of the Lord," would later motivate "America's pedagogue" to improve the classroom experience for future generations.

Just as Noah was beginning grade school, Hartford, like the rest of New England, was entering a period of economic retrenchment. At the conclusion of the Seven Years' War in 1763, the British had wrested control of Canada from the French. However, the burgeoning empire then faced the huge expense of maintaining a permanent military presence on the other side of the Atlantic. Attempting to force the colonies to foot the bill, King George III passed a series of tax laws such as the notorious Stamp Act of 1765. With levies imposed on various goods from coffee to wine, prices rose and the profits for most businesses, including farms, plummeted. These stark economic conditions darkened New England's mood. "This was a society," one historian has observed, "in which nobody played." For Noah Webster and his ilk, life meant sweat and toil. Fun and frolic were rarely on the agenda.

Noah would frequently hear his father, who had nearly lost his life in 1757 while fighting against the French, rail against British perfidy. The Websters' hometown paper, *The Connecticut Courant*, the oldest American paper still in business, was established in 1764 to give voice to these grievances. In the spring of 1766, the various Connecticut chapters of the Sons of Liberty—the protest organization that was then cropping up in all thirteen colonies—met in Hartford. As the *Courant* reported, "[they] . . . declare their respectful Approbation of . . . the . . . spirited Declarations and Resolves of the honorable House of Representatives of this Colony relative to the unconstitutional nature and destructive tendency of the late American Stamp-Act." Though Parliament soon repealed this dreaded piece of legislation, the local economy didn't improve. To fight for a better future, Noah Webster, Sr., would intensify his affiliations with neighbors oppressed by the same tyranny—British rule.

Noah would attend school just a few months a year, as work on the family farm—particularly during autumn harvests—took precedence. But even as a boy spending long hours in the fields, he showed a love of language. Ignoring his farm chores, he would often sit under the trees with his books, thinking about words and their origins. He was curious about exactly what they meant and how they related to one another. However, Noah's literary pursuits did not please his father, who would occasionally scold him, insisting that he get back to work.

In the summer of 1771, when Noah was twelve, he organized a singing group. After meeting with some success in a few performances, Noah and his friends began to sit together in church on Sunday to practice their craft. But much to his surprise and dismay, those in nearby pews didn't appreciate their efforts. Feeling humiliated, Noah knew not what to do nor where to turn. While another child might have sought out a parent, not so Noah, as he didn't have a close relationship with either his mother or father. However, the boy soon stumbled upon the next best thing: he would put his plight into words. This incident was the impetus for Noah's first publication, an anonymous letter to the editor that ran in *The Connecticut Courant* on August 21, 1771.

This turn to words was to be a lifelong pattern. Time and time again, emotional distress would compel Noah Webster to pick up his pen. His own words, he found, could both mitigate his anxiety and help him keep his mental equilibrium. To battle what the adult Webster called his "nervous affections," the socially awkward loner would take on a series of monumental intellectual labors. Through his flood of public communications, including his dictionary, America's most prolific freelance writer would express parts of himself that might not otherwise surface—his fears and his frustrations as well as his hopes and his dreams.

With no family letters or diaries surviving from his childhood, this compact missive of roughly four hundred words provides a unique window into Noah's developing mind. Many hallmark features of his adult personality are already in evidence—the arrogance, the obsequiousness and the hypersensitivity to perceived slights. Addressed to "Mr. Printer," the letter starts off like a legal brief: "After I have stated my case to you truly, I may then hope thro' your means for a redress of my grievance; the which if I obtain, will oblige several of your young friends as well as myself." Throughout his sixty-year literary career, Webster would look to his reader as a vital ally, who could both provide the empathy that he had never received at home and help him right what was wrong with the world. To convince the printer of his worthiness as an object of concern, Noah spends the first third of the letter boasting of his accomplishments. The boy touts his "natural good genius" and his "considerable degree of knowledge in the art of music." He then goes on to list the "advantages . . . flowing from this pleasant art," which include a "dutiful obedience to our parents" and "good manners." Finally, in his coda, he highlights the various injustices that have been heaped upon him and his fellow musicians. "But alas! There are but few comparatively," he concludes, "that openly encourage us. Some only deride us, and others are so silent or passive, as that we are greatly at a loss whether we please or displease the greater part, since the opposition we meet with from the envious and ill-natured cannot have passed unobserved, and yet no means have been used to prevent the growing mischief." Webster's complaint of both cold indifference and malevolence in his fellow churchgoers seems a bit far-fetched. Apparently, the boy was avidly seeking praise for his musical efforts and was crestfallen when it was nowhere to be found. Throughout his life, Webster's mercurial temperament would frequently leave him feeling like an aggrieved outsider. This persistent sense of outrage, which often had its roots merely in the battle going on inside his own head, would spark an equally persistent desire to be heard.

A LITTLE MORE THAN A YEAR LATER, on Wednesday, October 14, 1772, Noah, then just two days shy of fourteen, headed down Main Street with his family to attend a special service at the Fourth Church of Christ. It was a day of fasting and humiliation, then a common occurrence in Puritan New England, particularly on momentous occasions when God's aid was sought. The twenty-four-year-old Nathan Perkins was to be ordained as the new pastor, just the third in the church's sixty-year history. The West Division had gone without a full-time minister since the untimely death of the much beloved Nathaniel Hooker, Jr., two and a half years earlier. (The great-great-grandson of Connecticut's founder and the man who had baptized Noah, Hooker was just thirty-two when he died.) After auditioning sixteen local candidates and engaging in a fierce debate that caused deep divisions among the typically united towns- folk, the Ecclesiastical Society had finally issued an invitation to Perkins, an outsider, who had recently graduated from the College of New Jersey (today Princeton University). While the First Church of Hartford had offered nearly twice as much as the seventy pounds in base pay, Perkins, who came from a family of wealthy landowners, was convinced that the "good farms of West Hartford would be a better security . . . than the trade of Hartford town."

The short and stocky Perkins had already made a highly favorable impression with his thoughtful sermons, delivered entirely from memory, which he had been preaching as pastor-elect since the first Sabbath of the year. Perkins' theological views were strongly influenced by Jona- than Edwards, the Connecticut cleric who had ushered in the Great Awakening, a period of religious revival that lasted from 1730 to 1760. Edwards had combined a harsh Calvinism, which emphasized the de- pravity of human beings, with a belief in the need for deep religious feeling. Called New Lights, Edwards' followers, such as Perkins, advo- cated an intense engagement with spiritual concerns through personal Bible study.

On that bright October afternoon, the Fourth Church, which had been rebuilt in 1744 to accommodate the West Division's growing pop- ulation, was packed. The service drew not only local congregants but also visitors from towns throughout Hartford County—then the colony's largest, housing about a quarter of its two hundred thousand inhabitants— and from other neighboring towns as well. According to church custom, on this day the preaching was to be done not by the minister-elect, but by the church elders, the presbytery. The most influential clergymen from across Connecticut coordinated the service. Nearly all had close ties to Yale. Farmington's Reverend Timothy Pitkin, whose late father- in-law, Thomas Clap, had been Yale's first president, said the prayer before the sermon, which was given by the Reverend Andrew Lee, a recent Yale graduate from Perkins' hometown of Norwich. Lee read from the first book of Corinthians, "For the word of the cross is to them that perish foolishness; but unto us who are saved it is the power of God." The distinguished Reverend Elnathan Whitman, pastor of the Second Church of Hartford—the eldest of the elders, he was losing his hearing and spoke in a booming voice—delivered the charge, in which he highlighted the accountability of pastors both to God and to their parishioners. The Reverend Joseph Perry of Windsor concluded the service by giving the right hand of fellowship, officially welcoming Reverend Perkins into the fold. Summing up the day's events, *The Connecticut Courant* would report the following week, "The whole was conducted with decency and propriety." But few were more impressed by both the orderliness of the proceedings and the eloquence of the speakers than the impressionable adolescent Noah Webster.

As the crowd exited the church, its excitement was palpable. The new minister was partly responsible for this buoyant mood, but so, too, was the prospect of feasting, which was to follow the day of fasting. As the Websters dispersed to one of the celebratory meals prepared by the dozen householders whom the West Division's Ecclesiastical Society had appointed to keep "publick houses," Noah's mind wasn't focused on the sumptuous food he was to eat. The adolescent remained awestruck by the spectacle that he had just witnessed. This gathering of so many learned men in one place had inspired him. Though he wasn't sure he wanted to go into the ministry, these were the men whose ranks he wished to join. He suddenly began to envision a different sort of future for himself. Noah no longer saw himself spending the rest of his life engaged in manual labor on a farm, like his father or older brother, Abraham. Noah now wanted to follow in the footsteps of his mother's younger brother, Eliphalet, whom the late Nathaniel Hooker had fitted for Yale. Noah's uncle, who would be saddled with a nervous condition throughout his life, later became known for his bluntness and eccentricity—he would marry a woman he had never met. At the time, Eliphalet Steele was serving as a pastor in Egremont, Massachusetts (where, as Webster grew into adulthood, he would periodically visit him).

Shortly after Perkins' ordination, Noah approached his father, expressing a desire to study with the new pastor so that he could also attend Yale. Initially, Noah Webster, Sr., opposed his son's request for "more learning." Though Noah's father, too, revered education, he had one major reservation: the cost. College was not cheap. Tuition, room and board for a year at Yale in the 1770s—about twenty-five pounds—was more than half the annual salary of a skilled worker. But Noah Sr. soon gave in. With land suddenly at a premium in Connecticut, he realized that not all of his sons could go into farming. Additionally, Noah Sr. figured that in an emergency, he could mortgage the family farm (a measure that he would eventually take to pay for his son's education).

That autumn, Noah began meeting regularly with Nathan Perkins at either his house or the pastor's capacious quarters, also located on Main Street, which had originally been built for Reverend Hooker back in 1758. (Like Noah Webster's birthplace, this residence still stands; it is now the parish house of St. James's Episcopal Church.) To prepare Webster for Yale, Perkins would steep the adolescent in Latin and Greek, as Yale's rules then specified that "no person may expect to be admitted into this College, unless . . . he shall be found able . . . to read accurately . . . Tully [Cicero], Virgil and the Greek Testament and shall be able to write true Latin in prose." For this task, Perkins was eminently qualified. At the College of New Jersey, on account of his remarkable facility in translating those two canonical Latin authors, he had been selected as the class salutatorian, the top-ranking senior charged with giving a Latin oration at graduation.

While a breakdown would prevent Perkins from delivering that speech—in the spring of his senior year, he was so frail that he had to rely on his classmates for assistance whenever he left his residence—his undergraduate career had been distinguished. In 1770, after an experience of religious ecstasy revived him, Perkins established the Cliosophic

Society, a forerunner to today's Whig-Cliosophic Society, America's oldest college literary and debating club.

Though no longer unstable by the time he reached Hartford, Perkins possessed some odd quirks. Right after his ordination, he began keeping "a bill of mortality"—detailed records about the cause of death of every parishioner. He also held a rigid, doctrinal mind-set, which would lead him into tirades about "loose morals." Moreover, as one contemporary observed, Perkins "had little of the imaginative and rarely indulged in sallies of wit." And on those few occasions when he attempted humor, Perkins could be sarcastic. At the time of his ordination, the West Division pastor still received some of his salary in wood. When one parishioner asked Perkins to comment on his contribution, which consisted mostly of crooked scraps from the tops of trees, the pastor, annoyed by his stinginess, shot back, "That is a remarkable fine pair of steers you have on the lead, Colonel."

But Noah wasn't bothered by Perkins' lack of charm. The adolescent was thrilled to have found a father figure who could provide a steady supply of intellectual nourishment. Catholic in his interests, Perkins could discourse on almost any topic. Tutor and student would form a bond that would last a lifetime. As an adult, Webster would continue to rely on Perkins for advice. Commenting on his mentor's death in a letter to *The Hartford Observer* in 1838, Webster praised his special gifts as a classical scholar, adding, "To his instruction and example . . . I am . . . indebted for my taste for the study of languages." Webster became the first of more than a hundred students Perkins would prepare for Yale during the sixty-six years that he served as the West Division pastor—still one of the longest tenures of any minister in American history.

IN SEPTEMBER 1774, the not quite sixteen-year-old Webster, accompanied by his father, was excited to be making the forty-mile trek from Hartford to Yale, which would soon have a huge impact on his emerging identity. New Haven was then a budding commercial center with some 8,022 white residents plus another 273 blacks and Indians, according to a survey by the state legislature, which that fall both incorporated the town and named its streets. First laid out in 1638, New Haven consisted of a grid of nine squares; at the center was the sixteen-acre public square called the Green. Just above the Green—on the other side of College Street—was the square that contained the Yale campus. New Haven made quite an impression upon most visitors. Passing through a month earlier en route to the First Continental Congress in Philadelphia, John Adams called it "very pleasant." A lover of symmetry, Webster would go even further in his praise, later describing New Haven as "beautiful" because, along with Philadelphia, it was one of "the regularly built towns in America." This would be the first of many trips that father and son would take between what were then Connecticut's co-capitals. When traveling together, one would ride on the family horse, the other would walk. With the hardy Noah Webster, Sr., often feeling that he was more fit to go on foot, the incoming freshman may well have been the one who parked the horse at the Yale president's mansion, located on the edge of campus across from the surrounding farms.

Callow farmboy goes off to college to get educated: Noah Webster's coming-of-age journey was then the stuff of popular literature. Like Webster, "Tom Brainless," the adolescent protagonist of the satiric poem "The Progress of Dulness," written in 1772 by John Trumbull (at the time a Yale tutor), also exchanges grueling farmwork for books:

> The point's agreed; the boy well pleased,
> From country care and labor eased;
> No more to rise by break of day
> To drive home cows or deal out hay;
> To work no more in snow or hail
> And blow his fingers o'er the flail
> Or mid the toils of harvest sweat
> Beneath the summer's sultry heat

Serene, he bids the farm, good-bye,
And quits the farm without a sigh.

In his spoof of Yale, Trumbull, who would also serve as Yale's treasurer during Webster's undergraduate career, made fun of the college's
bland curriculum, which had traditionally pivoted around biblical studies.
Founded in 1701 for the "upholding and propagating of the Christian
Protestant religion," Yale—called the Collegiate School until 1718—was
originally designed to train its students for positions in local Congregational churches. Partly as a result of Trumbull's spate of satirical poems
and essays in the early 1770s, the college was more lively by the beginning of Webster's freshman year. Believing that Yale students were
"condemn'd each day to study, read, recite and pray," Trumbull had insisted on reducing the emphasis on Latin and Greek and adding English
literature and composition to the mix. Trumbull's reform efforts quickly
made their mark. Of the forty students in Webster's class of 1778, only
four would go into the ministry, as law suddenly emerged as the profession of choice. When editing a literary magazine a decade later, Webster
would pay homage to Trumbull by reprinting several of his poems, including this mock-epic that recounted the "rare adventures" of the Yale country bumpkin.

Though New Haven was up and coming—in 1763, a new state house
had been added to the Green, which already featured two churches—
Yale was in the sorriest state of any of the nine colleges then sprinkled
across the thirteen colonies. The students referred to its treeless campus
as a "Brick Prison" because it featured just three run-down buildings.
The Old College, constructed back in 1717 when Yale first moved to
New Haven from Old Saybrook, once aspired to grandeur, but this sky-
blue, three-story structure, crowned by a cupola, was teetering. (In 1782,
it would be demolished; Bingham Hall now occupies this site). The main
dormitory was the nearby New College—later renamed Connecticut
Hall, this Yale landmark, dating back to 1750, still stands—but it offered
few amenities. During the winter, Webster and his fellow Yale men would

The poet John Trumbull (1750–1831) was six years older
than his cousin of the same name, the celebrated painter,
who completed this portrait in 1793. In 1773, the precocious
Yale tutor—he had graduated from the college at
seventeen—moved to Boston, where he spent a year working
in the law office of John Adams. John Trumbull returned
to New Haven during Webster's freshman year.

have to spend their Saturday afternoons chopping wood to keep their
dorm rooms warm. Just to the south stood the small chapel—the first
on an American college campus—dwarfed by its 125-foot-high steeple,
an addition contributed by the citizens of New Haven. This 50-by-40-
foot building, where undergraduates congregated every day at sunrise
for morning prayers, also housed the library, a collection of three thousand books, which undergraduates could rent for sixpence per folio
volume—a fee steep enough to stave off much use.

And pre–Revolutionary War Yale wasn't exactly a hotbed of the En-

Yale in Webster's day was hierarchical. The man at the left wearing a black robe and a cocked hat is a professor, while the hatless figures dressed in plain clothes are freshmen.

lightenment. Less intellectually demanding than its British or Scottish counterparts such as the universities at Oxford or Edinburgh, the college resembled a modern-day preparatory school. The emphasis was on giving students a grounding in the classical languages (called "tongues") rather than on exhorting them to engage in probing scholarship. Freshman year focused on schoolboy Latin (Virgil's *Aeneid* and Cicero's *Orations*) and Greek (*The New Testament*). Sophomore and junior year consisted of more classical literature along with a smattering of geography, algebra, logic and natural philosophy. The seniors, in contrast, took courses in metaphysics and ethics, taught by the president, in which they read such cornerstones of Western philosophy as John Locke's *Essay Concerning Human Understanding*. For Webster, completing the requirements for his Yale degree would signify not that he was a learned man, but that he had acquired the necessary tools to become one.

Yale students grumbled about the food, which they washed down

with cider served in pewter cans, since the administration felt they could
not be trusted with glass. For the midday dinner, the commons fare
typically started with "Injun pudding"—cornmeal and broth—followed
by a few scraps of beef or chicken on a bone along with a couple of
potatoes and some cabbage. Transforming the discarded bones into hair-
raising projectiles, Webster and his classmates had their share of food
fights—both with one another and with the faculty, who ate on a raised
platform so that they could watch their charges' every move. Served at
five, supper was a lighter but less objectionable meal—often just brown
bread and milk. Students could find some supplemental nourishment
at the buttery, located in a corner room on the ground floor of the
New College. Manned by a butler, a recent college graduate, it sold
primarily fruit and baked goods. And to discourage students from bringing hard liquor into their rooms, this cozy gathering place also carried
beer and cider.

But to curb unruly behavior, the faculty relied much less on carrots
than on sticks. Traditionally, the punishment of degradation, which reduced the student's class ranking, had been a favored tool. However, a
decade before Webster's arrival, the administration began organizing the
class lists, which determined seating and various perks, alphabetically
rather than by social position. After ending this aristocratic arrangement, which had given the sons of governors and ministers preferential
treatment, the faculty began levying fines for standard college pranks.
While etching one's name on the shingles on top of the New College
could exact a toll between fourpence and one shilling and sixpence,
excessive drinking of spiced wine could cost from two to five shillings.
Likewise, the "crime" of traveling to New Haven on the Sabbath could
leave a student out twenty pence. And on occasion, physical punishment
was still used to keep order. For example, a few years before Webster's
arrival, Yale's instructors decided that the freshman who "was catched in
the act of ringing the bell atop the Old College at 9pm shall have his
ears boxed by the president." Freshmen, whom upperclassmen treated

as errand boys, also had to worry about excessive discipline from seniors, assigned the task of teaching them the "laws, usages and customs of the college."

Though Webster came from a family with a prestigious pedigree, he was a notch behind most of his school chums socially. And he initially felt some embarrassment about his father's relative lack of sophistication and wealth. In contrast to Webster, Oliver Wolcott, Jr., the Litchfield native who would later replace Alexander Hamilton as secretary of the treasury, didn't have to worry about paying his tuition each semester. Just as the fourteen-year-old Wolcott arrived in New Haven, his father, Oliver Wolcott, Sr., himself a Yale graduate, headed off to the Continental Congress as a Connecticut delegate. Of Wolcott Jr., who, like both his father and grandfather, would do a stint as the state's governor, Webster would later write, "He was in college a good scholar, though not brilliant. He possessed the firmness and strong reasoning powers of the Wolcott family, but with some eccentricities in reasoning." Other prominent members of the class of 1778 included Josiah Meigs, son of Return Meigs, Sr., a major in the Continental army, who became a professor of natural philosophy at Yale and president of the University of Georgia; Zephaniah Swift, a future chief justice of Connecticut; Uriah Tracy, who would serve as a Connecticut senator; and Abraham Bishop, later one of New Haven's richest men.

For the first time, Webster had companions with whom he could share his thoughts and experiences. Webster's best friend at Yale was Joel Barlow, whose deprived childhood had also resulted in a burning literary ambition. As Barlow wrote of his harsh early life on a farm in nearby Redding:

> From morn to noon from noon to night
> I dayly drove the plow
> And fodder'd like an honest wight
> Sheep, oxen, horse and cow.

The unexpected death of his father in late adolescence left Barlow with an inheritance of a hundred pounds, just enough money to attend Yale. Four years older than Webster, the dashing Barlow took his fellow farmboy under his wing. Following Barlow's lead, Webster would gain entry to a lively social circle in New Haven, which would include alluring representatives of the fairer sex. In contrast to Webster, Barlow had a keen sense of humor. During his stretch in the Continental army after Yale, in which he served along with the author of "The Progress of Dulness," Barlow would quip, "Trumbull grows red and fat, and I black and handsome."

Webster and Barlow were among the thirty-three members of the class of 1778 who joined the Brothers in Unity, a literary society. Its free-lending library had 163 books, which, as its leaders boasted, was a dozen more than could be found in the confines of its older rival, the Linonian Society. A center for debate and intellectual exchange, the Brothers in Unity, founded in 1768, also spiced up campus life every spring with dramatic performances, which had long been considered the devil's work in Puritan New England. (In fact, until the late 1760s, Yale students were fined three shillings for taking part in a play and one shilling for just attending.) Despite concerns from one Yale faculty member that dramas were "calculated only to warm the imagination," the upstart Brothers in Unity—a forerunner to Yale's present-day secret society, Skull and Bones—staged them in the chapel. During Webster's junior year, the group mounted the comedy *The West Indian* by Richard Cumberland. Webster's commonplace book—the notebook he began keeping at Yale, which features his favorite passages from literary works—includes dialogue from this play, and Webster presumably took part in this production. While showing occasional interest in the dramatic arts, Webster never strayed too far from the antitheater bias that reigned supreme in pre–Revolutionary New England. In 1823, he wrote, "Very few plays are, however, free from sentiments which are offensive to moral purity." And tragicomedy and opera he liked even less, labeling them "the inferior species of drama" in his 1828 dictionary.

When Webster matriculated, Yale housed one hundred students. Over the next few years, enrollment would expand by more than thirty percent, as students flocked to colleges to avoid the draft, just as they would during the Vietnam War almost two centuries later. In the mid-1770s, the entire faculty consisted of the president, Naphtali Daggett, who doubled as a professor of divinity; Nathan Strong, a professor of mathematics and natural philosophy; and four tutors, one for each class. Appointed as president *pro tempore* back in 1766, the overweight and clumsy Daggett, nicknamed "Old Tunker" by the students whom he failed to inspire, wasn't supposed to have remained on the job as long as he did. Daggett's distinguishing characteristic, which he shared with many clergymen of his day, was a biting sense of humor. When addressed by his official title, Daggett, who, like the rest of the faculty, walked around campus in a black robe, white wig and high-cocked hat, would retort, "But did you ever hear of a President *pro aeternitate* [for eternity]?" Among the tutors were Timothy Dwight, an accomplished poet and scholar, who would guide the class of 1777, and Joseph Buckminster, a renowned classicist, who, as the most recent Yale grad on the faculty, was assigned Webster's freshman class. Dwight and Buckminster, who would readily lapse into Latin quotation, would each have an immense influence on the intellectual development of the West Division farmboy.

Unfortunately, like Webster's hometown instructor, Nathan Perkins, both Dwight and Buckminster were tormented scholars who would wage intense internal battles for their own sanity. For the generation that had never learned how to play as boys and would come of age during the late eighteenth century, such emotional crises seemed to be a standard rite of passage. While Dwight had recovered from a nearly fatal attack of anorexia by the time Webster got to know him, Buckminster descended into despair right before his eyes. His tutor's bout with incapacitating depression would leave Webster shaken in his senior year. While Yale's professors would dazzle Webster with their intellectual prowess, they were too self-absorbed to provide much personal guidance. Upon graduation, when Webster became anxious about his own uncertain future, he would have no one to whom he could turn; and he, too, would veer toward a breakdown.

Webster and Barlow both learned versification from the precocious Timothy Dwight, a scion of one of New England's most illustrious families—Thomas Hooker was his great-great-grandfather and the pastor Jonathan Edwards his grandfather—who had taught himself Latin at the age of six and had graduated from Yale at seventeen in 1769. Appointed a tutor in 1771, Dwight considered employment the best antidote to melancholy, and he prided himself on studying fourteen hours a day and sleeping only four hours each night. A couple of years later, he suddenly became concerned that too much food was dulling his mind. He began to reduce his intake to twelve mouthfuls at each meal; after six months of this experiment, he upped the ante, cutting out all meat and eating only vegetables—primarily, potatoes. By the summer of 1774, Dwight was down to ninety-five pounds, and his father whisked him home to Northampton, Massachusetts, where he was expected to die. But under doctor's orders to avoid all study and to drink a bottle of Madeira per day, Dwight slowly regained his health over the next few months.

After his return to New Haven, Dwight would complete his epic, "The Conquest of Canaan," a biblical allegory in eleven books that recounted how Connecticut freed itself from British rule. In response, the eighteen-year-old Webster—who, like Barlow, then thought of himself as a poet destined for literary immortality—wrote "To the Author of the Conquest of Canaan," one of the few surviving examples of his youthful verses. Webster was often obsequious toward authority figures, but was particularly deferential to the instructor, who maintained a lifelong love affair with power, later earning sobriquets such as "the Pope" and "his Loftiness." Comparing Dwight to the giants Homer, Virgil and Milton, Webster harped on his teacher's likely impact on succeeding generations:

. . . o'er the land these glorious arts shall reign
And blest Yalensia lead the splendid train.

In future years unnumber'd Bards shall rise
Catch the bold flame and tower above the skies:
Their brightening splendor gild the epic page
And unborn Dwights adorn th' Augustan age.

Webster would eventually realize that Dwight's epic was too bombastic to have much of a shelf-life. A decade later, when sending a copy to George Washington, to whom Dwight had dedicated the poem, Webster alluded to the "faults . . . found in this performance."

Dwight's valedictory address, given to Yale's senior class in a private graduation ceremony on July 25, 1776, moved Webster deeply. Though America was officially only three weeks old, Dwight was convinced that "the greatest empire the hand of time ever raised up to view" already had a distinct identity. After describing the vast richness of the North American continent—its abundant forests, fields and mountains—Dwight homed in on the remarkable unity among Americans: "I proceed then to observe that this continent is inhabited by a people, who have the same religion, the same manners, the same interests, the same language and the same essential forms and principles of civil government. This is an event, which, since the building of Babel, 'till the present time, the sun never saw." From Dwight, Webster first began to appreciate how a shared culture could help Americans overcome their ethnic divisions and cement their national ties. Webster would dedicate his life to meeting Dwight's injunction to Yale men at the end of his address to "inform yourselves with every species of useful knowledge. Remember that you are to act for the empire of America, and for a long succession of ages." Later, when he became an author and editor, Webster would republish time and time again Dwight's 1776 speech; excerpts appeared both in the first issue of his literary magazine in 1788 and in the 1835 version of his reader for schoolchildren.

Ever since first meeting Dwight during their freshman year, Webster, Barlow and the rest of the class of 1778 were all convinced that he would evolve into an American hero. So enamored were they of Dwight that in September 1777, they petitioned the administration to have him re-place Buckminster as their tutor for their final year. The plan fell through, and the next month, the Continental Congress came calling, appointing Dwight chaplain for the Connecticut brigade headed by General Samuel Parsons. In 1795, Dwight would return to Yale as president.

Another reason that Webster's class preferred Dwight over Buck-minster is that their tutor's soul was slowly coming undone. Buckmin-ster's distress was partly rooted in a constitutional depression, which would plague him for the rest of his life. He was also racked by a deep sense of his own sinfulness. During his stint as a Yale tutor, Buckminster would traipse around New England, giving dozens of fast-day sermons, in which he gave voice to his obsession with his own personal failings. "Sin is an abominable thing," the pastor intoned, "which God's soul hates and it is no less offensive in his children than in others. Was there no such thing as sin in the world, suffering would be a stranger." Buck-minster's spiritual affliction was also partly related to matters of the flesh. In early 1778, he became engaged to the beautiful Elizabeth Whit-man, the daughter of Elnathan Whitman, the Hartford pastor who had preached at Perkins' ordination—a romance which he sealed with a ring of amethyst set in diamonds. However, Elizabeth, an aspiring poet, was tiring of her suitor's depression and hypochondria and ended the court-ship. She soon changed her mind, but Buckminster, having assumed a position as a pastor in Portsmouth, New Hampshire, that spring, would not have her back. In the year after his Yale graduation, Webster would continue to socialize with Whitman, by then smitten with Joel Barlow who, as she noted, put her "in mind of Buckminster."

During the breakdown at the end of his Yale career, Buckminster, who didn't fully appreciate the impact of his instability on others, leaned on his students for emotional support—and they felt that they had no choice but to provide it. A few months after his move, the pastor wrote to Webster, his pet: "The long acquaintance I have had with your class, the many favors I have received from them, the particular tenderness and respect with which most of them have treated me, joined to the peculiar share of genius and merit with which as a class, they were distinguished, have begotten and cherished such feelings in me as time can never totally remove and as I shall never feel for any other members of society."

Buckminster's assessment of his students' intellectual prowess would be echoed by historians, who would call Webster's class Yale's most distinguished until the Civil War. And of the class of 1778, Webster would be the most celebrated. In 1823, he received an honorary doctorate of laws from his alma mater, which, a century later, placed his statue atop Harkness Tower along with seven other "Yale worthies," such as its founder, Elihu Yale, and the novelist James Fenimore Cooper.

AMERICA'S STRUGGLE FOR INDEPENDENCE would shape every aspect of Webster's Yale career. With cataclysmic national events swirling around them, Webster and his classmates lived in a constant state of high anxiety. As Joel Barlow wrote to his mother their freshman year, "The students are sensibly affected by the unhappy situation of public affairs, which is a great hindrance to their studies." In the fall of 1774, just as Webster was acclimating himself to New Haven, the First Continental Congress was meeting in Philadelphia. Before adjourning at the end of October, the delegates had imposed a boycott on the importation of all British goods, which was slated to go into effect by December 1. That winter, Yale's student body, composed mostly of Patriots, did its part, ceasing its consumption of British tea.

By early 1775, the drums of war could already be heard in New Haven. In February, the undergraduates formed their own militia that began practicing and marching on the Green; so, too, did the Second Company of the Governor's Foot Guard, a sixty-man unit of New Havenites headed by Captain Benedict Arnold, then a local pharmacist and merchant. In March, a Yale senior reported to Nathan Hale, the 1773 Yale graduate who would be executed as America's first spy the following year, that "the Military Art just begins to dawn in the generous breasts of the Sons of Yale. . . . College Yard constantly sounds with *poise your firelock, cock your firelock, etc.*"

The war's first skirmish in April caused a near frenzy among Yale students. Though the "shot heard round the world" by the farmers on Concord's North Bridge took two days to reach New Haven, its impact was dramatic. On Friday, April 21, sophomore Ebenezer Fitch, later the first president of Williams College, wrote in his diary, "Today tidings of the battle of Lexington . . . filled the country with alarm and rendered it impossible for us to pursue our studies." That same afternoon, a handful of Yale upperclassmen joined the graying, thirty-four-year-old Benedict Arnold as he raided New Haven's powderhouse to seize the British ammunition held there. Arnold's cadets then dashed off to Boston to "assist their bleeding countrymen," as the *New York Journal* reported. The following day—two weeks before spring break was supposed to begin—classes were halted. Students didn't return to New Haven until the end of May. This was to be the first of many war-induced interruptions in Webster's Yale education.

The backdrop of war wreaked havoc upon Webster's psyche. Whatever tendency he had toward melancholy was greatly exacerbated. With the British ensconced in nearby New York City after the Battle of Long Island in the summer of 1776, the threat of a direct attack loomed large. In fact, a year after Webster's graduation, some three thousand British forces did descend on New Haven, burning and destroying property and mortally wounding "Old Tunker." Feelings of dread, coupled with thoughts of death and dying, would be frequent companions for Webster and his college chums. Elijah Backus, a member of the class of 1777, wrote the year of his graduation:

> I'm swiftly wafted down the Tide of Life:
> And soon shall enter on the endless scenes
> Of the huge Ocean of Eternity
> Where never ceasing rolls the vast Abyss.

To manage his dark moods and anxiety, Webster would discon-
nect from his innermost thoughts—a coping strategy he had begun in
childhood and would use for the rest of his life. This man of words never
cared much for introspection. Webster would always prefer doing—
whether it be rushing off to war or compiling a massive reference work—
to feeling.

THURSDAY, JUNE 29, 1775, was a radiant morning in New Haven, and
Webster, finishing up his freshman year, was up at the crack of dawn in
his room at the New College. At the time, Yale was also in session during the humid New Haven summers. Webster's morning routine had him
waking up at 5:30 a.m., then heading over to the chapel for an hour and
a half of prayers and recitations. And afterward, when the butler rang
the chapel bell as he did before every meal, Webster would sit down for
his usual breakfast of beer and bread. But today would be different. A
special guest was in town, and Webster had to rush off to another kind
of early morning engagement, one which required that he don his long
coat, knee breeches and cocked hat. Grabbing both his flute and flint-
lock musket, Webster marched down College Street toward the Beers
Tavern on Chapel Street, just a few hundred yards away.

Isaac Beers' elegant hostelry, located in a wing of his spacious home,
was a center of New Haven's cultural life. A bibliophile, Beers ran the
largest imported-book shop in North America on the College Street
side of the ground floor, where students would congregate and talk about
ideas. He also kept a general store, selling everything from pewter to
balloon hats. Ever the conversationalist, Beers would personally entertain his distinguished out-of-town guests such as John Adams and other
delegates to the Continental Congress. His current guest of honor was
George Washington, who just ten days earlier had been appointed general and commander-in-chief of the Continental army. On June 23,
Washington had left Philadelphia accompanied by his chief aides, Major

General Charles Lee and Major Thomas Mifflin; on the evening of the
twenty-eighth, they had all reached Beers' inn. On the following morning, Washington and his entourage would be setting out for Cambridge,
where they were to be stationed. But before leaving town, Washington
and Lee had a promise to keep. As soldiers-in-residence at Yale, they
had agreed to inspect the college's troops.

Arriving in front of the Beers Tavern, Webster fell in line with his
schoolmates. Soon, with Webster playing "Yankee Doodle Dandy" on
his flute, the entire Yale militia—a contingent of nearly a hundred students, forty of whom would later serve in the war—began marching in
unison. Smiling, Washington looked over at the students and expressed
his approval at the precision with which they carried out these military
exercises.

And then up College Street came two other military units. One was
a company of Minutemen and the other was the illustrious Second Company of the Governor's Foot Guard, led by Lieutenant Hezekiah Sabin,
Jr., just back from Boston where he had been serving under Captain
Benedict Arnold. Widely considered the best-equipped soldiers in the
whole Continental army, the Second Company was also the best dressed.
Despite the heat, Sabin and his men wore their complete uniforms, consisting of white breeches and vests along with scarlet coats, topped off
with collars of buff. And on their heads sat fur headdresses.

But these three groups of soldiers weren't the only ones to escort
Washington and Lee out of town. Suddenly, a throng of local residents
eager to express their support for the war effort started trailing them,
too. As New Haven's weekly paper, The Connecticut Journal, later described this procession, Washington "set out for the provincial camp
near Boston attended by great numbers of inhabitants of the town. . . .
by two companies dress'd in their uniforms and by a company of young
gentlemen belonging to the seminary of this place, who made a very
handsome appearance."

For the rest of his life, Webster would remain immensely proud of
his presence at the Beers Tavern that fateful day, which forever linked

him with America's resolve to take up arms against British tyranny. Sixty-five years later, in a July Fourth oration before a Sunday school class in New Haven, he spoke of that June morning in 1775 when "a company of students of Yale College" escorted Washington out of New Haven to the nearby Neck Bridge. Webster concluded this account, which fails to mention that the Yale militia was just one part of the cavalcade, with the line, "It fell to my humble lot to lead this company with music." But in fact, Webster never was at the head of the pack. The motivation for this embellishment remains unclear. While Webster's first biographer attributed it to "a pardonable little vanity," his granddaughter Emily Ford countered that Webster "inserted his own 'humble' share in the scene to make it more real to his auditors."

IT WAS FRIDAY, MAY 3, 1776, and it was sophomore Noah Webster's turn to step up to the podium. Public speaking then formed a key part of a Yale education, and the chapel galleries contained three raised platforms precisely because its undergraduates were expected to engage in frequent disputing and declaiming. While disputations (debates between students) could be done in either Latin or English, declamations (short speeches) could be given in either of those languages or in Greek or Hebrew (no modern languages were yet taught). Every Tuesday and Friday, eight students were chosen to address declamations to the faculty, and Webster's number had come up.

Webster's Latin speech, which he delivered from memory, focused on the relationship between youth and old age. Looking over at Buckminster, Webster began in his high-pitched voice: "We have all the arguments that it is necessary to use in proving that a well spent youth prepares for a happy old age. Young men of tender years who are averse to serious matters and those which pertain to the mind as if they were beyond all law are borne headlong to the enjoyment of passions and the gratification of earthly desires." Webster was arguing that a youth devoted to rigorous intellectual labors rather than sensual experience would pave the way for a peaceful adult life. He also made the case for the corollary, contending that the pursuit of pleasure in adolescence could later lead to regret and unhappiness. "But what foolishness, what madness it is," he declared, "to purchase youthful pleasure with the sorrow of Old Age!"

Though Buckminster and the other tutors were typically bowled over by Webster's ingenious compositions, not so on this occasion. His attempt to impress the faculty with his eloquence had come up short. Buckminster would later characterize his star pupil's effort that day as "second-rank."

Webster's remarks were uninspired because he himself didn't truly believe them. Unbeknownst to Buckminster, Webster had not been speaking from the heart. Over the past two years, a funny thing had happened to the Congregationalist farmboy; he had discovered the joy of letting go of his inhibitions.

Under the influence of the suave Barlow, Webster had been circulating with the fast crowd that chased women, drank and swore. And on account of this free-spirited behavior, he was the envy of his classmates. As the shy Zephaniah Swift, who was a year younger, noted in a letter written early in their junior year: "it appears that to be solely a man of Letters or a man of the world is not sufficient, for one pleases the learned, and the other the unlearned. . . . Your opportunities and the time you spend with the Ladies will enable you to reach both, but as for myself I fear I shall reach neither." Few documents remain from Webster's college years, so it's hard to determine exactly what pleasures he indulged in at Yale. However, at the age of fifty, in a piece published in a religious periodical, Webster would make some general allusions to these youthful indiscretions: "Being educated in a religious family under pious parents, I had in early life some religious impressions, but being too young to understand fully the doctrines of the Christian religion and falling into vicious company at college, I lost those impressions and contracted a habit of using profane language."

The split between Webster's morally upright public self and his pleasure-seeking private self would continue until his marriage in 1789. For the next decade, as he would acknowledge in the diary that he began keeping in 1784, he would divide his "time between the Ladies and books." But Webster would also at times feel ashamed of his keen interest in attractive young women. In a letter to Buckminster in 1779, he described his resolution to make himself "master of every evil passion and propensity."

Once married, Webster would stay faithful to his wife, but his youthful adventures would continue to haunt him. A year after his wedding, when endowing a Yale prize to the author of the best English composition, as judged by the faculty, he specifically excluded any person with a "well founded reputation of having been guilty of seduction." By thus sanctioning Yale essay writers of the future, Webster may well have been trying to atone for what he perceived to be his own wayward past. Likewise, thirty years later, Webster planned to compile an anthology of expurgated English poetry. Though he would abandon this project, he continued to feel that many canonical writers were too smutty. "It is mortifying," he wrote in 1823, "that [the seventeenth-century poet John] Dryden . . . should . . . regale the libidinous with his translations of Theocritus and Lucretius which I read when at college and which are vade mecums for a brothel." Just as Webster the sophomore had warned, Webster the old man would be tinged with sorrow about his adolescent flirtations with pleasure.

IN AUGUST 1776, Yale suddenly dismissed its students because a typhoid epidemic had swept over New Haven. And a few weeks after taking another trip back home with his father and the family horse, Webster found himself traveling once again. This time, there were two Websters and two horses, and Noah's companion was not his father but his older brother, Abraham, then nearly twenty-five. Abraham had to return to his army company, stationed in Skenesborough (today Whitehall), a small town on the eastern edge of New York State near the Vermont border.

Noah needed to trail along so that he could bring his brother's horse back to the West Division. For the first time, the seventeen-year-old Noah would observe war from close range.

His brother's harsh existence represented the road Noah had not taken. Without a Yale degree, Abraham had no choice but to become a farmer. In 1774, Abraham moved into his own house in the West Division, but with the price of land shooting up, Noah Sr. could manage to provide his eldest son with only half an acre. The following year, Abraham married Rachel Merrill. But in January 1776, tragedy struck. On the nineteenth, Rachel died in childbirth; a week later, their son, also named Abraham, was dead as well. In early February, the despondent Abraham attempted to bury his grief in a noble cause, signing up with Captain John Stevens' company in the Continental army, a decision that would soon bring on further hardship. For the rest of his life, Abraham, who would eventually settle on a farm in New York State, would struggle with loss, poverty and despair.

When Noah first saw his brother that summer, Abraham had just escaped a close brush with death. He had spent the spring in Quebec, where he had joined Benedict Arnold's forces. Initially, Abraham met with few difficulties. As he wrote Noah back on April 14, "I am through Goodness of God in good health, and tolerably contented with a soldier's life." Abraham was at first more anxious about the welfare of his family back home than about himself. Fiercely religious, he managed to keep calm by attending local church services, even though in Connecticut he had never been exposed to Catholicism. But in May, Abraham was captured by the enemy and thrown into a prison on the outskirts of Montreal. Paradoxically, he would then be saved by an illness that almost killed him. Concerned about the spread of the smallpox that Abraham had contracted, the British were forced to release him. Yet for a while, Abraham still feared for his life. As Noah later recalled, "It seemed to him his flesh would leave his bones." But after finding refuge in the cabin of a French woman who could offer him nothing but milk, Abraham somehow summoned up the strength to make it back to the West Division.

Now that he had regained his health, Abraham was ready to go back into battle.

From Hartford, the brothers rode to Bennington, Vermont, and then crossed over into forest land in New York State. Over the last twelve miles of their journey to Skenesborough—the New York town between Lake George and Lake Champlain—the Websters had to rely on marked trees as their guide.

After depositing Abraham with his unit, Webster faced a new round of travails. He needed to find a place to lay his head. Fortunately, he ran into Ashbel Wells, a classmate from his West Division schooldays, then serving in the army. He slept one night in Wells' tent. But Webster could hardly rest easy, as Wells had to fill the tent with smoke to fight off swarms of mosquitoes. The next night, Webster spent on a boat in South Bay, an inlet on the western shore of Lake Champlain. Webster then headed off to Mount Independence, where the army had built a fort. But he soon noticed that about half of the soldiers were suffering from dysentery. Terrified about having to breathe infected air, Webster made his way back to the Vermont forest, which was lined with tall pines and hemlocks. He hunkered down the following night on the floor of a farmhouse owned by a hospitable young stranger.

The next morning, Webster was greatly relieved to reach Wallingford, a Vermont town which had been settled just three years earlier by a former Connecticut pastor, Abraham Jackson, Sr. There Webster stayed with his aunt Jerusha—Mercy Steele's youngest sister—and her husband Abraham Jackson, Jr., the son of the venerable Deacon Jackson. The floor of the Jacksons' log cabin was nothing but bare earth sprinkled with a few sticks, and the walls were mud-plastered. The crude windows were placed high up so as to prevent wolves, bears or any other wild animals from jumping inside. But when compared with his previous Vermont rest stops, Webster's new quarters were sumptuous. "Here I was very comfortable," he would later write.

Though Jerusha Jackson was then busy raising several young children and in poor health, she accompanied Webster all the way back to

Hartford, riding one of the horses herself. She would die of consumption not long afterward.

IF YALE WAS IN A STATE of disarray when Webster first set foot in New Haven, it was literally crumbling when he came back to start his junior year. By the fall of 1776, two-thirds of the Old College had been torn down, leaving just its south end with the dining hall and kitchen. Now that the New College was the only dormitory, up to four students could be piled on top of one another in one of its dingy rooms. And that year, with wood in short supply, the undergraduates began relying on straw, causing some fire damage to their residence. By the beginning of December, with food prices also soaring, the campus was no longer inhabitable. On December 10, President Daggett had to call off classes because, as Webster later reported, "the steward . . . could not procure enough for the students to eat." Due to the various hardships caused by the war, Webster and his classmates would be denied the full benefits of a Yale education. "The advantages then enjoyed by the students, during the four years of college life," Webster would recall in his 1832 memoir, "were much inferior to those enjoyed before and since the Revolution, in the same institution."

Webster returned to Yale at the end of the extended winter break in early January 1777, but did not stay long. With the British threatening to attack New Haven, the college was forced to take drastic action. On March 29, Daggett shut Yale down. He then promptly resigned. At a meeting on April 1, the Yale Corporation decreed, "That in the opinion of this board, it is necessary to provide some other place or places, where the classes may reside under their respective tutors until God in His kind providence shall open a door for their return to this fixed and ancient seat of learning." Webster returned to his father's house, where he was briefly sidelined by smallpox, a disease that was then blanketing New England—often with lethal consequences. But he soon recovered, and in mid-May, he wrote his classmate Ichabod Wetmore about the possibility of rooming together during the summer term. Fond of Webster, Wetmore responded immediately, "Nothing can be more agreeable to me." Wetmore then set up the arrangements in Glastonbury, where the junior class was to be relocated. Continuing his course work under Buckminster, Webster stayed in Glastonbury, which was only a few miles from Hartford, until the fall recess began on September 10.

As Webster was packing up his belongings in Glastonbury, the Yale Corporation was still deliberating about how to keep the college running during the 1777–1778 academic year. Webster liked Glastonbury and would be disappointed when they finally made their decision in early November. As he later recalled, "The senior class to which N. W. belonged was ordered to repair to New Haven, although the other classes were permitted to remain in the country. This gave offense." But Webster ended up not having to spend much more time in the besieged New Haven. Classes didn't start until the end of November, and were suspended between the end of February and the end of June.

AND FOR A WHILE IT LOOKED as if Webster might never make it back to New Haven for his senior year. As soon as he returned to the West Division in September 1777, he was forced to confront some terrifying news. Lieutenant General John Burgoyne, described by *The Connecticut Courant* as "the chief and director of the King of Great Britain's band of thieves, robbers, cut-throats . . . and murderers" was on the march. In Canada, Burgoyne had been squaring off against the American general Horatio Gates and, in early July, had taken Fort Ticonderoga. Coming down from Lake Champlain, Burgoyne's force of 7,700 troops was now plundering northern New York State and Vermont. Even worse, despite Burgoyne's protestations to the contrary, the Indians under his command were murdering and scalping American women.

Horrified by British aggression, Patriots such as Noah Webster, Sr., then fifty-five, felt compelled to enter the fray. A captain of the alarm list—the emergency forces of the local militia, consisting of men over forty-five—Noah Sr. organized a band of soldiers from the West Division to head off Burgoyne's troops. Accompanying Noah Sr. were all three of his sons: Abraham, recently returned to Connecticut; Noah Jr.; and Charles, who had just turned fifteen. As Noah Jr. later wrote, "In the fall of the year 1777, when the British army under Gen. Burgoyne was marching toward Albany, all able-bodied men were summoned into the field. . . . I shouldered a musket and marched, a volunteer. . . . Leaving at home no person but my mother and a sister [Jerusha] to take charge of the farm." This time around, Noah Jr. would not just be trailing along, but he, too, would be marching off to war.

In late September, the quartet of Websters, along with the other Connecticut militiamen under the command of Lieutenant Colonel Hezekiah Wyllys, reached the east bank of the Hudson River near Kingston, New York State's new capital. The mission of the American troops was to prevent General Henry Clinton, then sailing north out of New York City (the former capital), from joining forces with Burgoyne. If the British could establish a line of posts along the Hudson, they could perhaps isolate New England from the rest of the colonies and bring a quick end to the war. The fate of the new nation hung in the balance— and so did Webster's. As he recalled some sixty years later, "In the most critical period of the Revolutionary War . . . when the companions of my youth were sinking into the grave, I offered to hazard my life."

As Webster scrambled to find a bed of straw to rest his head each night, Clinton's troops continued to advance. At dusk on October 6, on the left bank of the Hudson, the 2,100 men under Clinton achieved a major military victory, overcoming American resistance at Forts Clinton and Montgomery. While almost two hundred British soldiers were either killed or wounded, the American casualties were nearly twice as high. Hearing news of this defeat, Webster was rattled. In contrast, Clinton could smell victory and sought to encourage the embattled Burgoyne. From Fort Montgomery on October 8, Clinton dashed off a quick note on tissue paper, which he wrapped in a silver bullet, "*Nous y voici* [Here we are], and nothing between us and General Gates. I sincerely hope this little success of ours will facilitate your operations." But the Americans captured Clinton's messenger, and after being administered an emetic, he vomited up the missive, which thus never reached its destination.

Unaware of Clinton's success, the increasingly desperate Burgoyne, now in Saratoga, could no longer continue. In early October, Burgoyne had had to put his men on half rations. This want of provisions caused a sudden flurry of deserters. And at around noon on October 7, he had conducted a risky attack upon the Americans at Bemis Heights, a battle which was over in just a couple of hours. Benedict Arnold, wounded in the fray, had mounted a heroic charge. A worn-down Burgoyne was forced to abandon hundreds of sick and wounded soldiers in the field. Surrounded, Burgoyne retreated to Saratoga, where he would soon begin negotiating his surrender with General Gates.

When he heard these developments, Webster was greatly relieved. But just as he started to relax, he had to witness a frightening barrage of British terror from across the Hudson. With Burgoyne defeated, Clinton decided to sail back to New York City. To distract the enemy, he assigned Major General John Vaughan and his seventeen hundred troops the task of burning down Kingston. Calling the capital "a nursery for almost every villain in the country," Vaughan torched nearly all three hundred of its homes on October 16. This humiliating defeat turned Kingston into an ash heap. (New York would soon have to move its capital fifty miles further north to Albany.) As the British fleet retreated, Colonel Wyllys' regiment exchanged fire with a British sloop. The shots whisked right past the ears of Webster and his comrades, then beginning their march toward Albany.

That next day, Friday, October 17, would mark a watershed in the brief history of the new nation. As one Saratoga-based Connecticut soldier recorded in his journal, "The hand of providence worked wonderfully in favour of America this day. . . . At three o'clock [Burgoyne and his army] marches through our army . . . with a guard for Boston." Within a few hours, Webster received word. He later recalled, "Before the regiment reached Albany, it was met by an express upon a full gallup brandishing a drawn sword exclaiming as he passed the regiment, 'Burgoyne is taken, Burgoyne is taken!'" With "the chief cut-throat" subdued, the militiamen were no longer needed, and Webster returned home. America's first major victory would soon convince France to join the fight against the British. Keenly aware that his brief tour of duty had helped to turn the tide of the war, the adult Webster would be moved to tears whenever he reminisced about the courier's shouts. On his list of the forty most "remarkable events" in America's history, which he appended to the back of his speller, Webster would include both the Battle at Bemis Heights and Burgoyne's surrender.

AT THREE THIRTY ON THE AFTERNOON of Thursday, July 23, 1778, the College Chapel bell tolled. This was the signal that Ezra Stiles had been waiting for. Yale's new president was now ready to convene the Presentation Day (today Class Day) exercises for the graduating seniors.

That morning, Webster and the rest of the class of 1778 had all passed two sets of public examinations. First came a grilling in Latin and Greek; and then, after a recess of half an hour, came a barrage of questions about the sciences. Those were the final requirements for the bachelor's degree and the honorific "Sir" that went with it. All that now stood between Webster and his Yale diploma was the cliosophic (on the arts and sciences) oration that he was slated to deliver that afternoon.

After being closed all spring, Yale had reopened on June 23, with Stiles at the helm. Back in March, Stiles had accepted the Yale Corporation's offer of a hundred sixty pounds—only forty of which were to be paid in cash; the rest were to come in the form of corn, pork and wheat—for his services, but the imminent threat of capture by the British had delayed his relocation to New Haven for three months. With Buckminster in Portsmouth where he had replaced Stiles as pastor, the new president personally supervised the instruction of the seniors. As with Buckminster, who considered Stiles "an honor to mankind," Webster and his classmates took an immediate liking to the eminent biblical scholar, who impressed them with both his vitality and his command of Hebrew, Arabic and Aramaic. On June 30, the seniors engaged in their first forensic disputation under Stiles, discussing the question of whether "learning increaseth happiness." So much did they enjoy his tutelage that the next day they asked Stiles to double their dose to two disputations a day until graduation.

Focusing his penetrating dark gray eyes on the seniors and guests gathered in the chapel auditorium, the short and compact Stiles began in his mild yet energetic voice, "*Ut nostra cura Gradibus academis conferendis innotescat* [As our concern for those taking academic steps becomes known]. . . ." After finishing his Latin introduction, Stiles ceded the floor to the ten top-ranking seniors. At exactly 3:47, as Stiles would later note in his factoid-filled diary, Sir Meigs began his cliosophic oration in Latin. Twelve minutes later, Sir Barlow delivered the commencement poem, "The Prospect of Peace," which concluded with his utopian vision:

THEN Love shall rule, and Innocence adore,
Discord shall cease, and Tyrants be no more;
'Till yon bright orb, and those celestial spheres,
In radiant circles, mark a thousand years.

Barlow was expressing the millennial thinking that had first gained wide currency with the publication *Of Plymouth Plantation,* the journal of Webster's ancestor, the early Massachusetts governor William Bradford. For the optimistic Barlow, the American Revolution was the signature event that signified the end of Satan's nefarious influence. Having inspired his Calvinist listeners with his dream of a glorious future for America, Barlow sat down to a round of applause. Barlow's patriotic composition, published later that year, would make a lasting impression. "Your poem does you honor in this part of the country," Buckminster wrote Barlow from New Hampshire that fall, "and every person that has seen it speaks very highly of it."

Though Webster's remarks weren't as heralded as Barlow's, they do reveal something about the arc of his own intellectual career. The sixth student orator that afternoon, Webster addressed the state of natural philosophy (the objective study of nature) in his sixteen-minute address. "There are few subjects," he began, "in the whole circle of literature that present a larger field for the exercise of genius or furnish more sublime and rational satisfaction for a speculative mind." Webster proceeded to cover the discipline's history, starting with the Egyptians and the Greeks. Classical philosophers like Plato and Aristotle, he argued, were stuck in "a maze of irregular discoveries which their own strength of genius was insufficient to understand, much less to explain." But then came the Dark Ages during which all learning declined. In the Renaissance, scientific progress resumed and Isaac Newton managed to put the field on a solid empirical footing.

While Webster had initially toyed with the idea of becoming a poet like Barlow, by the end of his senior year at Yale, he saw himself as a budding philosopher. The "immortal" Newton, who had discovered "the nice order and regularity observed by those stupendous bodies that compose the solar system," was the intellectual hero whose example he wished to emulate. Webster's literary ambition now focused on acquiring and organizing knowledge: "Those who design to distinguish themselves in the literary world may, by a proper degree of application, make themselves masters of the arts and sciences, which during the earlier ages of civilization, were scarce known to mankind, and which have been advancing, with some interruption, to their present degree of perfection for more than 4000 years." Like Dwight in his valedictory address two years earlier, Webster also reminded his fellow graduates of the need for "uncommon acquisitions of knowledge." Having completed his "liberal education," Webster was thoroughly steeped in the ideals of the Enlightenment. He was committed to bringing order to the world through his intellectual labors, though he hadn't yet figured out exactly what those labors might be.

Sir Tracy gave the last speech of the day, the valedictory address. The class tutor typically addressed the seniors, but Buckminster did not wish

to return to Yale. In a letter to Barlow sent from Portsmouth, Buckminster had mentioned the difficulty of traveling to New Haven, adding, "I
am really disconnected from College." Sir Tracy finished his remarks at
5:28. How Webster and his classmates celebrated the end of their undergraduate days is not known. Ezra Stiles' diary—the only surviving
account of the festivities—is vague: "Decency in amusements recommended & observed in the day and evening."

TWO MONTHS LATER, on Wednesday, September 9, in a brief private ceremony in the Yale chapel, Stiles handed out diplomas to Webster and
the other seniors. (Commencement services, as the term implies, were
initially held at the beginning of the academic year.) Like most of his
classmates, Sir Webster gave President Stiles a gratuity of ten dollars,
while the impoverished Sir Barlow could manage only eight. But the
total of $351 contributed by the thirty-five new graduates wasn't worth
much. As Stiles noted in his diary next to this tally, five dollars in paper
currency was then equal to just one silver dollar.

   In September 1778, rampant inflation was blanketing the colonies.
The price of a subscription to the *Courant* had nearly tripled since early
1777, shooting up to eighteen shillings per year.* To help finance the
war, the Continental Congress had authorized the states to print their
own money, and the economically devastated Connecticut had been the
first to do so. By October, the state would be printing its first set of fifty-
dollar bills; by early 1779, it would have to introduce sixty-five-, seventy-
and eighty-dollar bills as well. But printing additional denominations of
currency just exacerbated the problem. "The depreciation of [our money]
has got to so alarming a point," wrote George Washington in April 1779,
"that a wagon load of money will scarcely purchase a wagon load of
provisions."

---

* Until the Coinage Act of 1792, which stated that "the money of account of the United States shall
be expressed in dollars" and thereby created a uniform national currency, Americans used several different types of currency—including pounds, dollars and silver dollars—issued by the states.

Looking for his first job in a period of hyperinflation, when many Americans were resorting to barter, Noah Webster was feeling lost and confused. And he was suddenly separated from the beloved classmates with whom he had shared his hopes and dreams. As he contemplated his future back at the family farm, all he knew was that he had to keep reading and writing. As a Yale undergraduate, Webster had developed a love of intellectual discovery; exploring the ideas running around inside his own head made him feel thoroughly alive. The thought of going into business repelled him. "What is now called a liberal education," he later wrote, "disqualifies a man for business." According to Webster, business required mechanical thinking, and once a young man was exposed to books, there was no turning back.

But Webster had no idea how he could earn a living. Barlow found himself in a similar predicament, writing Webster from New Haven shortly after their graduation, "We are now citizens of the world . . . no longer in circumstances of warming the soul and refining the sensibility by those nameless incidents that attend college connection. . . . I am yet at a loss for an employment for life and unhappy in this state of suspense." While Barlow and Webster both held fast to their literary ambitions, they felt hopeless about ever achieving them. As the two Yale men well knew, war-ravaged America did not yet harbor any professional writers.

Webster had hoped that his father might provide some wise counsel, but that's not what he got. One day that fall, while he was pacing up and down the pine-planked floor of the family parlor, Noah Sr. pulled out one of those hardly inflation-proof eighty-dollar Connecticut bills and told him, "Take this; you must now seek your living; I can do no more for you."

The twenty-year-old was stunned. He felt, as he later wrote, "cast upon the world." Webster promptly raced up the stairs to the second floor and threw himself headfirst onto the straw mattress in his boyhood bedroom. For the next three days, he hardly came out—even for meals. He did little but read *The Rambler,* the collection of moral essays penned a generation earlier by his idol, Samuel Johnson (then still living in London off the special pension granted by King George III). "This book," Webster would later note in his third-person memoir, "produced no inconsiderable effect on his mind." In Johnson's maxims—such as the one that would grace the title page of his dictionary a half century later, "He that wishes to be counted among the benefactors of posterity must add, by his own toil, to the acquisitions of his ancestors"—the new graduate found the fatherly advice he longed for. Johnson advocated approaching life with a scrupulous exactness, and that's the path that Webster resolved to take.

Graduation from Yale unmoored Webster, separating him from everything he held dear. As he later recalled, "Having neither property nor powerful friends to aid me, I knew not . . . by what way to obtain subsistence. Being set afloat in the world at the inexperienced age of 20, without a father's aid which had before supported me, my mind was embarrassed with solicitude and gloomy apprehensions." To avoid lapsing into abject despair, Webster would turn to his favorite companions—words.

Spelling the New Nation

AUTHOR, n. 1. One who produces, creates or brings into being; as God is the *author* of the Universe. 2. The beginner, former, or first mover of any thing; hence the efficient cause of a thing. It is appropriately applied to one who composes or writes a book, or original work, and in a more general sense, to one whose occupation is to compose and write books; opposed to compiler or translator.

On Saturday, February 20, 1779, a distraught Webster placed an advertisement in New Haven's newspaper, *The Connecticut Journal*: "Lost on the road between New Haven and Wallingford a neat pair of men's shoes almost new. Whoever shall find them and give information to the printers either of New Haven or Hartford will be handsomely rewarded, and much oblige their humble servant." That winter, Webster was working as a schoolteacher in Glastonbury and making occasional weekend visits to New Haven to visit Joel Barlow, who had stayed on at Yale to pursue graduate studies. Nothing seemed to be going right. He couldn't even manage to keep his belongings from falling off his horse.

Though Webster was pleased to be back in Glastonbury, where he had spent the second half of his junior year, his first job was far from satisfying. Then a lowly occupation often held by alcoholics and former convicts, teaching paid less than two pounds per month. The working conditions were also harsh, as schoolmasters typically had to stare down rambunctious students in dilapidated and overcrowded classrooms. Webster complained of his unhappiness in frequent letters to Barlow. While Webster's half of the correspondence does not remain, Barlow's responses provide a picture of his mounting angst. On December 31, 1778, he wrote, "It appears by your letter that you indulge yourself much in serious contemplation upon the disorderly jumble of human events and are at a loss how you shall make your course from the college to the grave." Barlow continued to offer encouragement. "I have too much confidence in your merits," he reassured Webster a month later, "both as to greatness of genius and goodness of heart, to suppose that your actions are not to be conspicuous." While Webster would languish in dead-end jobs for a couple of years, Barlow's prediction turned out to be true long before either man expected. Soon after the publication of his speller in 1783, Webster would become a household name across New England.

EAGER TO INCREASE HIS EARNING POWER, Webster decided to leave Glastonbury at the end of the winter term and become a lawyer. During the Revolution, for a young man with a bachelor's degree, admission to the Connecticut bar required two years of study with a practicing attorney. In the spring of 1779, Webster moved into the Hartford home of Oliver Ellsworth, then serving as both the state's attorney from Hartford County and as a delegate to the Continental Congress. Having also started a private practice, the thirty-four-year-old Ellsworth had already established himself as one of the state's busiest and richest lawyers. His docket consisted of between a thousand and fifteen hundred cases. Though Ellsworth could be gruff in both his speech and his manner—if he tired during an oral argument, he might resort to wiping his trousers with a handkerchief—he had a knack for driving his points home in the courtroom. Webster would later describe Ellsworth, who in 1796 became chief justice of the U.S. Supreme Court, as "a mighty" of the Connecticut bar.

While in Hartford, Webster was burdened by a grueling schedule.

Unlike his well-to-do classmate Oliver Wolcott, who could afford to study law full-time, Webster had to take on a day job. From Monday through Saturday, he instructed students at the elite Brick School. During the evening, he struggled both to help Ellsworth with his cases and to make his way through his host's vast law library. Within a few months, the strain led to acute depression and anxiety. He couldn't sleep nor could he concentrate. With considerable shame and embarrassment, Webster told Ellsworth that he had to quit.

The breakdown of the twenty-year-old Webster in the summer of 1779 closely parallels the plight of the twenty-year-old Samuel Johnson a half century earlier. In 1729, Webster's hero had to leave Oxford after just one year because his father could no longer foot the bill. That winter, according to his biographer James Boswell, Johnson "felt himself overwhelmed with an horrible hypochondria, with perpetual irritation, fretfulness, and impatience; and with a dejection, gloom and despair, which made existence misery. From this dismal malady he never afterward was perfectly relieved; and all his labours, and all his enjoyments were but temporary interruptions of its baleful influence." Though Johnson bounced back from this lapse into incapacitating mental illness several years later, he was never again the same. Immersing himself in monumental literary works such as his *Dictionary of the English Language* and *Lives of the Most Eminent English Poets* could mitigate his depression, but not cure it. "My health," Johnson observed at seventy-two, "has been from my twentieth year such as has seldom afforded me a single day of ease."

Webster, too, wouldn't feel quite right after the age of twenty. While his descendants have maintained that Webster would soon overcome his early bout with depression, this conventional wisdom is not accurate. Of Webster's aborted first stab at legal training, his granddaughter wrote, "At this time and for two years he was troubled with a distressing nervous affection, which he eventually outgrew." But in fact, Webster, like Johnson, waged a lifelong battle with mental illness. In a letter to one of his adult children dated June 26, 1818, the fifty-nine-year-old Webster wrote that "my nervous affections . . . which I have had for *forty* years seem to increase with age" (italics mine). Like Johnson, Webster would have to learn how to live with his nervous condition. And Webster would stumble upon the same creative solution: He, too, would make use of his legendary capacity for nonstop intellectual labor, which he could perform with an obsessive exactitude.

After leaving Ellsworth's house, Webster went back to his father's farm to regain his stamina. But Webster was no longer an adolescent who could depend on his father for subsistence. To pay for his room and board, he did some teaching at a local parish school. Unfortunately, the winter of 1779–1780 was the coldest in a century and also one of the snowiest. "For a week or ten days past," *The Connecticut Courant* reported in early January, "there has been a greater body of snow on the ground than has ever been known, at one time, during the remembrance of the oldest man." Years later, Webster would vividly recall that commuting to work that winter required walking four miles a day through "drifts of snow which completely covered the adjoining fences."

33 Miles to Hartford.
102 Miles to New York.
J. STRONG

IN EIGHTEENTH-CENTURY NEW ENGLAND, it was a common practice for affluent citizens to place milestones on major thoroughfares in their community. While most were of red sandstone, the one Jedediah Strong, the register of deeds in Litchfield, erected on Bantam Road near his residence, a half mile west of the courthouse, was of sleek marble.

In the summer of 1780, Webster tried once again to become a lawyer. This time, he selected as his mentor Jedediah Strong, in whose Litchfield home he would live for nearly a year. The son of Supply Strong, who owned an eighth of Litchfield when the town was first settled in 1721, Jedediah Strong had graduated from Yale in 1761. Though trained to be a minister, he switched to law and then to politics. In 1770, Strong was appointed a selectman. The following year, he was elected to the Connecticut state legislature, where he would eventually serve during some thirty sessions. In 1779, Strong was named a delegate to the Continental Congress, but he declined the appointment because of what was called "an inveterate complication of nervous disorders."

Thus, lawyer and trainee would both be on the mend from mental afflictions at the same time. Strong was then under considerable stress. In 1777, this small man with the unbecoming face and limp had lost his wife of three years. By the time of Webster's arrival in 1780, the aggrieved widower was raising his five-year-old daughter, Idea, by himself. Strong hired Webster because he needed an assistant to help him with compiling and recording public records. An exacting man with beautiful handwriting, he was good at what he did, but he was also overwhelmed by the demands of daily life.

Webster had heard about the opportunity from Titus Hosmer, a family friend from the West Division who was then serving in both the state senate and the Continental Congress. Webster jumped at the chance to move to Litchfield, then one of Connecticut's four largest towns, with a population of about four thousand. Two of his Yale classmates, Oliver Wolcott and Uriah Tracy, were already studying law there under Tapping Reeve. Married to Aaron Burr's sister, Sally, the brilliant but humble Reeve counted the future vice president, whom Webster would soon meet, among his many devoted students. Though Reeve had a genial manner, he was self-absorbed. He once was observed walking around town with a bridle but no horse; not realizing that the animal had run off, he proceeded to tie the bridle to a post. Webster occasionally attended the law lectures that Reeve gave in the basement of his two-story home. To accommodate his growing number of students, Reeve would soon construct an addition to his residence. This building, in turn, became the Litchfield Law School, the nation's first private law school.

By March 1781, Webster was ready to take the bar exam in Litchfield. Much to the surprise of Webster and his twenty fellow candidates, no one passed. But Webster didn't give up. In early April in Hartford, he tried again and was successful. Though he was now Noah Webster, Esquire, his new title, which he would soon proudly affix to his byline, wasn't much use. With the Revolutionary War still in full swing, Webster couldn't find any work as a lawyer. As he later recalled, "the practice of law was in good measure set aside by the general calamity."

Webster would forever remain loyal to his Litchfield employer, who met a particularly tragic end. In 1788, Strong got remarried, to Susannah Wyllys, the daughter of Connecticut's secretary of state, George Wyllys. But just two years later, Strong was arrested for horrific cruelty toward his new wife. Newspapers throughout New England covered his scandalous divorce trial: "It appeared in evidence that the accused had often imposed unreasonable restraints upon his wife, and withheld from her the comforts and conveniences of life; that he had beat her, pulled her hair, kicked her out of bed, and spit in her face times without number." Presiding over the case in the Litchfield courthouse was Judge Tapping Reeve, who pronounced a fine of a thousand pounds and bound Strong to his good behavior. As the papers also reported, this punishment was satisfactory to his acquaintances "in Litchfield and elsewhere who have long known the infamy of his private character." But Webster was one of the few who stood by Strong. In fact, a year later, Strong hired Webster, then living in Hartford, as his attorney. On July 12, 1791, Webster wrote in his diary, "Mr. Jedh Strong in town; engages me to negotiate with his wife for a release of all claim to her dower; she declines." With Webster's legal maneuvering unsuccessful, Strong sank deeper into debt and drink. A decade later, Strong went mad and a guardian had to take over his affairs. Upon his death in 1802, his remains would be placed in an unmarked grave in a cemetery just west of Litchfield. All that would be left of Strong was his elegant milestone.

It was seven thirty on Monday evening, October 1, 1781, and the Sharon Literary Club, America's first literary society, was in session.

Founded in January of 1779 by Cotton Mather Smith, the town's pastor, who served as chairman, and his son, John Cotton Smith, then a thirteen-year-old preparing for Yale, who became its secretary, the group was designed to "promote a taste of belles lettres and of logic and to gain some skill in the useful freeman's art of debate." The weekly meetings, which were suspended from the beginning of May to the end of September so that the townsfolk could attend to pressing agricultural duties, ran for an hour and a half. At precisely nine o'clock, refreshments were served. An hour of dancing typically followed—except on nights such as this one when the meeting, which rotated among more than a dozen local residences, was held at the parson's large stone house, constructed by a Genoese mason, on the east side of Sharon's main street. As Parson Smith's ebullient twenty-year-old daughter, Juliana, editor of the club's magazine, *The Clio, a Literary Miscellany,* once explained, "Papa does not think dancing to be wrong in itself, but only that it may be a cause of offending to some."

That spring, Noah Webster had moved to Sharon. In this western Connecticut town across the border from New York's Dutchess County, he opened a small private school, in which, as he put it in an advertisement that ran on June 1 in *The Connecticut Courant,* "young gentlemen and ladies may be instructed in reading, writing, mathematics, the English language, and if desired, the Latin and Greek languages—in geography, vocal music, etc." An instant success, Webster's academy had already attracted numerous students from the area's prominent Whig families such as the children of Mrs. Theodosia Prevost (later Mrs. Aaron Burr) and of the lawyers John Canfield and Zephaniah Platt. Living in one of the perfectly proportioned square rooms in Pastor Smith's three-story house, he conducted his classes upstairs in the roomy attic with its oak rafters. All summer long, Webster had been toiling away for the three dollars a month that he was clearing from the six and two-thirds dollars he charged each student per quarter. His only break had been a brief trip to New Haven to pick up his master's degree. With advanced degrees not requiring any additional classes, all Webster had

A man who was fastidious about his appearance, Webster was a natty dresser.

to do was to give a lecture at the September 14 graduation, Yale's first public ceremony in seven years. On the afternoon of his talk, entitled "Dissertation in English on the universal diffusion of literature as introductory to the universal diffusion of Christianity," he also handed over another twenty-five dollars to President Stiles.

Juliana, her older sister, Elizabeth, and her mother, Temperance, helped the roughly one hundred guests settle in their seats in the three rooms set aside for the occasion—the parson's study, the parlor and the kitchen—which were all heated by a large fireplace. The granddaughter of William Worthington, one of Oliver Cromwell's colonels, Temperance Gale had captured Parson Smith's heart with her sharp intelligence and her stunning beauty. In 1758, right after the death of her first husband, Dr. Moses Gale of Goshen, she was caught in a rainstorm while riding on horseback through Sharon. Finding temporary shelter in Cotton Smith's magnificent home, she never left.

The three Smith women remained mostly silent while, as Juliana later put it in her diary, "the slower half of creation was laying down the law." As the hostesses picked up their knitting needles, they noticed that Webster, Parson Smith and Dr. Joseph Bellamy, a cleric from neighboring Bethlehem, were having a heated discussion regarding the proper translation of Plutarch's *Life of Hannibal*. The animus, they assumed, came from the large and stout Bellamy, an eminence grise with a reputation for terrorizing his interlocutors with sharp words. Mrs. Smith herself had recently had her own run-in with her mild-mannered husband's mentor, which required her, as she later wrote, to show "pretty plainly that I was not beholden to him for his opinions or permission." However, the precise nature of the dispute between the two pastors and the future lexicographer has been lost to history. Of this encounter, all that remains is Juliana's report that "they became as heated over a Greek word as if it were a forge fire."

According to protocol, the main event of the evening was a reading of the complete contents from the latest issue of *Clio*. Juliana was an enterprising editor who managed to garner literary forays from a wide variety of contributors. Chief among them were her brother's Yale classmates such as Abiel Holmes (later a pastor whose son was the writer Oliver Wendell Holmes, Sr.); James Kent (a future chancellor of New York State); and David Daggett (later a U.S. senator from Connecticut). As a critic, Juliana was hard to please. Just because she printed something, it didn't necessarily follow that she liked it. As she once wrote her brother, "Oh my dear Jack, I fear me there is very little promise that any of your friends will prove to be Shakespeares or Miltons."

As the evening wore on, Webster stepped into the kitchen, which, situated behind the two other rooms, gave speakers a view of the entire assemblage. He then read his latest, a moral essay, which took the form of a dream. The full text no longer remains, but the acerbic Juliana did bequeath to posterity a blanket assessment of Webster's writings for *Clio,* comparing them unfavorably to the imagined cogitations of the family's horse, Jack:

> Mr. Webster has not the excuse of youth (I think he must be fully twenty two or three), but his essays—don't be angry, Jack—are as young as yours or brother Tommy's, while his reflections are as prosy as those of our horse, your namesake, would be if they were written out. Perhaps more so, for I truly believe, judging from the way *Jack Horse* looks around at me sometimes, when I am on his back, that his thoughts of the human race and their conduct towards his own, might be well worth reading. At least they would be all *his own* and that is more than can be said of N. W.'s. In conversation, he is even duller than in writing, if that be possible, but he is a painstaking man and a hard student. Papa says he will make his mark.

Despite her sharp edge, Juliana Smith was touching on what would emerge as a central feature of Webster's literary activity. Over the course of his long career, Noah Webster, Jr., would rarely dazzle his readers with breathtaking originality. He would, indeed, make his mark on posterity but not so much for his writing as for his rewriting. His monumental contribution to American letters would be to redo the leading British works on language for a native audience. Lexicography was a perfect fit for Webster's personal tics, as it required collecting and examining ideas that were not one's own (of all the entries in his dictionary, only "demoralize" would be of his own coinage). And no one could analyze the words of others more scrupulously or with greater élan than Webster.

That night was the last time Webster would address the Sharon liter-

ary society. A week later, just as the fall term was beginning, he suddenly
closed up his school and skipped town. While Webster didn't explain his
surprising decision in his memoir, it appears that he was distraught over
a failed romance. That summer, in addition to his full load of teaching
duties, the musically accomplished Webster also directed a choir one
evening a week. And before long, he fell in love with one of his students,
Rebecca Pardee, a local beauty to whom he proposed marriage. At the
time, Rebecca was unattached, but in the fall, her former beau, Major
Patchin, who had been serving abroad in the army, returned to Sharon.
With Rebecca unable to choose between the two appealing bachelors,
she deferred to the wishes of the local clergy—a rare move even for the
times. The church elders decided in favor of the major because he had
first won her affection. Webster never wrote about this loss, but it must
have devastated him. Commenting on Webster's "pretty love romance"
with Rebecca Pardee a century later, *The Saturday Evening Post* quipped,
"Unlike most disappointed swains, he did not turn to puerile poetry for
relief. It took a whole dictionary to express his feelings."

AFTER WANDERING ACROSS Connecticut in a fruitless search for employment, Webster returned to Sharon early the following year. Back at the
Smith house, he soon began a lively correspondence with the pastor's
son, John Cotton Smith, then finishing up his junior year at Yale. A half-
dozen years younger than Webster, Smith was honored by Webster's
"condescension in writing." Perhaps attempting to soften the blow of the
rejection by Pardee, in January 1782 Smith reported on the negative
impact of marriage on Josiah Meigs, Webster's Yale classmate, who was
now his tutor: "he appears no more possessed of that vigour, sprightli-
ness and vivacity, but on the contrary anxieties and solicitudes seem to
brood upon him. . . . if this be the effect marriage produces . . . may I
get the wrong side of thirty before I put on its shackles." Steering the
dialogue away from personal concerns, Webster wrote Smith of his
dreams for himself, his friends and his nation:

American empire will be the theatre on which the last scene of the stupendous drama of nature shall be exhibited. Here the numerous and complicated parts of the actors shall be brought to a conclusion; here the impenetrable mysteries of the Divine system shall be disclosed to the view of the intelligent creation. . . . You and I may have considerable parts to act in this plan, and it is a matter of consequence to furnish the mind with enlarged ideas of men and things, to extend our wishes beyond ourselves, our friends, or our country, and include the whole system in the expanded grasp of benevolence.

For Webster, emotional setbacks resulted not in mourning, but in a ratcheting up of his fierce ambition. Doing something noteworthy, he felt, could help him regain his self-esteem. And fortunately for Webster, his grandiose fantasies surfaced at a crossroads in world history. With the Revolutionary War now winding down—that October, Lord General Cornwallis had surrendered to Washington at Yorktown—and a new nation needing to be built, Webster would soon have ample opportunity to satisfy his itch for fame and glory.

In fact, that January Noah Webster, the scribe of American identity, made his debut and, by the end of the month, had emerged as a public figure with a significant following. In late 1781, *Rivington's Royal Gazette* tried to do what British had failed to do—convince Americans to renounce their independence. The loyalist New York City newspaper carried a series of letters by Silas Deane, a former Connecticut delegate to the Continental Congress, which leaned on a recent pamphlet by Abbe Raynal, a French philosopher, to make the case for reconciling with the British. Hearing of this attempt to, in his words, "twist the meaning of the Abbe . . . in order more effectually to disunite the Americans," Webster was apoplectic. He immediately shot back with an editorial, "Observations on the Revolution," first published on January 17 in *The New York Packet* and republished two weeks later in the prominent New England paper, *The Salem Gazette*. Webster offered a different reading of Raynal's work: "A philosopher like the Abbe . . .

must see that the astonishing opposition of America to the attacks of Great Britain cannot be the fortuitous ebullition of popular frenzy; but the effect of design—the calm result of daring zeal, tempered with reason and deliberation." Over the next couple of months, Webster published three more articles, stressing that the break with Britain was permanent. "America," he emphasized, "is now an independent empire. She acknowledges no sovereign on earth, and will avow no connexions but those of friend and allies."

In the spring of 1782, Webster considered giving teaching another try in Sharon. On April 16, he distributed a prospectus, announcing his plan to open another school on May 1 in which "any young gentlemen and ladies, who wish to acquaint themselves with the English language, geography, vocal music, etc. may be waited upon for that purpose." A couple of days later, the Smith family suffered a huge loss. Thomas Mather Smith, the brother of Juliana and John Cotton Smith, died of consumption at age nineteen. And then, for the second time, Webster abandoned both his plans to teach school and his room in the Smith household under mysterious circumstances.

Webster didn't account for this hasty retreat from Sharon in his memoir, either. Though the death of Thomas Smith was not sudden—as Webster put it in a touching poem to Pastor Smith, the youth's family and friends had suffered "the pangs of six months' slow decay"—its finality may have jolted the Smiths, who perhaps no longer felt prepared to put up a houseguest. But another failed romance may also have played a role. Toward the end of his stay in Sharon, Webster had fallen for Juliana Smith, and she, too, would reject his advances. While Webster soon gave up his pursuit of the discerning editor, who, in 1784, would marry Jacob Radcliff, later the mayor of New York City, he never forgot about her. When putting together his reader a couple of years later, Webster included a brief moral essay, "Juliana: A Real Character," which reads like a love letter to the real Juliana Smith. In fact, composing these few pages made him ill. In his diary on November 1, 1784, he noted, "Writing the character of Juliana. PM very sick with a headache." "Juliana," the piece begins, "is one of those rare women whose personal attractions have no rivals." Webster goes on to heap twenty-seven paragraphs of lavish praise upon this "elegant person." Juliana possesses all those qualities that Webster holds most dear. She has "engaging manners. . . . to her superiors she shows the utmost deference and respect. To her equals . . . the most modest civility." Juliana, Webster adds, also "pays constant and sincere attention to the duties of religion" and has a "strong desire for useful information" (an attribute that was particularly enticing to the future lexicographer). In the last paragraph, Webster uncharacteristically expresses abject romantic longing: "If it is possible for her to find a man who knows her worth, and has a disposition and virtues to reward it, the union of their hearts must secure that unmingled felicity in life, which is reserved for genuine love, a passion inspired by sensibility, and improved by a perpetual intercourse of kind offices." Juliana was clearly the type of woman Noah Webster—a twenty-six-year-old bachelor when he wrote these words—was looking for in a wife. A decade later, Webster would pay another tribute to this Sharon love by naming his second child Frances Juliana.

After leaving Sharon in the spring of 1782, Webster also lost touch with Juliana's brother, John Cotton Smith, who would go on to have a distinguished career in Connecticut politics. From 1812 to 1817, Smith served as the state's last Federalist governor. Afterward, he became president of the American Bible Society and would dabble as a wordsmith. Surprisingly, after the publication of Webster's dictionary, the retired lawyer would issue harsh attacks upon the man he once revered as a teenager. In an essay "The Purity of the English Language Defended," published in *The New York Mirror* nearly six decades after Webster's Sharon sojourn, Smith would write, "It is from orthography that language receives its form and pressure; and as ours has been settled by respectable authority, and sanctioned by the best usage, the chief merit of a lexicographer . . . consists in suffering it to remain precisely as he finds it. Unfortunately, our author [Webster] thought otherwise." Smith was knocking Webster for his unique contribution to American letters—the creation of a distinct language for the new nation. That Webster first formulated this goal while living in Smith's own house didn't soften the ex-governor's stance toward his former literary society colleague. In fact, it had been to the teenage John Cotton Smith that the young Sharon teacher complained about his frustration with the leading British speller, the grumblings that eventually led to Webster's spectacularly successful school text.

IN APRIL 1782, while Webster was winding up his second sojourn in the Smith house, General George Washington moved into Hasbrouck House in Newburgh, a town in upstate New York, just across the Hudson River from Sharon. There Washington set up the new headquarters for the Continental army. While the United States had succeeded in neutralizing British forces, New York City was still in enemy hands and the war was not yet over. Though the new nation faced many challenges, Washington had to focus largely on the disbanding of the Continental army's seven thousand troops. Under the Articles of Confederation—hastily passed in 1777 and ratified in 1781—the national government had little leverage. It could not, for example, raise tax revenue. Frustrated by this arrangement, some sought quick fixes. On May 22, 1782, Colonel Lewis Nicola wrote to Washington, suggesting that he take matters into his own hands and declare himself king. Washington would have no part of this scheme. "Let me conjure you then," the General wrote back that same day, "if you have any regard for your country, concern for yourself or posterity, or respect for me, to banish these thoughts from your mind, and never communicate, as from yourself, or any one else, a sentiment of the like nature." As he waited for Benjamin Franklin and the other diplomats in Paris to complete the peace negotiations, Washington, like most of America's leaders, wasn't sure exactly what kind of country he wanted; however, the General knew what traps he wished to avoid.

After leaving Sharon, Webster spent a day in Newburgh with a friend who was an officer in Washington's army. He then moved on to the neighboring town of Goshen, located in Orange County, where he opened a classical school for the children of prominent local families. Down to his last seventy-five cents, Webster felt he could no longer afford to teach in a public school. Fortunately, his new pupils—the scions of well-to-do parents such as the pastor Nathaniel Kerr and Henry Wisner, New York's lone signer of the Declaration of Independence who would later help found the State University of New York—paid not in paper currency, but in silver dollars. This arrangement gave Webster, he later noted, "an advantage rarely enjoyed in any business at this time."

Yet Webster still longed to earn a better living in his chosen profession—law. He was also feeling lonely in this strange town outside of his native Connecticut. "In this situation of things," Webster recalled in his memoir, "his spirits failed, and for some months, he suffered extreme depression and gloomy forebodings." With the nation's overall economic picture bleak, Webster was not alone in feeling desperate. But he managed to shake himself out of despair through a creative solution. "In this state of mind," Webster added, "he formed the design of composing books for the instruction of children; and began by compiling a spelling book on a plan which he supposed to be better adapted to assist the learner, than that of Dilworth."

The Reverend Thomas Dilworth was the author of the eighteenth century's most widely used speller. Until about 1700, English spelling was all a jumble, particularly in the New World. As late as 1716, "general" was spelled "jinerll" in official Hartford documents. But soon after the first standards began to be set, a series of spellers appeared. Dilworth's *A New Guide to the English Tongue* was first published in London in 1740. Seven years later, Benjamin Franklin printed the first American edition. Focusing more on pronunciation than on orthography (correct spelling), Dilworth explained to children how to divide words into syllables. As noted in the preface, he sought to give "each letter its proper place, each syllable its right division and true accent and each word its natural sound." This was the alphabet method of teaching reading. By 1782, Dilworth's speller had reared the vast majority of English speakers on both sides of the Atlantic. As Joel Barlow once observed, Dilworth's was "the nurse of us all." Though the cleric had died in 1780, sales showed no signs of slowing down; a new edition consisting of tens of thousands of books continued to come out every year.

Having used Dilworth as a school instructor, Webster was keenly aware of its shortcomings and inconsistencies. But in revising Dilworth, Webster would grapple not only with pedagogy but also with cultural politics. During his sojourn in Goshen, the new nation's identity remained a huge question mark. Just as Americans were debating what kind of ruler they should have, they were also debating what language they should speak. After all, the English of King George III was now the language of the oppressor. Some proposed replacing it with German, then the country's unofficial second language, spoken by nearly ten percent of the population. Others advocated even more radical ideas. As the Marquis de Chastellux, a member of the French Academy and a major-general in the French army, reported on the chatter among some Bostonians in 1782, "They have gone even further, and have seriously proposed introducing a new language; and some people, for the convenience of the public, wanted Hebrew to take the place of English, it would have been taught in the schools and made use of for all public documents." And if nothing else, perhaps a name change was in order. "Let our language . . . be called the Columbian language," stated a letter that ran in newspapers across the country that year. "Let us make it as familiar to our ears to say that a foreigner speaks good Columbian, as it is to say that he speaks good English. The dignity and habits of independence can only be acquired by a total emancipation of our country from the fashions and manners of Great Britain." A new speller, Webster realized, could quickly put an end to this debate, as it would be destined to shape the speech habits of Americans for generations to come. "A spelling book," he would later write, "does more to form the language of a nation than all other books." The emotionally fragile and often despondent Noah Webster, Jr., was compelled to think big. This project with its potentially vast repercussions could well meet his pressing need for both fame and silver dollars.

Dilworth's *New Guide* contained five parts. The first part, which covered about half of the book, included syllabariums (lists of syllables) followed by tables of related words and short readings. Dilworth began by presenting columns of syllables such as "ma, me, mi, mo, mu" and "ab, eb, ib, ob, ub"; a few pages later, he provided various monosyllabic words such as "an," "as," "at," "ax" and "ay." And then to give children a chance to practice what they had learned, he featured "some early lessons on the foregoing tables." Lesson I featured the following reading:

No man may put off the Law of God.
The way of God is no ill way.
My joy is in God all the day.
A bad man is a foe to God.

Adhering to the same format, Dilworth went on to teach the pronunciation of words containing more and more syllables. The second part of Dilworth consisted solely of "a large and useful table of words that are the same in sound, but different in signification." While the third part contained a grammar, the last two parts were readers that featured fables and prayers, respectively.

Webster would eventually rework the five parts of Dilworth's speller into three separate books—the three volumes of his *A Grammatical Institute, of the English Language, Comprising, an Early, Concise, and Systematic Method of Education, Designed for the Use of English Schools in America.* The first volume, his speller, roughly paralleled the first two parts of Dilworth—consisting largely of syllable lists and the tables of homonyms. Likewise, Webster's second and third volumes—his grammar and reader—revised the third, fourth and fifth parts of Dilworth. Webster's grammar, published in March 1784, never sold too well, and he abandoned it in 1804 (though he later wrote an academic treatise, *Philosophical and Practical Grammar of the English Language*). His reader, which first appeared in February 1785, fared better, and lasted until it was superseded by the McGuffey reader in the late 1830s. But Webster's so-called blue-backed speller—the nickname derives from the thin blue paper that covered later editions—was a sensation that would stay on the market for more than a century. Its initial print run of five thousand copies was more than the total number of spellers sold in a year throughout the colonies back when Webster was a West Division schoolboy. In 1784, the second and third editions of the 120-page text were published. Nearly four dozen more editions—some with print runs as high as twenty-five thousand—would come out by the end of the eighteenth century. The tiny speller—it was about six and a quarter inches long and three and a half inches wide—was the cash cow that enabled Webster to devote the second half of his life to the dictionary. To use the nautical metaphor of his granddaughter Emily Ford, "it was the little steam tug that conveyed the large East Indiaman laden with spices and silk, or the man-of-war bristling with cannon."

Webster was not the first person to revise Dilworth, nor the first to challenge its dominance in the American marketplace. In 1756, the British author Daniel Fenning published his *Universal Spelling-Book*. Its tenth edition—the first one printed on the other side of the pond—appeared in Boston in 1769. Modeled closely on Dilworth, the text by Fenning also contained five parts, including a grammar and reader. But it also featured some material not found in Dilworth, such as a dictionary of five thousand easy words and some historical information about the kings of England.

To compose his speller, Webster did some cutting and pasting from both Dilworth and Fenning, and then added his own American touches. But though Webster's text was not entirely original, it was a seminal contribution to pedagogy. His method of instruction was the most user-friendly to date. Simple yet rigorous, Webster's book spoke directly to children in a language they could easily understand. Soon after its publication, Timothy Pickering, then the quartermaster general based in

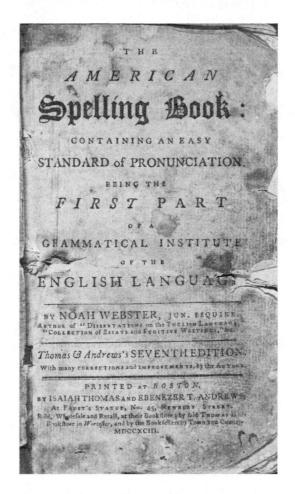

Upon the recommendation of Yale president
Ezra Stiles, Webster selected the long-winded
A Grammatical Institute of the English Language as the
title for the first edition of his speller. (This was a nod
to the Protestant theologian John Calvin, whose
seminal work was *Institutes of the Christian Religion.*)
In 1787, Webster renamed it *The American Spelling
Book,* which was close to his original title,
The American Instructor.

Newburgh and later Washington's secretary of state, stayed up all night
reading it, reporting to his wife: "The author is ingenious, and writes
from his own experience as a schoolmaster, as well as the best authori-

ties; and the time will come when no authority as an English grammarian will be superior to his own." But Webster had done more than just improve on the spelling books of his British predecessors. He had also helped give birth to a new language, which in turn would soon unite a fledgling nation. Though he didn't yet use the term "American English," his speller was a linguistic declaration of independence: "It is the business of *Americans* to select the wisdom of all nations, as the basis of her constitutions. . . . to prevent the introduction of foreign vices and corruptions and check the career of her own. . . . to diffuse an uniformity and purity of *language*—to add superiour dignity to this infant empire and to human nature." Americans, Webster asserted, would speak English, but it would be an English of their own making.

Webster consistently improved on Dilworth by supplying a greater degree of clarity. For example, Dilworth's definition of a syllable as "either one letter; as a; or more than one; as man" was confusing. In contrast, Webster's left nothing in doubt: "one letter or so many letters as can be pronounced at one impulse of the voice, as a, hand." Likewise, Webster, like Fenning before him, critiqued Dilworth's method of dividing up words according to abstract principles borrowed from Latin grammar. Webster argued that it made more sense to divide them up according to their pronunciation. "The words," he wrote in the preface, "*cluster, habit,* Mr. Dilworth divides *clu-ster ha-bit*; according to which, a child naturally pronounces the vowel in the first syllable, long. But the vowels are all short. . . . In order to obviate this difficulty, he has placed a double accent thus, *clu"ster, ha"bit.* . . . Let words be divided as they ought to be pronounced *clus-ter, hab-it.* . . . and the smallest child cannot mistake a just pronunciation." Furthermore, Webster also objected to Dilworth's insistence that "ti" before a vowel be considered a separate syllable. For words such as "na-ti-on" and "mo-ti-on," Webster preferred "na-tion" and "mo-tion," thus opting for two syllables rather than three. Besides these methodological tweaks, Webster also tailored his text for an American audience. Axing the dozen or so pages that Dilworth devoted to the spelling of English, Irish and Scottish towns, Webster inserted a list of all the states and principal towns and counties in the United States of America. In addition, for every Connecticut town, he included both its population as well as its distance in miles from the state capital, Hartford (then still the center of his own personal universe). Webster's recent addresses also crept into the book as he stuck in entries such as "Litchfield, 1509, 32" and "Sharon, 1986, 59." For towns throughout the other twelve states, he failed to feature any analogous statistical addenda.

Webster saw his rewriting of Dilworth as a necessary follow-up to the American Revolution. Just as the American military had taken on the tyrannical British government, the American literati, he felt, now had to strike out against the unwieldy English language. Their charge: to bring order to its underlying chaos. As Webster well understood, the sounds of English letters "are more capricious and irregular than those of any alphabet with which we are acquainted." In English, as opposed to many other languages, while a given vowel or consonant can denote a variety of different sounds, the same sounds can be represented by a variety of different combinations of letters. Americans, Webster believed, could create a better form of English than the British. "This country," he stressed, "must in some future time, be as distinguished by the superiority of her literary improvements, as she already is by the liberality of her civil and ecclesiastical constitutions."

His overriding linguistic goal was that Americans should adopt "one standard of elegant pronunciation." Though Webster now knew where he wanted to take the English language, he wasn't yet sure how to get there. In that 1783 first edition of his speller, he proposed only some general guidelines. Citing the greatest man of letters of ancient Rome, Cicero, the icon upon whom Benjamin Franklin and Alexander Hamilton also drew inspiration, Webster argued that "*usus est norma loquendi*" [usage should determine the rules of speech]. But he didn't specify whether the usage of one group—say, the highly educated—should take precedence over another—say, country folk. At this stage of his career, he identified the problems with regional dialects without discussing how to adjudicate between them: "I would observe that the inhabitants of New England and Virginia have a peculiar pronunciation which affords much diversion to their neighbors. . . . The dialect of one state is as ridiculous as that of another; each is authorised by local custom; and neither is supported by any superior excellence."

Though Webster pled neutrality, that's not what he felt. In fact, after a quick allusion to "a flat drawling pronunciation" among some New Englanders, he went on to describe several vulgar pronunciations commonly heard in the South, such as "reesins" for "raisins" and "woond" for "wound." In later editions, Webster would make his preference for the New England way explicit.

In this first salvo on behalf of his native tongue, Webster didn't include the spelling changes, which he would later insist on in his dictionary, and for which he became best known. Calling "Dr. Johnson's dictionary my guide," Webster here argued against expunging "superfluous letters" such as the "u" in "favour" and "honour." He supplied the following rationale: "Our language is indeed pronounced very differently from the spelling; this is an inconvenience we regret, but cannot remedy. To attempt a progressive change is idle." Webster would go back and forth on this point over the next few decades before settling on the need for limited spelling reform. But in his 1783 text, Webster did break a little new ground. For example, the speller is where Americans first learned to pronounce the twenty-sixth letter of the alphabet "zee" rather than "zed."

While Webster's speller was well suited to curry the favor of a struggling new nation, it would have not sold so well were its author not also a marketing genius. As would often be the case, Noah Webster's personal failings would be instrumental to his literary success. Precisely because of his shaky self-esteem, Webster turned out to be a natural at self-promotion; after all, talking (or writing) himself up was his way of being in the world. The first book printed in the new United States of America would benefit from the publicity tools that later became the staples of the publishing industry, including blurbs from prominent people (many of which Webster wrote himself), prepublication buzz, heated media controversy and the book tour. In the late eighteenth century, authors—not publishers—typically arranged for the financing, printing and distribution of books, and Webster would handle these practical challenges with remarkable aplomb. Over the next century, only the Bible would sell more copies in America than Webster's speller.

However, the soon-to-be literary sensation would continue to struggle with intense feelings of anxiety and alienation.

3

Traveling Salesman

PUBLICITY, n. The state of being public or open to the knowledge of a community; notoriety.

Already a seasoned networker by his early twenties, Webster tried to cash in on his connections with the well-heeled. In the fall of 1782, he headed south from Goshen to the nation's capital, Philadelphia, armed with a letter of introduction by Henry Wisner, then a prominent member of the New York State Senate, which began, "Mr. Noah Webster has taught a grammar school for some time past in this place, much to the satisfaction of his employers. He is now doing some business in the literary way, which will, in the opinion of good judges, be of great service to posterity." Webster had just completed a draft of his book, and the purpose of his business trip was twofold: "showing my manuscripts to gentlemen of influence and obtaining a law for securing to authors the copy-right of their publications." From scholars and statesmen, Webster sought both advice and endorsements as well as help in protecting his intellectual property. Piracy was then common. As Joel Barlow had warned him that summer, "The printers make large impressions of it [Dilworth] and afford it very cheap." To become America's first self-sustaining freelance writer, Webster would take it upon himself to become the father of American copyright law.

In Philadelphia, he briefly intersected with such luminaries as the Virginia delegates Thomas Jefferson and James Madison, from whom he learned that the Congress of the Confederation lacked the authority to pass a national copyright law. Webster then tried to take his campaign to the state legislatures of both Pennsylvania and New Jersey, but neither was in session. But though he had ready access to the corridors of power—in Trenton, he met personally with Governor William Livingston—he came up empty-handed. Upon his return to Goshen in October, all he had to show for his travels was an endorsement from Dr. Samuel Smith, a professor of theology in Princeton, who wrote of "the many useful improvements" in his speller. That month, he turned his attention to the state legislature in his native Connecticut. To make the case to his friend John Canfield, a state representative, Webster solicited a recommendation from the Litchfield legal scholar, Tapping Reeve, who characterized the work as "well conceived and judiciously executed." In January, he confessed to Canfield that his trilogy was leaving him close to another breakdown: "I have been indefatigable this winter; I have sacrificed ease, pleasure and health to the execution of it, and have nearly completed it. But such close application is too much for my constitution." But public acceptance soon came. Later that month, Connecticut passed America's first copyright law. By the end of the year, with additional prodding by Webster, New York, Massachusetts, Maryland, New Jersey, New Hampshire and Rhode Island all fell into line.

Giving up his teaching post, the twenty-four-year-old Webster moved back to Hartford, then still a farming village of just three hundred houses and twenty-five hundred residents, to arrange for publication of his speller. He initially stayed with John Trumbull, who had recently completed the transition from poet to high-powered attorney. In Connecticut's co-capital, Webster was pleased to reconnect with his Yale classmates Oliver Wolcott, then beginning his legal career, and Joel Barlow, who continued to write poetry while working as a publisher. Webster's first order of business was to negotiate a deal for his speller with Hudson and Goodwin, the firm that published *The Connecticut Courant*. To pay the printing costs, Webster relied on the largesse of his friends. Showing what Webster later called "generosity [that] far exceeded his means,"

Barlow helped out with five hundred dollars; Trumbull made an even more substantial donation. For the rest, Webster submitted a promissory note, which the company agreed to accept in return for the author's promise to let them print subsequent editions. On September 16, 1783, just two weeks after the Treaty of Paris, which officially ended the American Revolution, Webster placed an ad in the *Courant,* highlighting the distinguishing features of his forthcoming text: "The sounds of our vowels which are various and capricious are ascertained by the help of figures. . . . words are so divided as to lead to a just pronunciation . . . the irregular and difficult words are collected in an alphabetical table with the true spelling in one and the true pronunciation in another." While individual copies cost fourteen pence, to promote sales to schools, Webster offered a bulk discount of fourteen shillings per dozen—a marketing strategy that would work splendidly.

But Webster was just beginning his media campaign. On October 14, 1783, a week after the official publication date, his *Grammatical Institute* commandeered the front page of the *Courant.* Webster had placed a long endorsement signed by several key local officials, including George Wyllys, Connecticut's secretary of state; his brother Samuel Wyllys, the major general of the Connecticut militia; Thomas Seymour, soon to become Hartford's first mayor; and Nathan Strong, the influential pastor at the First Church of Hartford. Also lending their names to Webster's cause were Trumbull and Barlow, as well as his former tutor, Nathan Perkins. And next to this ad, under the byline N.W., appeared an essay on the state of language in America which began, "It is surprising to consider how much the English language has been neglected and how little understood by those who have undertaken to compile dictionaries, grammars and spelling books." Though Webster was still two days removed from his twenty-fifth birthday, he was already comparing himself to the greats in the history of English lexicography. Then finishing up the second part of the trilogy, Webster here focused on some of the key points in that volume such as the faults of prior grammars such as Dilworth's. But he concluded with his sweeping vision: "The author's design is to publish a general system of English education. . . . we should remember that unless the Greeks and Romans had taken more pains with their language than we do with ours they would not have been so celebrated by modern nations." With his trilogy, which would bring order to his native tongue through rules and standards, Webster hoped to help America become a worthy successor to the Roman Empire.

Webster's promotional campaign oscillated between invoking such lofty goals and issuing harsh critiques of his predecessors. Though Webster raised many valid objections to works such as Dilworth's, his tone was contemptuous. While partisan attack was the lifeblood of late eighteenth-century American journalism, Noah Webster fell into vilifying his opponents more easily than most. A by-product of his tempestuous temperament, ad hominem assault worked its way into nearly all his writing, not just his newspaper editorials. With his speller, as with his dictionary, the man whose father had emotionally abandoned him at twenty would attempt to slay his literary forefathers. In the preface, Webster shredded Dilworth: "In short, though his spelling book was a great improvement upon former methods of education, yet almost every part of it was originally defective." Webster was no more respectful toward his other sources. At the back of his speller, he inserted "The Story of Tommy and Harry" from Fenning's *Universal Spelling-Book,* adding in a footnote, "In the original, the language is flat, puerile and ungrammatical; for which reason I have taken the liberty to make material alterations." Noting such zealousness, Webster's supporters gently chided him. Writing from New Hampshire a month after the speller's publication, Buckminster opined, "I am pleased with the spirit and stile of your introduction, think however you are a little too severe upon our friend, Mr. Dilworth. . . . it is a wonder if an ill natured world does not ascribe some of the observations not so much to his deficiencies as to a desire to give a currency to your Institute." As Buckminster predicted, critics would soon jump on Webster for his arrogance. But once again, Webster's character flaw came in handy. The charged attacks on Webster created a media frenzy, which, in turn, put the spotlight on his books and boosted their sales still further.

———

WEDNESDAY, MAY 19, 1784, was to be a day of reckoning for both Webster's state and his country. The Lower House of Connecticut's General Assembly was slated to consider the subject of the national impost. And Noah Webster was eager to witness both the dramatic debate and the ensuing vote, which would also be a referendum on the power of his own words.

That afternoon, Webster walked out of his rented room at the house of Captain John Skinner and headed up the recently renamed Main Street (formerly King's Highway), which was still all there was to Hartford. As the Marquis de Chastellux reported during his visit in the early 1780s, Hartford "did not merit much attention" because the whole town was then little more than this "long street parallel with the river." Webster's destination was the state house, located on Main Street's north end. Built in 1720, when Connecticut's steadily growing legislative bodies could no longer fit snugly into taverns, the two-story structure was just seventy feet long and thirty feet wide. Dubbed the "Court House" by locals, it was divided into two equal-sized chambers—the Lower House and the Upper House. As Webster made his way through the side door up to the gallery, already filled with anxious spectators, he could not help but notice that the building was in ill repair. A year earlier, during a celebration that marked the end of the Revolution, a fire had coursed through the balcony and singed most of the cupola. Settling back in his seat, Webster began to replay in his mind the key moments in the yearlong controversy—one in which he had been a central participant—that had led up to this fateful moment. In his memoir, he described the backstory:

> In the summer of 1783, commenced a popular opposition to the act
> of Congress which granted extra pay to the officers of the American
> army, to indemnify them for the losses they had incurred by being

paid in a depreciated currency. This opposition was most general and violent in Connecticut. . . . To oppose this grant of Congress, the citizens, in many towns, appointed delegates for the purpose of holding a convention at Middletown. In the first meeting there was not a majority of the towns represented; but at the second meeting, more than fifty towns, being five sevenths of the state, were represented. In this convention, some resolves were proposed against the act of Congress. . . . In this crisis N.W. commenced writing a series of papers with different signatures.

Though the Middletown Convention, as Webster also noted, "ended in smoke" early that spring, opposition to the officers' pension, which was to be funded by a national impost—a value-added tax of five percent—still ran high among Connecticut denizens. Under the Articles of Confederation, the passage of any amendment required unanimous approval by all thirteen state legislatures; thus, Connecticut's final verdict on this new national tax had vast repercussions. As James Madison and other members of the Continental Congress warned, should Connecticut succeed in thwarting the will of the other twelve states that supported the measure, anarchy could well result across the new country.

Siding with Madison, Webster had been busy firing off dozens of editorials since the previous August. His mission, he later wrote, was "enlightening and tranquilizing the minds of his fellow citizens." His first piece, "An Address to the discontented people of America," published in *The Connecticut Courant* on August 26, 1783, began with the disclaimer, "I am not fond of scribling [*sic*] in public papers. It is a business by which little good is to be done and less reputation to be acquired." But Webster the writer often denied what Webster the man was thinking and feeling. In fact, Noah Webster, Jr., loved nothing more than to voice his opinion in the newspaper, and he never failed to aim high.

For the petulant Webster, by defending the actions of Congress, he was standing up against both chaos and evil itself. Going into his natural attack mode, he identified those he disagreed with as enemies to his country. Failing to express any empathy for the protesters who met at Middletown, he portrayed them all as violent thugs. In one of several pieces written under the pseudonym "Honorius,"* (the name of the Whig protagonist, modeled on John Adams, in the 1775 mock-epic poem "McFingal" by John Trumbull), Webster declared in September that "the resolves of some towns in this state . . . amount to high treason against the United States and render the leaders liable to an impeachment." But though Webster's vitriol may have been unwarranted, his political judgment proved remarkably astute. He was way ahead of the curve in understanding that the Articles of Confederation hadn't created a strong enough central government. In "An Address to the *thinking judicious* inhabitants of Connecticut," published on September 30, 1783, "Honorius" attempted to win over the unthinking and foolish: "There is one consolation, however, that must ease the mind of a well wisher to his country—which is that these convulsions will terminate in a general conviction of the necessity of a supreme power and a more peaceable acquiescence in their decrees."

Throughout the fall of 1783, Webster cast aspersions on Connecticut's rebels. In November, he published an unsigned letter to the editor of the *Courant*, addressed "To Mr. Respondent, Probus, Agricola, & c." His purpose, he claimed, was to protect "Honorius" from an "ambuscade" by these myriad writers, whom he assumed to be the same person. However, Webster's missive was more offense than defense. He maintained that the writing of his enemy lacked "some little degree of respectability." While Webster charged his interlocutor with hiding behind "different garbs," he also went on to assume a variety of different identities. On December 30, two weeks after the third Middletown Convention, Webster took to an anonymous poem to ridicule his foes as Tories eager to destroy the fruits of the Revolution:

---

* Throughout the eighteenth century, journalists often used pseudonyms to express political opinions.

How every member of Convention,

Tortures his brains and racks invention,

To blast good men and in their place

Foist knaves and fools with better grace:

O'erturn our happy constitution,

Reduce all order to confusion,

With want of laws make mankind groan,

And on their miseries raise a throne.

Putting "Honorius" to rest after a final send-off in January 1784, Webster resurfaced as the officers' prime defender in two editorials signed "A.Z." published that January and February.

But early in 1784, Webster suddenly changed his tack. Steering clear of polemical prose, he began making broad appeals for American unity in a series of unsigned essays entitled "Policy of Connecticut" that would run both in the *Courant* and in New London's *Connecticut Gazette* throughout the first half of 1784. Few of Webster's contemporaries realized that these sober assessments of Connecticut affairs were written by the same person who had penned the vituperative "Honorius" essays. In fact, many assumed that Jonathan Trumbull, the outgoing governor of Connecticut (and father of the celebrated painter John Trumbull), was the anonymous author. Nicknamed "Brother Jonathan," the popular Trumbull, who was the only Colonial governor to stay in power after the Revolution, firmly backed the officers' pension. In March, sounding much like Connecticut's seventy-three-year-old sage, who was also known for his discriminating way with words, Webster conceded that the national impost was a necessary evil: "And I have no doubt that after people become acquainted with the utter impossibility of opposing the whole continent, they will ultimately close those wild schemes with this rational reflection; that of the two evils, they ought to choose the least. . . ." Calm reason had also come over Webster himself.

As the debate began in the Lower House, Webster was feeling hopeful. After all, the fourth meeting of the Middletown Convention in mid-March had been a bust. Likewise, the results of the statewide election, held on May 11, augured well. Of the new Assembly delegates, some three-quarters now expressed support for the government. At the same time, Webster had some cause for concern. In February, the impost had been defeated by a vote of 69 to 37, with only delegates from the commercial centers such as New London and Norwich showing much enthusiasm. Likewise, in the election the previous week, Trumbull's loyal longtime lieutenant governor, Matthew Griswold, had received just 2,192 out of the 6,853 votes cast by the freemen. While the Assembly voted Griswold into the governor's office a few days later, his failure to attain a majority suggested lukewarm support for Trumbull's policies. Though both the Upper House and new governor were squarely behind the measure, there was no guarantee that the Lower House would come through.

And when Erastus Wolcott, who had served as brigadier general during the Revolution, took to the floor to argue for a state impost rather than a national impost, Webster became anxious. One of fourteen children of the Colonial governor Roger Wolcott, Erastus Wolcott was a well-to-do farmer from East Windsor. But unlike his brother, Oliver Wolcott, Sr., and his nephew, Oliver Wolcott, Jr., Webster's college classmate, Erastus Wolcott had only a grade-school education. However, the general was skilled in representing the interests of Connecticut's agrarian majority and its small manufacturers. As Wolcott argued, the state impost, by taxing articles made abroad such as hats and clocks, would shift more of the financial burden to the state's growing professional and commercial class.

The debate pitted both the rural inland communities against the coastal towns and Noah Webster's past against his present. While Webster was of the land, he was now a proud hat-wearing Connecticut professional. Leading the other side was General Samuel Holden Parsons, a New London native who had also emerged as a celebrity due to his war record. A Harvard graduate and respected lawyer, Parsons had served on the board of officers that had condemned to death Benedict Arnold's accomplice in treason, Major John André. The nephew of the new governor, Parsons, who would later endorse Webster's speller, countered Wolcott by emphasizing the importance of national unity.

At five o'clock, the question was finally put to all the delegates. Webster and the other spectators all held their breath. And then just like that, the controversy was all over. Yeas were 93. Nays were 42.

Of this vote, Webster, who was rarely jubilant, noted in his journal, "A happy event!"

As Webster returned home from the state house, he came across Stephen Mix Mitchell, then a newly elected member of the governor's twelve-man Council of Assistants and later the chief justice of the state supreme court. "You Sir," Mitchell told him, "have done more to appease public discontent and produce a favorable change, than any other person." Two days later, at a retirement ceremony in which a vast retinue accompanied "Brother Jonathan" back to his family home in Lebanon, the governor also personally thanked Webster for his service to his state and his country.

Webster the public scribe would have the last word on this historic vote. In an anonymous article published the following Tuesday in the *Courant*, he wrote, "Never did people in general feel more satisfaction at any public measure than in consequence of this act."

LESS THAN TWO WEEKS LATER, on June 1, 1784, the very day that the second printing of the speller was released, Webster rode from Hartford to the small Connecticut town of Canterbury. He was off on a promotional tour around New England to meet with scholars, publishers and booksellers. Over the next week, he would weave back and forth between Providence, Worcester, Newport and Boston. To mark his arrival in a new venue, he would place an ad in the local newspaper, in which he mentioned where his book was to be sold. News of the speller appeared in several papers that month, including *The Massachusetts Spy: Or*

Worcester Gazette, The Providence Gazette and Country Journal and *The Newport Mercury*. In Boston, he drank an evening tea with James Bowdoin, then a Massachusetts state legislator. The future Bay State governor held considerable influence among the literati, as he was also the first president of the newly established American Academy of Arts and Sciences. In Cambridge, Webster's after-dinner host was Joseph Willard, the president of Harvard, who had recently penned an endorsement of the speller. After a brief stop in Newburyport, Webster rode on to New Hampshire. On Sunday, June 13, he saw his former Yale tutor, Joseph Buckminster, give a sermon at the North Church in Portsmouth.

During his week in Portsmouth, Webster's quest for a bride was often on his mind. Throughout his twenties, Webster was constantly surveying the landscape for attractive women, and it didn't take long for him to be smitten. But he wasn't winning over too many hearts. Shortly before leaving Hartford, he had written in his diary, "If there were but one pretty girl in town, a man could make a choice, but among so many, one's heart is pulled in twenty ways at once. The greatest difficulty, however, is that after a man has made *his* choice, it remains for the lady to make *hers*." Of his second night in Portsmouth, he was filled with more romantic longing: "Took a view of the town. Drank tea at Dr. [Joshua] Bracketts. At evening attended a ball and was agreeably entertained; had a fine partner, but she is engaged." A couple of days later, Webster was also wistful after spending an evening in the elegantly wainscoted home of Colonel John Langdon and his striking wife, Elizabeth. As a commander of light horse volunteers at Saratoga, Langdon had personally witnessed Burgoyne's surrender; then a leading member of the New Hampshire state senate, Langdon would later take a turn as both the state's senator and governor. Of Mrs. Langdon, whom the Marquis de Chastellux had described a couple of years earlier as "young, fair and tolerably handsome," Webster jotted down in his diary, "a most beautiful woman, 20 years younger than her husband."

Webster returned home to Hartford on July 3. The following week, he moved into his new Main Street lodgings, the home of Dr. Eliakim

Fish, an eminent physician who later became the first president of the Hartford County Medical Society. Though he apprenticed himself to his Yale mentor, John Trumbull, he found little legal work. His only gainful employment was promoting his own books. Webster spent most of his time reading. But the lack of purposeful activity left him feeling anxious and depressed. On Saturday, August 7, he lamented in his diary, "Did nothing worthy of particular notice." Without a new literary project, he soldiered on as best he could. A few days later, he noted, "Read a little law and some poetry, if a man lays up a few ideas every day and arranges them, it is enough." The following day, he added, "*Ibidem*" [the same]. His taste in books extended to history, politics and literary criticism. Fiction, which in the late eighteenth century was not to be confused with literature—that term was reserved for the classics or scientific writing—rarely made much of an impression. After finishing *Betsy Thoughtless,* a popular Bildungsroman by Eliza Haywood about an independent woman who leaves her abusive husband, he observed, "Novels will not bear reading but once. It would be well if people would not permit children to read romances, till they were arrived to maturity of judgement."

Unlike his idol Samuel Johnson, Webster did not have a literary sensibility. Stories rarely captivated him. His commonplace book illustrates the analytic detachment with which he read fiction. This notebook, to which he added for about two decades after his Yale graduation, includes a few passages from Henry Fielding's bawdy 1749 novel, *The History of Tom Jones.* What Webster found worth recording was not any moving adventure, but the author's definitions. At the beginning of the sprawling novel, one character dies of "a broken heart," an affliction which Fielding describes as "a distemper which kills many more than is generally imagined, and would have a fair title to a place in the bills of mortality, did it not differ in one instance from all other diseases, viz., that no physician can cure it." Above this passage, Webster superimposed in big, block letters the word that Fielding has just defined—"DESPAIR." For Webster, reading great works of literature could prove relaxing to the extent that it gave him a chance to classify and arrange concepts. He would follow his own dictum, mentioned in a 1790 essay, to "always endeavor to read with some particular object."

The one activity that Webster relished during the summer of 1784 was responding to the speller's most vociferous critic, a man who called himself "Dilworth's Ghost." Though the Ghost, who sometimes went by D.G., never revealed his true identity, he appears to have been a retired schoolteacher from Dutchess County named Hughes. He first surfaced in a letter addressed to "Mr. N—W——, A.M. alias Esq." that was published in *The Freeman's Chronicle* on June 24, 1784. The Ghost mounted a vigorous campaign to assassinate Webster's character. Standing up for the author of Dilworth's speller, his supposed bodily incarnation, the Ghost accused Webster of engaging in a sleight of hand: "You accuse me very invidiously and without sufficient cause of absurdity and falsity, and afterward adopt what you had censured in me." While the Ghost's first piece rambled, it kept coming back to the charge of plagiarism. In addition, the Ghost was incensed by Webster's lack of modesty. Mocking Webster's pride in his titles, the Ghost wondered: "As from A. M. in part the first, you have risen to Esquire in part the second, may it not be expected that you will appear benighted in the third part and dub yourself Sir N—h &c. or perhaps, from 'We' to 'We ourself,' which must undoubtedly entitle you to all the respect that can be due to an imperial despot." On account of his New England peregrinations, Webster didn't see the Ghost's handiwork when it was first published. In his absence, Barlow, calling himself "Thomas Dilworth," fired back a widely circulated letter that characterized the Ghost "as abusive a scribbler as ever disgraced the annals of literature."

Not known for his playfulness, Webster nevertheless had some fun when he finally got around to his own rebuttals. Quickly realizing that every manifestation of the Ghost would help to move his product, he encouraged "his Ghostship" to keep writing. Webster also came up with a few choice barbs of his own. "That the publication referred to is the publication of a Ghost," he wrote in early July, "I have no doubt for no being on this earth is capable of such a ghostly performance." On July 22, Webster penned a long letter to *The New York Journal* in which he went point by point through all of the Ghost's attacks. Regarding the Ghost's chief complaint, he mused: "I am accused of compiling and transcribing. The accuser ought, however, to remember that every grammar that was ever written was a compilation. The materials of all English grammars are the same, and that man who arranges the principles of the languages in the best form and reduces the ideas to the easiest method compiles the *best* grammar." Here, Webster was not only fending off the Ghost, but he was also saying something fundamental about the obsession that would drive his literary output for the remaining six decades of his life. His grammar, like his dictionary, required that he be a compiler, arranger and organizer. For Webster, this vocation was no shame—far from it. In fact, he considered bringing order to the raw materials of others a divine calling.

Much to Webster's delight, over the next nine months, other critics took up the Ghost's mantle and kept attacking the *Grammatical Institute* in the Connecticut papers. In its first issue published on November 21, 1784, *The Litchfield Monitor* ran letters signed "A Learner of English Grammar" and "Entity" that also challenged Webster's ideas about pronunciation. Undaunted, Webster gleefully responded a couple of months later, "The Ghost has now appeared in a different shape. From a substantial spectre in a state of probation, he has transmigrated into an Entity, a mere physical existence. . . . But under whatever shape or name my enemies are introduced to notice, they will answer all my purposes if they will rail at the Institute as much as possible." An anonymous poet would have the final word about the controversy in March 1785:

He Dilworth's Ghost? Tis all a fiction! . . .
Could Dilworth see his name thus stolen . . .

His wrath sink Entity to non-existence
And strike the grammar learning dabster
A deadlier blow than he's struck Webster.

With Dilworth's Ghost and his allied spirits improving his visibility throughout New England, Webster also had to combat charges that he himself had composed their invectives.

The net result of the Ghost's efforts to smear Webster was that sales of the speller doubled, from five hundred to a thousand copies a week. By early 1785, as the public wrangling was starting to die down, Webster had sold some twelve thousand books—an astounding number in a country of just three million. He then began selling new publishers the rights to market his book in other states, and the sales figures began to rise exponentially. But the impoverished Webster was forced to ask for cash up front—a move that would cost him dearly in the long run. If he had been able to hold out for a decent royalty rate, he would have become inordinately wealthy. As Webster lamented several years later, "Could I have kept my copyright in my own hands . . . I might now have rid in a chariot." In 1786, Benjamin Edes of Boston paid five pounds, ten shillings per every thousand copies. Two years later, Philadelphia's William Young and New York's Samuel Campbell also finalized contracts with Webster. While Young published the speller in Pennsylvania, Delaware, Maryland and Virginia, Campbell took over operations in New York, New Jersey, North Carolina and South Carolina. Campbell got a bargain, paying just eighty pounds (two hundred dollars) for a five-year period, during which he would sell nearly two hundred thousand copies.

A few other regional deals for the speller ensued, but in June of 1788, New Hampshire made the Constitution the law of the land, and as Webster was quick to observe, he was suddenly confronting an entirely new marketplace. On June 25, 1788, Webster, putting all patriotic sentiment aside, wrote Isaiah Thomas, the Worcester printer and publisher: "This day we have received the intelligence that the *ninth* state has

ratified the federal constitution. This constitution will place the regulation of literary property in the power of Congress and of course the
existing laws of the several states will be superseded by a federal law.
This will enable me to enter into new contracts with regard to the publication of the Institute." As it turned out, the U.S. Congress didn't pass
the national copyright law until 1790. From that time on, authors held
the rights to their books for fourteen years. In 1804, after the initial term
for his speller expired, Webster began working out new contracts with
his publishers for an updated edition, *The American Spelling Book, Revised.* Between 1783 and 1804, Webster managed to sell some eighty-
eight different editions of his speller. Sifting through all the contracts
with various publishers, one historian has estimated that a typical edition
translated into about twelve thousand copies, meaning that Webster sold
about a million books by the time he filed for that second national copyright. During his lifetime, Webster would peddle nearly thirteen million
copies.

But after his death in 1843, *The Elementary Spelling Book* (the title
for all editions published after 1829) would enter its heyday, with sales
averaging more than a million a year. By the 1840s, the publisher, George
Cooledge, was so concerned that he wasn't printing Webster's book fast
enough that he constructed a new steam press. Cooledge eventually
bumped up his rate to 525 copies an hour or 5,250 a day. Summing up
the career of Webster's 1783 creation, H. L. Mencken wrote in the early
twentieth century, "The influence of his Speller was really stupendous.
It took the place in the schools of Dilworth's . . . [book], the favorite of
the Revolutionary generation, and maintained its authority for nearly a
century."

Along with the speller's wide circulation came enormous cultural
influence across the nation. Speaking at a hundredth birthday celebration for Webster in September 1858, Jefferson Davis, then a Mississippi
senator, declared, "Above all other people we are one, and above all
books which have united us in the bond of a common language, I place
the good-old spelling book of Noah Webster. We have a unity of lan-

guage which no other people possess and we owe this unity above all to Noah Webster's Yankee spelling book." And even when the North and South started slaughtering each other on the battlefield a few years later, southern leaders such as Davis, later the president of the Confederate States of America, never wavered in their attachment to this cornerstone of Yankee culture. During the Civil War, Confederate publishers such as the Macon, Georgia, house of Burke, Boykin and Co. put out their own versions of *The Elementary Spelling Book,* which were virtual reprints except for a few minor changes "to suit the present condition of affairs." This Georgia rendering of "the cheapest, the best and the most extensively used spelling book ever published" sold so briskly that by 1865, it was already in its third printing.

Webster's speller also gave rise to America's first national pastime, the spelling bee. Before there was baseball or college football or even horse racing, there was the spectator sport that Webster put on the map. Though "the spelling match" first became a popular community event shortly after Webster's textbook became a runaway best seller, its origins date back to the classroom in Elizabethan England. In his speller, *The English Schoole-Maister,* published in 1596, the British pedagogue Edmund Coote described a method of "how the teacher shall direct his schollers to oppose one another" in spelling competitions. A century and a half later, in his essay, "Idea of the English School," Benjamin Franklin wrote of putting "two of those [scholars] nearest equal in their spelling" and "let[ting] these strive for victory each propounding ten words every day to the other to be spelt." Webster's speller transformed these "wars of words" from classroom skirmishes into community events. By 1800, evening "spelldowns" in New England were common. As one early twentieth-century historian has observed:

> The spelling-bee was not a mere drill to impress certain facts upon the plastic memory of youth. It was also one of the recreations of adult life, if recreation be the right word for what was taken so seriously by every one. [We had t]he spectacle of a school trustee stand-

ing with a blue-backed Webster open in his hand while gray-haired men and women, one row being captained by the schoolmaster and the other team by the minister, spelled each other down.

From New England, "spelling schools" migrated to the Midwest. As Edward Eggleston wrote in his 1871 novel, *The Hoosier Schoolmaster,* "In fact, spelling is the 'national game' in Hoopole County. Baseball and croquet matches are as unknown as Olympian chariot races. Spelling and shucking are the only competitions." This regional interest fed into today's Scripps National Spelling Bee, established in 1925. In a tribute to the prime mover behind the tournament, *Webster's* has always served as its dictionary of record.

IN THE FALL OF 1784, a year after the publication of his speller, Webster had considerable cachet but little cash. He was a well-connected and respected member of the Hartford community, but his professional life was going nowhere. A novice lawyer who wouldn't plead his first case before a jury until February 1785, Webster would often go to the courthouse just to watch the proceedings. In September, he heard the case of General Erastus Wolcott, who had sued a neighbor for flooding his property. "Verdict for the defent," Webster wrote in his diary that night. Gradually he picked up a few clients of his own. In November, he represented the West Division's Stephen Bidwell in a case in which the judge was none other than Noah Webster, Sr. But while he was still trying to get his legal career off the ground, Webster continued to move in elite social circles. On October 12, when the Marquis de Lafayette, then on his nineteen-hundred-mile victory tour around America, came to Hartford, Webster attended the ceremonial dinner held at David Bull's tavern—known to locals as "Bunch of Grapes"—on the west side of Main Street. Though he enjoyed rubbing elbows with George Washington's adopted French son, Webster couldn't shake his financial anxiety. That night, he wrote in his diary, "Money is so scarce that I cannot

borrow 30£ for a few weeks, giving 12 pr cent interest and good security." But the impoverished Webster was not despondent, as he could
always fall back on his string of literary successes. Four days later, he
summed up where he stood, "My birthday. 26 years are past. I have lived
long enough to be good and of some importance."

What also boosted Webster's spirits was his favorite hobby—dancing.
Though his search for a permanent partner wasn't proving successful, he
kept jumping back out onto the dance floor. On October 26, he arranged
a dance at his house, reporting the next morning in his diary, "Much
fatigued." In mid-November, he attended a family dance at the house of
Joel Barlow, recently married to his college sweetheart, Ruth Baldwin.
A few weeks later, Webster participated in a ball at William Collier's
tavern; "25 Gentlemen and 53 Ladies" was his summary of the evening
in his diary. At the end of the year, Webster and Barlow helped put together a subscription assembly, which held biweekly dances through the
end of March. On December 31, the day following the first assembly,
Webster noted, "Feel exceedingly well after dancing; close the year." In
a 1790 essay, "Address to Young Gentlemen," Webster described dancing as a necessary outlet for a budding writer: "Its excellence consists in
exciting a cheerfulness of the mind, highly essential to health; in bracing
the muscles of the body and in producing copious perspiration. . . . The
body must perspire, or must be out of order." While Webster the public
scribe would later advise women not to take dancing too seriously—"No
man ever marries a woman for her performance on a harpsichord or her
figure in a minuet"—Webster the private citizen may well have felt otherwise. He kept an eye out for beauty, grace and talent. During the
winter season, his landlord's daughter, Rebecca Fish, made quite an impression: "At evening attend Assembly, very agreeable. Saw Miss Becca
Fish dance a minuet for the first time; of 3 ladies, she did best."

ON FEBRUARY 5, 1785, Webster finished going over the page proofs for
the third part of his *Grammatical Institute*. Two and a half weeks later, he

announced its publication in the *Courant,* stating that his new book contained "the rules of *reading* and *speaking* . . . calculated to form the morals and improve the understanding of youth." Though Webster briefly alluded to the rules of elocution, this volume was largely a reader, which included selections from both "British writers of eminence" and some American men of letters. With American literature then little more than a concept, Webster had to improvise. He drafted a few short compositions of his own (including "Juliana," that essay about his former love interest, Juliana Smith) and threw in a few unpublished poems from his Yale friends Joel Barlow and Timothy Dwight. As an inveterate compiler and arranger, Webster was once again not so much creating as revising. In this case, his models were books such as the 1780 text *Exercises in Elocution,* by British minister William Enfield, then in use in several American colleges, and *The New England Primer,* the primary school reader that dated back to the late seventeenth century. The various editions of *The New England Primer* were awash with religious tales and maxims, and as Webster wrote in the preface, he objected to this practice because the "common use of Bible is a kind of prostitution of divine truth to secular purposes." Webster retooled his reader in 1787 under the title *An American Selection of Lessons in Reading and Speaking Calculated to Improve the Minds and Refine the Taste of Youth and also to Instruct Them in the Geography, History and Politics of the United States.* This version included a fiercely patriotic epigraph from the French statesman Mirabeau: "Begin with the infant in his cradle: Let the first word he lisps be Washington."

Just as Webster was bringing his reader to press, he was starting on another project, a political treatise inspired by discussions with his fellow writers in Hartford, a circle that would soon gain national recognition as "the Connecticut wits." On December 28, Webster reported in his diary, he "formed regulations for the literary club." This group, which would distinguish itself by its satire-laced federalism, would eventually include Barlow, Timothy Dwight, John Trumbull and David Humphreys (Washington's aide-de-camp during the war), as well as the physicians Lemuel Hopkins and Elihu Smith. At the next meeting, the club "converse[d] upon the great question: What are the means of improving and establishing the union of the United States." Just a month later, Webster dashed off his own pamphlet on the subject that he entitled *Sketches of American Policy.*

As Webster noted in the *Courant* ad of March 8 that announced the publication of his *Sketches,* the fifty-page pamphlet consisted of four "heads":

I. Theory of Government

II. Governments on the Eastern Continent

III. American States; or the principles of the American Constitutions contrasted with those of the Eastern States

IV. Plan of policy for improving the advantages and perpetuating the union of the American states

Webster later admitted that the first three sections contained "chimerical notions" and were "general." The first sketch borrowed heavily from Rousseau's *Social Contract,* which he had just read and whose "visionary ideas" he would later reject. In the second, Webster lamented that most European governments were despotic and relied on superstition and military force to command their subjects. The third highlighted the unique opportunity possessed by Americans to design a new government during "the most enlightened period of the world." In contrast, Webster would consider the fourth, which advocated handing over more power to the federal government, one of his crowning achievements. Reflecting back on all his political writings on American unity during the mid-1780s, Webster would later contend that he played a pivotal role in designing the Constitution. "I know of no other person," he wrote in 1804, "who took the same active part in or who devoted half the time to the subject [proving the necessity of a new federal compact] as I did."

In that final sketch, Webster offered his prescriptions for his struggling and fragmented nation. The centerpiece of his plan to ward off anarchy was to transform the "Policy in Connecticut"—the title of his anonymously authored series in the *Courant* published the preceding year—into "American policy." If the country as a whole could be run like his Congregationalist haven, Webster argued, it could be just as harmonious, "like nature in the planetary system." For Webster, Connecticut's particular nexus of executive, legislative and judicial authority, in which his father had served proudly (albeit in a small role), was a model of peaceful governance. "The state," he wrote, "elects a governor or supreme magistrate and cloaths him with the whole power to make the laws. . . . Thus the whole power of the state is brought to a single point—united in a single person." While a new executive called a "president" did make it into the Constitution, not so for some of Webster's other recommendations—namely, his pleas for the abolition of slavery and "a general diffusion of knowledge among all classes of men."

Most leaders of the early Republic would later concede that Webster's efforts were instrumental in shaping the contours of the new central government. In 1804, James Madison, then Jefferson's secretary of state, wrote to Webster:

> It is certain that the general idea of revising and enlarging the scope of the federal authority, so as to answer the necessary purposes of the union, grew up in many minds, and by natural degrees, during the experienced inefficacy of the old confederation. The discernment of General Hamilton must have rendered him an early patron of the idea. That the public attention was called to it by yourself at an early period is well known.

Besides Madison and Hamilton, the two chief authors of *The Federalist,* other key advocates for a stronger union were Thomas Paine, Patrick Henry and Pelatiah Webster, Noah's older cousin, a Pennsylvania merchant who had authored an influential but little-read 1783 essay, *Dissertation of the Political Union and Constitution of the Thirteen United*

States of North America. But while Webster had not produced something entirely original, he had made his singular contribution by his thoughtful compiling and arranging, as well as his clear articulation of critical points.

Webster's highly regarded fourth sketch also argued for cultural unity—to wit, a uniformity of manners between North and South. He professed to take a neutral stance toward all cultural practices. "Particular districts," he wrote, "have local peculiarities, but custom gives all an equal degree of propriety." But this claim, like his allegedly nonjudgmental approach toward southern pronunciation in the speller, didn't come from the heart. By maintaining that improvements in education would ultimately produce national standards, Webster was suggesting that Southerners should do the accommodating. As he stressed in a footnote, little learning in America occurred outside of New England. "In the southern states, gaming, fox hunting and horse-racing are the height of ambition; industry is reserved for slaves. In the northern states, industry and the cultivation of the arts and sciences distinguish the people." While Webster hadn't yet been any further south than New York, he still felt he knew enough to offer these generalizations.

But south was where Noah Webster was now headed. In April 1785, as New England, after enduring a brutally cold winter, was still shrouded by two-foot snowdrifts, Webster began making preparations for an extended tour of the southern states. Over the next thirteen months, he would take his copyright campaign to the remaining state legislatures. Steady book sales, he figured, could provide him with the financial stability that he sorely lacked. Assuming he could find a suitable bride, his sporadic legal work wasn't bringing in enough money for him to marry. Though Webster was often lonely, he was proud of his literary accomplishments. As he observed on the fast day of April 20, he felt neither "plunged in calamities nor overwhelmed with the blessings of heaven." A week and a half later, the twenty-six-year-old New England celebrity left Hartford to seek renown all across the new nation, which he had already helped to define.

PART TWO

Founding Father

FEDERALIST, n. An appellation in America, given to the friends of the constitution of the United States, at its formation and adoption, and to the political party which favored the administration of President Washington.

Counting His Way across America

COUNT, v.t. To number; to tell or name one by one, or by small numbers, for ascertaining the whole number of units in a collection; as, to count the years, days and hours of a man's life; to *count* the stars. Who can *count* the dust of Jacob? *Numb. xxiii.*

On Monday morning, May 2, 1785, as the melting snow pushed the water in the Connecticut River to dangerous heights, Webster headed off to the other end of America.

By midafternoon, he had completed the first leg of his southern journey, the familiar forty-mile trek to New Haven. Upon his arrival, Webster headed directly for Chapel Street, where he spotted Yale president Ezra Stiles. Webster's former classmate, Josiah Meigs, who had recently completed a stint as Stiles' science tutor, was about to inaugurate the age of American air travel. Like Stiles and the rest of the crowd gathered on the Green, Webster, too, was eager with anticipation.

Webster looked over at the eleven-foot-wide sphere that was destined for the sky. Made of paper, the balloon was decorated with a figure of an angel, which in one hand bore a trumpet and in the other, an American flag and the motto "*Nil intentatum nostri liquere poetae*" [There is no theme that our poets have not tried]. The immortal words from Horace's *Ars Poetica* were also painted in seven other languages, including Greek, Hebrew, Chaldee and English.

Shortly before three o'clock, Meigs, now publisher of the new newspaper *The New Haven Gazette,* began stuffing the kindling shavings into the one-foot hole at the base of the balloon. A few minutes later, the flaming metal basket took off.

Craning their necks, Webster and the rest of the spectators looked straight up.

The balloon traveled just over the weathervane of the Brick Church on the Green, falling down on Mr. Marshfield's house nearby. But soon Meigs was gearing up for a second launch. This time, the pyramid of fire rose a few hundred feet higher, but its descent was much more rapid; sensing that New Haven was under attack, some militiamen accidentally shot three balls right through it.

In his diary, Webster accentuated the positive, "See a balloon ascend ingenuity of Mr. Meigs. It rises several hundred feet."

New Haven was just a one-night stopover. Within a few weeks, Webster was zigzagging across the South, where his daily life would be filled with uncertainty. To finance his travels, he would have to find work as he went along. A foreigner in his own country, he would battle headaches, boredom and despair. He would miss his native New England. Early in 1786, he noted in his diary, "An eminent merchant in Alexandria informed me that of 50 planters in Virginia who sold him tobacco, only 4 or 5 could write their names but made a mark on the receipts. O New England! How superior are thy inhabitants in morals, literature, civility and industry." Though Webster rarely mingled with the hoi polloi—he met the most prominent people in nearly every town he visited—the feelings of alienation persisted.

After completing his southern tour in mid-1786, Webster went back on the road to give another round of talks on the English language in the Middle (mid-Atlantic) and New England states. While he would dutifully record his thoughts about his two-year trans-American odyssey in his diary, in his public writing he said little—with one exception. In 1788, at the end of one of his articles, Webster appended the list:

	Houses
Portsmouth, NH	450
Newbury-Port	510
Salem	730
Boston	2200
Providence	560
Newport	790
Hartford, city	300
New Haven	400
New York	3340
Albany and suburbs	550
Trenton	180
Philadelphia and suburbs	4500
Wilmington	400
Baltimore	1950
Annapolis	260
Frederick's Town	400
Alexandria	300
Richmond	310
Petersburg	280
Williamsburg	230
Charleston	1540
Savannah	200

As he traveled across America in 1785 and 1786, Webster would personally count every house in its major towns and he wanted the world to know his final tallies.

This compulsion to count links Webster with his lexicographical brethren. As a teenage medical student in Edinburgh in the early 1790s, Peter Mark Roget of *Thesaurus* fame would count all the steps he took to class every day. Likewise, Webster's hero, Samuel Johnson, once remarked that he took recourse in "the study of arithmetic" whenever he

Webster reexamined his house counts before publishing
the final list in his 1788 article in *The American Magazine*.
While here he records a total of 4,600 houses in
Philadelphia—including an additional eighty-two "allowed
for mistakes"—in his final tally, he reported 4,500.

felt "disordered." While heading toward his breakdown at Oxford, Johnson produced a chart in his journal listing the total number of lines of
Latin poetry he would translate in a week, month and year, if he did a
certain number per day (say, ten, thirty or sixty). For Webster, too,
counting could help mitigate the angst that lurked within. In the mid-

1780s, most of America's biggest metropolitan areas were still small enough that he could count all the houses during one leisurely walk. But this one-man data collection agency didn't focus just on America's residential real estate. For the next few years, an often nervous and distraught Webster kept track of a wide range of data, including demographic information, temperature readings, wind currents and voting records.

THE MAN WAS BLIND, yet he was an international authority on optics.

His name was Dr. Henry Moyes. At a few minutes before seven on the evening of Monday, May 16, 1785, the professor was standing before a packed house of nearly two hundred at Baltimore's St. Paul's Church, located in the center of town, about a mile north of the harbor. The eminent scientist was then barnstorming across America's major cities, giving lectures four nights a week. His twenty-one-lecture course in Baltimore, for which he charged gentlemen a guinea and ladies a half guinea, covered "all those astonishing discoveries which must forever distinguish the 18th century."

Seated in a pew at the front, Webster was eager to hear Moyes talk about light, the subject of his remarks that night. A year earlier in Boston, Webster had attended Moyes' lecture on electricity, which he found instructive. And having been introduced to the professor the day before, Webster was most impressed, characterizing America's newest celebrity as "blind, but sensible."

Webster had arrived in Baltimore just two days earlier. From New Haven, he had sailed to New York City, where he stopped off just long enough to have tea with Colonel Aaron Burr, then a young trial lawyer, at his town house on Maiden Lane. At the time, Webster knew Burr's new wife, Theodosia Prevost, better than the colonel himself, as back in Sharon, Webster had taught the two boys from her former marriage. En route to Baltimore, Webster also passed through Philadelphia, where he enjoyed a lively dinner with his cousin, the author and merchant Pelatiah Webster, who commented favorably on his *Sketches*. Webster also considered his older relative, a 1746 Yale graduate, "very sensible," and the two writers would remain close until the Philadelphian's death a decade later.

Though Baltimore was a boom town, Webster felt uncomfortable in his new surroundings. The housing stock of Maryland's commercial center, which had doubled since 1782, was, as Webster would personally determine that fall, approaching two thousand units. And rents near the harbor had risen to a guinea per square foot. However, this town of some ten thousand residents was still run-down and dirty. Only its main thoroughfare, Market Street (today Baltimore Street), was paved. The French politician and writer Jacques Pierre Brissot noted a few years later, "the great quantity of mud after a rain, everything announces that the air must be unhealthful. However, if you ask the inhabitants, they will tell you no." Despite his uneasiness in Baltimore, Webster would make it his base of operations over the next six months.

Webster was often sad and homesick. Missing the orderliness of Connecticut, he longed for news from his friends and family back in Hartford. That summer, he would write in his diary, "Lament that I am in Baltimore." To keep up his spirits, Webster would surround himself with fellow New Englanders such as Dr. James Mann, a prominent army surgeon during the Revolution, who accompanied him to Dr. Moyes' lecture that night.

As Webster well knew, Moyes had a distinguished academic pedigree, despite having lost his sight at three due to smallpox. As a boy in Kirkaldy, Scotland, Moyes had accompanied the economist Adam Smith, then writing his masterpiece, *Wealth of Nations,* during his afternoon walks. Through Smith's prompting, Moyes had studied under two of the world's greatest philosophers, those architects of the Scottish Enlightenment, Edinburgh's David Hume and Glasgow's Thomas Reid.

As Moyes began to speak, Webster was struck by the clarity of his language and exposition. The doctor divided his lecture into six parts. After discussing ignition and combustion, he moved on to the production of light. With help from his assistant, a Scotsman named Mr.

Frasier, he then performed an experiment demonstrating the materiality of light. The professor, who himself could not see the light of day, concluded by discussing sunlight and light particles. Between his scientific points, Moyes interspersed moving anecdotes. Describing his reaction when he was once thrown off a stagecoach, Moyes observed, "I was quite at home in the dark ditch. The inversion of the order of things was amusing. I that was obliged to be led about like a child, in the glaring sun, was now directing eight persons to pull here and haul there." His cheerful disposition moved Webster. He was not alone. Reviewing Dr. Moyes' performance, *The Maryland Journal* reported, "Charmed to see a gentleman whom cloud indeed. . . . surrounds, . . . his auditors have expressed the highest satisfaction in his abilities and the agreeable manner in which he delivers himself on these truly admirable and important subjects."

The next day, May 17, Webster moved into Mrs. Sanderson's lodging house off of South Street, where Dr. Mann and another New Englander, Josiah Blakely, a Hartford merchant, were also staying. That night, he went back to St. Paul's to hear Dr. Moyes lecture on phosphorus. A week later, after returning from his overnight stay in Mount Vernon, where he had passed on a copy of his *Sketches of American Policy* to General Washington, Webster caught a few more installments of the professor's lecture series. On May 24, Webster wrote in his diary, "The Dr. has 190 hearers generally." Impressed by the size of the crowds, Webster began toying with the idea of emulating Dr. Moyes. To pay for his book tour, he would soon become America's first homegrown celebrity speaker.

ON SATURDAY, MAY 28, Webster made provisions to take his copyright campaign to the Deep South. His ultimate destination: the South Carolina port city of Charleston (known as Charles Town until the British evacuation at the end of the war).

Catching the sloop *George* from Baltimore on May 30, Webster stopped off at Norfolk, Virginia, on June 1, where he was delighted to eat cherries for the first time—the fruit would later be a mainstay of his New Haven garden. He was surprised by the fertility of the soil, in which green peas were so plentiful. But after dropping off three dozen spellers with a local bookseller, he couldn't wait to get out of town, writing in his journal, "Little attention is paid to religion, education, or morals. Gentlemen are obliged to send their children to the northward for education. A shame on Virginia!" Though Webster didn't complete a count of Norfolk's houses, he came up with a rough estimate, adding that the town "consisted of two or three hundred houses well built of brick; but it was burnt by the British troops and has not recovered its former elegance." Squalls alternating with calm seas made sailing on to Charleston trying. This leg of the trip, which was supposed to take a few days, lasted a few weeks. As the boat stalled, Webster's nerves started to fray. On June 14, he observed, "Wind continues contrary. O how disagreeable! We make but 10 or 12 miles a day." Whenever a favorable breeze came along, Webster and his fellow passengers would express relief by singing and dancing on the quarterdeck.

Soon after reaching Charleston at 8 a.m. on Sunday, June 26, Webster dashed off to hear Parson Smith's sermon at St. Michael's Church. After the services, Webster stayed for a musical performance by Miss Maria Storer, an English opera singer then giving a series of concerts in Charleston. With the local newspaper, *The Columbia Herald,* criticizing her for singing Italian songs, which its correspondent called "at best an exotic entertainment," she had recently switched to more traditional fare. But even so, Webster objected. "Miss Storer," he recorded in his journal, "sings part of Handel's Oratorio—very odd indeed! A woman sings in public after church for her own benefit! I do not like the modern taste in singing!" Slipping a quarter into the plate, Webster grudgingly acknowledged her talent, "She sung *well* in the modern taste, but I cannot admire it."

Over the next week, Webster met with a host of local dignitaries including General Christopher Gadsden, who had been a delegate to the Continental Congress and a brigadier general in the Continental army, and Charleston's first mayor, Richard Hutson. The town's inhabitants appealed to him: "The people in Charleston are very civil and polite. They behave with great decency in church. The slaves are kept in good order, they are remarkably attentive in church."

Webster was pleased to celebrate America's ninth birthday in Charleston. Independence Day festivities began precisely at one o'clock in the afternoon as the militia fired thirteen volleys, one for each state in the union. Afterward, Governor William Moultrie hosted a lavish dinner at the City Tavern. Fourteen toasts were drunk, most of which struck a deep chord with Webster, such as number ten, "Unanimity to the American States," and eleven, "May the arts and sciences flourish in America." After dinner, Webster and the other celebrants endured a brief scare, as one of the thirteen hot air balloons went up in flames as it headed toward the beef market. The fire was quickly extinguished, and no further balloons were launched. As Webster put it in a letter to his publisher, Hudson and Goodwin, the fire "put an end to this boyish amusement."

That evening, Webster walked back over to St. Michael's Church to get a view of the city from its steeple. Modeled on the English churches designed by Christopher Wren, St. Michael's, completed in 1761, stood on the site of a seventeenth-century Anglican church, the first built south of Virginia. The tower featured an exquisitely wrought clock and eight bells (which the city's Loyalists had had shipped back to England during the war). "They have," Webster noted in his diary, "a good chime of the bells."

After walking up the nearly two hundred steps to the top of the steeple, Webster looked out and was impressed by the town's orderly layout: "Charleston is very regular; the most regular of any in America, except Philadel and New Haven."

Charleston would soon return the compliment. The following day, Webster donated three hundred copies of his *Grammatical Institute* to the Mt. Sion Society, which administered South Carolina's newly created Winnsborough College. Later that summer, the society's secretary published a letter of thanks to Webster in *The State Gazette of South Carolina,* which included a glowing tribute, "That your exertions for the advancement of useful knowledge may meet with merited success and applause must be the wish of every friend to science in the rising states of America." The speller would soon be a staple of education throughout South Carolina and, when the state's copyright law passed a few months later, Webster would reap the profits.

As Webster got ready to leave Charleston, he reported to his publisher that his southern journey, though expensive, was "the most useful and necessary I ever undertook."

AT SIX O'CLOCK ON WEDNESDAY, October 19, Webster fought off the rain to make his way to Baltimore's First Presbyterian Church on Fayette Street.

Three days earlier, Webster had celebrated his twenty-seventh birthday. With his efforts to burnish his national reputation proceeding slowly, the fiercely ambitious author was feeling that life was passing him by. In his diary, he articulated his fears: "The revolution of a few years sweeps us away. . . . a few revolutions more with accelerated motion will turn me off the stage."

Webster's last few months in Baltimore had been rocky. The May advertisement in *The Maryland Journal* announcing his intention of opening a language school had attracted little interest. Forced to find another means of support, he taught singing according to a "regular scientific method." And with the locals short of cash, he was forced to accept articles of clothing—gloves, shoes, slippers and silk stockings—for his tutelage. Though Webster managed to "astonish all Baltimore with ten scholars," his heart wasn't in his singing school. In early October, he got into a nasty "miff" with a singer by the name of Mr. Hall. "People in Baltimore," he lamented in his diary, "have not been accustomed to my rigid discipline." What's more, his voice was losing its timbre. Regarding his instruction at his school on October 15, he was forced to acknowl-edge, "Sing bad this evening."

In early October, the ever resourceful Webster sought to become the "American Dr. Moyes." He, too, would now try to fill up lecture halls night after night.

Fortunately, Webster had recently gathered some new material on which he could draw. During a lonely weekend in late August, when he was feeling bored and disgusted with Baltimore, he had picked up his pen. As was often the case, emotional distress prompted a burst of cre-ativity. As he later recalled, "While I was waiting for the regular sessions of the legislatures in those states which had not passed laws for protect-ing literary property, I amused myself in writing remarks on the English Language, without knowing to which purpose they would be applied." Now, nearly two months later, he had figured out a way to make use of these musings.

Webster got to the church at six thirty, just as the doors opened. The five lectures that he was slated to give over the next week would all begin at seven. For the entire series, he charged seven shillings, sixpence. The fee for one lecture was a quarter.

Over the last few months, Baltimore's First Presbyterian Church, a brick building recently expanded to accommodate fifty pews, had be-come like a second home. Using the space for his singing school, Web-ster had forged a cordial relationship with its pastor, the Reverend Patrick Allison. Called "a man of substance" by his peers, the erudite Allison had a taste for belles lettres, championing the work of British writers such as Alexander Pope and Joseph Addison. A personal friend of George Wash-ington, Allison had served as chaplain for both the Continental Congress (during its brief tenure in Baltimore) and the Continental army. Webster and Allison were frequent breakfast companions, and a few days earlier over tea, Webster had given Allison a preview of his remarks.

Due to the inclement weather, the church was less full than he had hoped. Surveying the crowd of about thirty, Webster launched into his introduction: "The principal design of this lecture is to point out the origin of the English language. It begins, however, with general remarks on the importance of the subject—finds fault with the mode of education, which leads us to study the Hebrew, Greek, Latin, French and German languages, to the almost entire neglect of our own." National pride would be Webster's central theme. Americans, he argued, needed to devote more attention to one of their prized possessions, their own language. After giving a brief history of America's tongue, Webster stressed its richness: "The English language is exceedingly copious; it is said to contain about 20,000 words. For the most part, the same idea, or nearly the same, may be expressed by two different words."

While his listeners found Webster's ideas engaging, if not enthralling, something about his manner rubbed them the wrong way. A veteran of the classroom, Webster was used to teaching children, not adults. Appearing to talk down to his audience, Webster came across as an annoying "know-it-all." Catching Webster's road show several months later in Philadelphia, the future secretary of state Timothy Pickering, who had been so moved by Webster's speller, observed: "In truth there was so much of egotism, especially in a young man, apparent in his communications, as to prevent his hearers, receiving the satisfaction which might otherwise have been derived from many ingenious observations. . . . diffidence in a public lecturer, especially in a young man, [is] essential to the art of pleasing." Diffident, Noah Webster would never be. To counteract his deep-seated social anxiety, he projected an unbecoming arrogance. A few years later, the writer William Dunlap, then Webster's colleague in a New York literary society, satirized his awkwardness at the podium in *Cuttgrisingwoldes,* a play in which a character named Noah Cobweb exclaims:

> My rules, my lectures, ev'ry night repeated
> Began to talk sometimes ere they were seated
> To show my zeal I ev'ry night held forth

And deep imprest th'Idea of my worth
Not soon forgot.

Webster was no affable crowd-pleaser like Dr. Moyes. Unskilled in forging human connections, he acted as if he were the only person in the room. Paradoxically, though he wasn't sensitive to the perspective—or even presence—of his auditors, Webster would seek from them validation of his own worthiness. Admiration, he could never get enough of.

Not only was Webster's manner overbearing, but he also didn't have much of a stage presence. Speaking in a high-pitched monotone, his body language betrayed his inner turmoil. As one correspondent noted in *The New York Packet* in April 1786, "[Mr. Webster] appears to be enraptured when he speaks, but his raptures seem forced. The motions of his hands are rather unpleasing." Though mortified by such observations, Webster would eventually acknowledge that his critics had a point: "That my delivery was ungraceful may be true. I was never taught to speak with grace. I know of no institution in America where speaking is taught with accuracy." But to those who found fault with his use of language, he would not back down. For Webster, words were much more means than ends. He no longer had any poetic aspirations. To the New York writer who charged that his style was "divested of what are commonly called the flowers of rhetoric," Webster shot back, "My design is of more importance. I wish to express my sentiments with clearness." The accurate definer also poked holes in the phrasing of this reviewer, "How, Sir, can a style be *divested* of what it never possessed? I suppose the correspondent meant *destitute*."

Back at the First Presbyterian Church two nights later, before a slightly larger audience, Webster addressed errors in pronunciation in various local communities. While he professed not to play favorites, he tended to find fewer faults with the practices of New Englanders than with those of other Americans. As in his speller, so, too, in his lectures, Webster was obsessed with creating linguistic order in America. In a report back to his Baltimore landlady, Mrs. Coxe, a few months after this first round of lectures, Webster wrote that his plan was to "effect a uniformity of language and education throughout the continent."

In his fourth Baltimore lecture, delivered on Monday, October 24, he took on poetry, discussing the rules of poetic verse such as line breaks and pauses. Ever the critic, Webster could not resist commenting on the slip-ups committed by the world's greatest poets: "Homer, Shakespeare, and Milton are incorrect in regard to these pauses, but they are great geniuses; their souls were engaged upon sublimer subjects, which occasioned them frequently to overlook these minutiae." In his last Baltimore lecture on October 26, Webster formulated his thoughts on education. Once again, he aimed to instill national pride: "The tour of America is more necessary to an American youth than the tour of Europe. Let it be remembered that a Washington, a Franklin, a Jay, an Adams and many other Americans of distinction were educated at home." Webster was here talking as much about himself as about any hypothetical youngster, since he was then rounding out his own education by circling around America. In a rare moment of introspection, Webster later acknowledged that the lecture series first begun at Dr. Allison's church may well have served his own emotional needs above all. "The readings were," he acknowledged in 1789, "probably more useful to myself than to my hearers."

While many listeners were irked by Webster's style (or lack of it), few opposed his message. The night of his final Baltimore lecture, a relieved Webster wrote in his diary, "The lectures have received so much applause that I am induced to revise and continue reading them in other towns." He would end up delivering them in a total of twenty towns. The substance was mostly the same, but as he moved back North, he sneaked into his literary musings some of the demographic information that he had unearthed while down South. On July 1, 1786, the day after Webster's sixth lecture on English at the Connecticut State House in New Haven, Yale president Ezra Stiles recorded in his journal, "Last evening I attended Mr. Webster's . . . last lecture. From him [Webster] I learn.

Virginia: 650 thousands souls whites and blacks: ratio 10 to 11, i.e. ten Blacks to eleven Whites. Maryland: 90 thousand taxables, 150 thousand souls black, 200 thousand souls whites."

An expansion of the ideas Webster first laid out in his *Grammatical Institute,* Webster's lectures would form the basis of his 1789 book, *Dissertations on the English Language.* To Benjamin Franklin, then the recently retired president (governor) of Pennsylvania, Webster dedicated this volume, citing both the Doctor's greatness as a scholar, but also his "plain and elegantly neat" prose. Franklin was the paragon of clarity Webster hoped to emulate. As in the speller and in his *Sketches,* here, too, Webster sought to unite Americans:

> All men have local attachments, which lead them to believe their own practice to be the least exceptionable. Pride and prejudice incline men to treat the practice of their neighbors with some degree of contempt. . . . Small causes, such as a nick-name or a vulgar tone in speaking, have actually created a dissocial spirit between the inhabitants of different states, which is often discoverable in private business and public deliberations. Our political harmony is therefore concerned in a uniformity of language.

To combat local "pride and prejudice"—Webster lifted the phrase not from Jane Austen, then just entering her teens, but from novelist Fanny Burney—Webster recommended the adoption of national pronunciation standards. While not dictating specific norms, Webster urged Americans to eschew the lead of British authors who looked to the "stage." Rather than relying on those versed in the dramatic arts, whom he abhorred, Webster suggested turning to the common man, since "the general practice of a nation is the rule of propriety."

But Webster's framing of this debate as one pitting the experts against the people was slightly disingenuous. After all, a principal objective of his *Dissertations* (and the lectures upon which the volume was based) was to promote his textbooks. And Webster also made a direct appeal to his fellow Americans to spend more money on his pedagogical tools: "Nothing but the establishment of schools and some uniformity in the use of books can annihilate differences in speaking and preserve the purity of the American tongue."

LESS THAN TWO WEEKS after his final Baltimore lecture, Webster set off for Richmond to take his copyright campaign to Virginia's state legislature. But he first stopped off at Mount Vernon, where he spent another night as Washington's houseguest. As Webster left on November 6, Washington handed him letters of introduction to Virginia's governor and the speakers of its two houses, which included the following remarks: "[Mr. Webster] is author of a Grammatical Institute of the English Language—to which there are very honorable testimonials of its excellence and its usefulness. The work must speak for itself; & he better than I, can explain his wishes." Missing among those testimonials was one from Washington himself. In a letter dated July 18, Webster had asked Washington for "the addition of your name, Sir, to the catalogue of patrons." The perennial straight shooter, Washington had declined, explaining that "I do not think myself a competent judge." On purely literary matters, Washington preferred to remain outside the fray. Even so, the General understood the political implications of Webster's textbooks and was eager to lend a hand.

Washington's clout proved to be considerable. In Richmond, Webster renewed his acquaintance with James Madison and dined with Benjamin Harrison V, the longtime state legislator who had just ceded the governor's office to Patrick Henry. (Harrison's son, William, and his great-grandson, Benjamin, would both grow up to be U.S. presidents.) At Harrison's suggestion, Webster gave his lecture series in the capitol building. In December, Webster reported back to Washington that he had succeeded in registering his books for copyright in Virginia, adding, "For this success I acknowledge myself indebted . . . to your politeness."

During this legislative session, as Webster later recorded in his memoir, Virginia's delegates issued an invitation to all the other states to meet in Annapolis to "form some plan for investing Congress with the regulation and taxation of commerce." The Annapolis Convention the following September, which consisted of twelve delegates from five states, was the forerunner to the Constitutional Convention. As an elder statesman, Webster took fierce pride in recalling even his tangential connections with such seminal events in America's founding.

Having completed his business in Richmond, Webster crisscrossed the state, moving on to Petersburg, Williamsburg and Alexandria. The layout of Virginia's principal towns, which placed theaters rather than churches at the center, left him dismayed. He described Petersburg as an "unhealthy place" with some three hundred houses, the same number as in Richmond. Only Williamsburg appeared tolerable. As he wrote in his diary, the former state capital, though decaying, "consists of 230 houses well built and regular." But a small turnout for his readings at the "large and elegant" College of William and Mary soured him on all the state's inhabitants. On December 7, he observed, "Read my second lecture to the same number. . . . the Virginians have little money & great pride, contempt of Northern men & great fondness for dissipated life. They do not understand grammar." In an effort to combat sagging attendance, Webster dashed off reviews of his own lectures. In an "Extract of a letter from a Gentleman in Virginia to a friend in this town," which appeared in Baltimore's *Maryland Journal* on January 3, 1786, an "anonymous" reporter noted, "Mr. Webster has paid us a visit—his lectures in support of his plan were delivered and much approved by the first characters . . . I think it is high time to dispossess ourselves of prejudice in favour of Britain so far as to act ourselves."

On January 20, a lame Webster—he had hurt his leg when his horse slipped on an icy road—was back in Baltimore, catching up on his correspondence. Since the New Year, he had lectured in both Annapolis and Frederick as he attempted to curry favor with Maryland legislators. Webster took a liking to Annapolis, whose 260 houses he considered "more elegant . . . in proportion than in any town in America." Maryland's state capital also offered ample opportunities for dancing with "a brilliant circle of ladies." On January 11, his last night in town, Webster noted in his diary, "Visit the ladies; tell them pretty stories."

After a week of meetings and lectures in Frederick, Webster had reached Baltimore on the nineteenth. The following day, he explained the purpose of his trip to Timothy Pickering, who had introduced himself to Webster a few months earlier in a letter praising his *Grammatical Institute*. To the recently retired quartermaster general, whom he was looking forward to meeting soon in Philadelphia, Webster wrote, "I shall make one *general* effort to deliver literature and my countrymen from the errors that fashion and ignorance are palming upon Englishmen." For Webster, his personal quest to sell more books was synonymous with the heroic effort to rescue America and its language from the clutches of the fashion-loving, theater-addicted British. Though this stance was self-serving, it also had a ring of truth. By 1786, America's union was in a state of disarray. As David Ramsay, the South Carolina delegate who was the acting president of the Continental Congress, put it that February, "There is a languor in the states that forbodes ruin. . . . In 1775 there was more patriotism in a village than is now in the 13 states." His language reforms, Webster sensed, could be instrumental in restoring national pride.

However, the usually confident Webster wasn't convinced that he could pull off this daunting feat. Aware that he lacked the charisma of more dynamic speakers such as Moyes, who attracted as many as a thousand listeners to his talks, he confided his fears to Pickering: "Two circumstances will operate against me. I am not a *foreigner*; I am a *New Englandman*. A foreigner ushered in with titles and letters, with half my abilities, would have the whole city in his train." But Webster's cri de coeur to Pickering had little to do with the precise nature of the challenge he faced. A foreigner could never have succeeded in his mission, which was to reshape America's language. In fact, now that Webster had left the South, his distinguished New England pedigree was bound to

open doors. Yet Webster tended to see himself as a beleaguered outsider
even when he was a respected insider.

Before heading to the big stage of Philadelphia, then America's largest city with some forty-five hundred houses (as he himself would soon
determine), Webster stopped off in Delaware. Unfortunately, he arrived
in Dover just as the legislature was ending its session. However, his visit
to the capital would not be in vain, as a committee was appointed to
look into a copyright law, and a bill was passed during the next session.
Webster was greatly relieved to be out of the South, which he would
never visit again. Of the response to his lectures in the four-hundred-
house town of Wilmington, he observed, "More taste for science in these
states than below." In Wilmington, Webster also hobnobbed with John
Dickinson, who had just finished a term as governor of both Delaware
and Pennsylvania, and would later represent Delaware at the Constitutional Convention. Using his favorite encomium, in his diary Webster
described the so-called Penman of the Revolution—before the war,
Dickinson had authored the influential essay "Letters from a Farmer in
Pennsylvania"—as "a very sensible man."

Webster's month in Philadelphia was memorable. On February 15,
his second night in town, he enjoyed the first of several dinners with
Pickering, whom he characterized as "one of the best of men." The following evening, from his perch at Mrs. Ford's lodging house on Walnut
Street, he wrote a letter, introducing himself to Benjamin Franklin:

> Mr. Webster presents his respects to his Excellency President Frank-
> lin and begs him to peruse the enclosed papers and correct any mis-
> take in the principles. It is designed to collect some American pieces
> upon the discovery, history, war, geography, economy, commerce,
> government, &c. of this country and add them to the third part of
> the *Institute,* in order to call the minds of our youth from ancient fa-
> bles and modern foreign events, and fix them upon objects immedi-
> ately interesting in this country. A selection for this purpose should
> be judicious, and the compiler feels his need of assistance in the

undertaking. He will do himself the honor to call in a few days and take the advice of his Excellency.

This consummate compiler didn't actually need Franklin's help in putting together a new edition of his reader. But having won over America's most influential citizen a year earlier over dinner in Mount Vernon, Webster was now eager to move on to number two. While he lacked the social skills necessary to form intimate friendships, he was adept at ingratiating himself with the powerful. Flattery he knew. And Franklin, who, as the newly elected president of Pennsylvania, also headed the board of trustees of the University of Pennsylvania, quickly grew fond of Webster. As a fellow polymath who was also obsessed with education, Franklin, then eighty, would anoint Webster his intellectual heir. For the remaining four years of his life, Franklin would prove to be Webster's steadfast colleague.

The day after composing his note, Webster met Franklin for the first time. The elder statesman immediately gave Webster permission to use a room in the university for his lectures. Franklin also talked about one of his pet projects, his plan for spelling reform. For years, the former printer and publisher, who had recently returned from France, had been interested in establishing a new English alphabet based on phonetic principles. Webster, too, was intrigued by aligning spelling more closely with pronunciation. Under a purely phonetic system, Webster would later note in his diary, "every man, woman and child, who knows his alphabet, can spell words . . . without ever seeing them."

Shortly after those initial meetings with Franklin, Webster reported back to George Washington: "I am encouraged by the prospect of rendering my country some service, to proceed in my design of refining the language and improving our general system of education. Dr. Franklin has extended my views to a very simple plan of reducing the language to perfect regularity. Should I ever attempt it, I have no doubt that I should be patronized by many distinguished characters."

Webster was thrilled by the possibility of collaborating with Franklin. He hoped thereby both to serve his country and to improve his chances of finding more support ("patrons") for his own work. Webster was keenly aware of what the ability to drop such big names as both Washington and Franklin could mean for his future. On May 24, after he had left Philadelphia for New York, he shared with Franklin some thoughts on the latter's proposed orthographic changes, noting that Washington was likely to be supportive of their efforts. "Could he be," Webster stressed, "acquainted with the new alphabet proposed, [the General] would undoubtedly commence its advocate." In a postscript to this letter, Webster asked Franklin to endorse his *Grammatical Institute*. By the summer of 1786, Webster and Franklin were making plans to confer on spelling reform in Philadelphia in the fall.

Webster's trip to Philadelphia in early 1786 proved fruitful in other ways as well. Shortly after his arrival, he enjoyed another round of discussions with both Pelatiah Webster and Dr. Moyes, who was winding up his American tour. Webster also met Dr. Benjamin Rush, a signer of the Declaration of Independence then settling in as a physician at Pennsylvania Hospital. A social activist, Rush hoped to "remake America" by revamping both education and medicine, and he would develop into one of Webster's favorite correspondents. Though Rush respected Webster's intelligence, he had some qualms about his character. Rush would enjoy repeating to friends what Webster said to him after he had congratulated him upon his arrival in Philadelphia: "Sir, you may congratulate Philadelphia upon the occasion!"

On February 27, Webster was introduced to Rush's old friend Thomas Paine, the author of the famous Revolutionary pamphlet, whose title, thanks to Rush, had been changed from *Plain Truth* to *Common Sense*. Paine was then soliciting comments on his engineering prowess, as he had just completed a design for a new suspension bridge. Examining Paine's model, Webster rendered the following verdict in his diary, "Executed, in miniature, with success."

Webster's language lectures at university hall on Fourth Street, which he considered "a large clumsy building," drew consistently good crowds; the hundred and fifty "mostly literary characters" in attendance at his sixth and final lecture on March 11 expressed their approval with "great applause." But while Webster achieved many of his objectives—he also registered his speller under the state's new copyright law—his sojourn in Philadelphia was not without disappointment. In late February, he noted in his diary, "Go to the Assembly; the ladies will not dance with strangers if they can avoid it—polite indeed!" Though Webster was running in elite circles, his failure to find dancing partners that night made him feel like a social outcast. "People in high life," he added, "suppose that they have a right to dispense with the rules of civility." A month later, after hosting a farewell Sunday dinner for his newfound Philadelphia friends, he was gone.

From Philadelphia, Webster moved on to Princeton, where he stayed at the home of Samuel Stanhope Smith, the president of the College of New Jersey, whom he had first met nearly four years earlier. Discovering that most of the students, then busy preparing for exams, were too impoverished to pay for tickets, Webster nixed his plan to deliver lectures. On March 24, he scurried out of town after just three days. He did have time for a quick house count: The small college town had just ninety. Of this stop, his diary mentions a couple of dinners with Dr. Smith, a tea at the home of the local parson and some scattered data, "48 rooms in College, 70 students, Presidents salary £ 400. Professor of moral philosophy £ 200. Tutors £ 150 currency."

With anxiety about pounds and pence racing through his mind, Webster began thinking about how to garner some solid gate receipts in the nation's capital.

UPON ARRIVING IN NEW YORK on Saturday, March 25, Webster found a room at Mrs. Ferrari's lodging house at 56 Maiden Lane—then a string of small shops and elegant houses. (A few years later, Secretary of State Thomas Jefferson would live at 57 Maiden Lane). He was residing down the street from Aaron Burr and his family, whom he visited on his first day in town, just as he had the year before. On Monday the twenty-seventh, Webster met New York's mayor, James Duane, who personally procured the use of city hall for his lectures. This was a major coup because the three-story building, located at the corner of Wall and Nassau Street, where Federal Hall now stands, had since 1785 doubled as the halls of Congress. Following in the footsteps of other distinguished guests such as Dr. Moyes, Webster would give his series of six lectures in its second-floor assembly chamber, whose walls were adorned with paintings of Columbus, Washington and France's King Louis XVI, then America's closest foreign ally.

Despite some severe snowstorms in early April, Webster maintained an active social schedule. He enjoyed numerous teas and dinners with several national leaders, including Dr. David Ramsay, who presided over Congress during John Hancock's illness, and the New York delegate Judge Zephaniah Platt, the father of Jonas Platt, the future congressman whom he had taught in Goshen. Webster's mood was largely buoyant, even when attending the theater. After seeing *The Provoked Husband,* a Restoration comedy by John Vanbrugh, Webster reported in his diary that the actors performed well. However, he also alluded to some irritation, adding, "Some low scenes and indelicate ideas interspersed here and there are very exceptionable [objectionable]. Every exhibition of vice weakens our aversion for it." In point of fact, Vanbrugh's farce, which featured characters such as the simpleton Sir Francis Wronghead, contained nothing racy. But Webster never did take to social satire. A decade later, beneath a newspaper clipping of an eighteenth-century poem, "The Bunter's Wedding," which spoofed the dregs of London society, he would pencil in the following comments, "Too low for the sublimity of my genius and the elegant taste of N. Webster."

On the morning of April 27, at the invitation of Dr. Ramsay, Webster attended a special breakfast in honor of Captain O'Beal, the Seneca Indian chief, who was then negotiating with federal authorities. "The Seneca Chief & five others," Webster wrote in his diary, ". . . behave with great civility, & took tea and coffee with decency and some appearance of breeding. When they left the house they shook hands with men & women, without any bow, wearing strong marks of native independence and dignity." Webster, who donated one sixth of the receipts from his New York lectures to the poor, would forever be concerned about the plight of the downtrodden.

That evening, Webster gave his final lecture before an appreciative crowd of two hundred, which included Dr. Ramsay as well as many other congressional delegates.

As Webster awoke on Friday the twenty-eighth, he was filled with pride. His twice-weekly lectures at city hall, in which he had advocated purifying America from "the principles and effects of a modern corruption of language in Great Britain," had been a resounding success.

Having decided to move on to Albany on Monday, May 1, he had just one final weekend in New York. This was the morning, he decided, when he would begin his count. With his broad hat and walking stick, the impeccably dressed Webster marched out onto Maiden Lane.

The entire city was then confined to today's financial district, so Webster figured he needed only a day to complete his task. Along the East River, the city ran a total of about two miles; Grand Street was at its northern tip, above which began a highway called "Road to Boston." Along the Hudson (or North) River stood just a mile of paved roads. From the city's west bank to its east, the distance was on average three-quarters of a mile; its entire circumference was thus about four miles.

The New York that Webster was about to circumnavigate was still suffering from the aftereffects of the seven-year British occupation, which had ended just two and a half years earlier. The rubbish and detritus from the Great Fire of 1776, which had destroyed some five hundred houses as well as Trinity Church, the city's first Episcopal church, were still evident. As Webster headed down from Maiden Lane to the Battery, he noticed that many of the brick buildings with tiled roofs could use a coat of fresh paint, and that vacant lots were everywhere. The city wouldn't get its much-needed face-lift until the following year when its population—about twenty-four thousand at the time of Webster's walk—

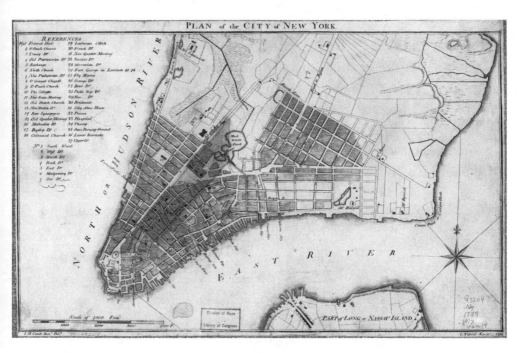

This 1789 map was by John McComb, Jr., Manhattan's most prominent architect, who later designed both Gracie Mansion and The Grange, Alexander Hamilton's retreat.

would begin to swell. The pavements upon which Webster trod on that spring day were also by and large not yet mended.

Two years later, Webster wrote up what he saw on that spring day. In the March 1788 issue of *The American Magazine,* a New York literary journal that he began editing in late 1787, Webster published an article, "General Description of New York." In this twenty-page piece, Webster provided a complete inventory of New York, which was so admired by historians that it was republished a century later as the preface to a facsimile edition of David Franks' *New York Directory for 1786.* New York's first directory, Franks' eighty-page volume consists primarily of the street addresses of the city's residents and businesses (e.g., under "Lawyers, Attornies and Notaries Publics &c" are listed about forty names, including "Aaron Burr, Esq., 10 Little Queen Street, and "Alexander Hamilton, Esq., 57 Wall-st.") While Franks' lists of individuals provide a micro-level view of New York's contents, Webster's prose furnishes the macro-level view.

As Webster examined the houses on Broadway, he basked in the street's grandeur. As he put it in the 1788 article: "But the most convenient and agreeable part of the city is Broadway. This street runs upon the height of land between the two rivers, beginning at the fort, near the south of the city and extending to the hospital in front of which it opens into an extensive plain or common." The hospital just north of Chambers Street marked the end of the developed area on New York's west side. On the fields in front, Webster spotted about two hundred horses and cows that were grazing. Behind the hospital was an out-of-the-way orchard where a week earlier, Webster had witnessed a duel that fatally wounded George Curson, an Englishman accused of seducing a woman from a prominent Old New York family. While Webster also considered Wall Street "elegant," he lamented that "most of [the other streets] are irregular and narrow." New York would never appeal to Webster as much as the orderly New Haven and Philadelphia.

As Webster walked, he also paid close attention to New York's churches, which then constituted its skyline. He was impressed by the neatness of its Protestant edifices—namely, the three Dutch, three Episcopal and four Presbyterian churches. In his article, he included detailed descriptions of all ten, which highlight their precise dimensions. "The Third Presbyterian Church," he remarked, "was erected in the year 1768, is a genteel stone building, sixty-five and a half feet long and fifty-five and a half feet wide; and stands in Little Queen-street." Of the city's other churches, his article would note just his count:

German Lutheran 2
Roman Catholic 1
Friends' Meeting 1
Anabaptists 1
Moravians 1
Jews Synagogue 1

Webster completed his tallying by the early evening, leaving him enough time to have tea with Peter Vandervoort, the sheriff of Kings County.

That night, Webster wrote in his diary, "Take the number of houses—3500 nearly." In his 1788 article, in which he included his house count data from across the country along with a host of other demographic information about the city, he would publish an exact figure: 3,340.

In his published account of New York, Webster would also supplement his raw data with some general comments about its citizens. Webster cited William Smith's 1757 *History of the Province of New York*, which carried the following assessment: "The people, both in town and country, are sober, industrious, and hospitable, though intent on gain." While noting that many changes had taken place since the Revolution, Webster concurred: "Notwithstanding, in point of sociability and hospitality, New York is hardly exceeded by any town in the United States." Webster remarked how in New York, the members of the principal families mingle freely with other well-bred citizens. He contrasted this warmth, which he himself had experienced, to the "affectation of superiority" that governs the behavior of the leading families in Philadelphia. Webster attributed this difference to the manners of each town's prevailing sect; while America's largest city took after the reserved Quakers, its capital adopted the personality of the neat and parsimonious Dutch.

Webster's 1788 urban portrait would forever define Manhattan during the early days of the Republic.

WHILE WEBSTER WOULD ALWAYS ENJOY keeping track of facts and figures, a chance meeting the following year would reduce his reliance on this particular means to manage his anxiety. Falling in love would bring to an end his days as an aimless wanderer.

Courtship at the Constitutional Convention

COURTSHIP, n. 1. The act of soliciting favor. *Swift*. 2. The act of wooing in love; solicitation of a woman to marriage. *Dryden*. 3. Civility; elegance of manners. *Obs. Donne*.

After finishing a series of lectures in Albany, Webster returned to Connecticut, arriving back in Hartford on May 27. Two days later, he dined with Joel Barlow. On May 30, he rode on to the West Division and was reunited with his family. That evening, he wrote in his diary, "Meet my friends with joy."

Webster immediately made arrangements to take his lecture tour around his native New England. His primary objective was to raise the funds needed to print new editions of *The Grammatical Institute*. And by fraternizing with the community leaders and school officials who attended his talks, as well as the booksellers who sold the tickets, he also hoped to boost sales. While Webster would still focus on the future of American education, he would now also share the experiences and factoids that he had gathered during his visits to other parts of the country. He decided to start in his hometown. On June 5, he placed the following ad in *The Connecticut Courant*: "Mr Webster will read some remarks on the government, the population, agriculture, literature, slavery, climate and commerce of the United States; exhibiting a comparative view of each of those views in the eastern, the middle and the southern states; with some observations of manners." At the North Meeting House the following evening, Webster was rudely interrupted. Angry that he had provided free tickets to members of the state legislature, but charged an admission fee to everyone else, a contingent of local farmers mobbed the Presbyterian church, breaking a few windows. Having climbed to the top of the social ladder, Noah Webster, Jr., was now viewed with envy and contempt by those who, like his father and two brothers, spent their lives toiling in the fields. The antipathy went in both directions. "Let it be remembered," Webster wrote in his diary, "that in the year 1786, there are people in Hartford so illiberal, that they will not permit public lectures to be read in a church because they cannot be admitted without paying two shillings." Over the next two nights, he completed this brief lecture series in more friendly confines—Mr. Collier's dance studio. But only a few friends showed up.

Webster fared better in New Haven, where he was also pleased to reconnect with Ezra Stiles and Josiah Meigs. After counting New Haven's four hundred houses on Saturday, June 17, he gave the first of his six well-attended lectures at the state house the following Monday. On June 30, he delivered his last lecture "avec éclat." That same day, in a letter to Pickering, he quantified exactly how this reception compared with what he had experienced elsewhere: "In New Haven, I have about 70 hearers . . . a greater number in proportion to the size of the town than I have had before."

Though publicly Webster was animated, in private he was feeling despondent. Upon his return to Hartford in early July, he reported being "oppressed with *vis inertiae*" [the force of inertia]. Caught in what he perceived to be a never-ending search for a wife, he was also spiritually adrift. While attending a Quaker meeting during his next round of touring, he recorded the following mental meanderings: "Not a word spoken . . . a whisper or two among the Ladies excepted, I was very attentive to the silent exhortations of a pretty girl of sixteen. Such blushes, such lips made one feel devotion." And summing up another silent meeting a day later, he reported, "Saw a sweet girl."

Over the next four months, Webster's barnstorming took him to Boston (twice), Salem, Portsmouth, Newburyport, Providence and Newport. Webster was disappointed with the typically low turnouts. The one bright spot was a subscription lecture before ninety literary men—including the revolutionary journalist turned state senator, Samuel Adams—at Faneuil Hall on his second trip to Boston. And Webster was honored that Franklin himself had acknowledged the importance of his efforts. In response to Webster's June 23 letter, the Doctor wrote back on July 9: "I think with you that your lecturing on the language will be of great use in preparing the minds of people for the improvements proposed, and therefore would not advise your omitting any of the engagements you have made, for the sake of being here sooner than your business requires, that is in September or October next. I shall then be glad to see and confer with you on the subject."

Webster's lectures, which had started out as supplements to his own *Grammatical Institute,* had evolved into a prologue for his upcoming collaboration with Franklin. But with Franklin at the height of his national fame, Webster didn't mind second billing.

In Salem, Webster crossed paths with John Gardner, a South Carolina businessman who had accompanied him on his first house-count in Baltimore back in September 1785. The two statistically obsessed men pooled their data on America's housing stock. A nephew of Timothy Pickering, Gardner was proving to be a dedicated sidekick. On June 16, as a wave of fires ravaged Charleston, Gardner had exhorted Webster, "I am much obliged to you for the return of the houses of the several towns in your letter. . . . I must request you to persevere in counting houses wherever you have leasure [*sic*]." In that same letter, Gardner, whose family's fortune would be funneled into Boston's Gardner Museum a century later, also offered his immediate assessment of the conflagration's impact on his Charleston tally: "The number stood 1560 but was yesterday reduced 19 by a terrible Fire which broke out near Broad Street." Buoyed by their meeting in mid-August, Webster was more dedicated than ever to completing this national survey.

As he traveled around Massachusetts that summer, the discontent of the state's farmers reached a fever pitch. The previous year, the Bay State had enacted a new tax of a pound per poll (head), which was roughly four times the rate of its New England neighbors. Also burdened by declining land prices, the aggrieved denizens of rural Massachusetts demanded that the state government print paper money. Considering the rebels morally reprehensible, Webster repeatedly mocked their so-called grievances. On August 14, Webster wrote Pickering from Salem, "The best way to redress grievances is for every man when he gets a sixpence, instead of purchasing a pint of rum or two ounces of tea, to deposit his pence in a desk, till he has accumulated enough to answer the calls of the collector."

A couple of weeks later, a band of farmers in western Massachusetts, led by Daniel Shays, took up arms. The next month, the movement that later became known as "Shays' Rebellion" shut down the state supreme court in Springfield, which had been sending scores of debt-ridden farmers to prison. Webster the businessman would have to start making concessions to the economically distressed rural New Englanders. In its ads for his books at the end of that summer, his publisher Hudson and Goodwin noted that in lieu of cash, it would also accept "grain of any kind, bees-wax or flax."

However, the popular unrest was making Webster so uncomfortable that he now felt it necessary to abandon New England. On September 14, as he was winding up his second visit to Boston, he wrote a friend, the New York merchant James Watson, "In the course of autumn, I shall take up my bed and walk out of Connecticut. . . . These eastern states are in tumult." Noting that "I am the son of a New England farmer—an honest man," Webster stressed that the disposition of the current generation of New Englanders is "not natural—it is all habit and the effect of credit." Waxing nostalgic for a past that never was, he argued that repayment of debts should be simply a matter of honor. Webster's moralistic stance heaped the blame solely on the victims of America's struggling economy.

While lecturing in Providence in late September, Webster learned that mobs were also forcing the hand of the Rhode Island legislature, which had recently authorized the printing of a hundred thousand dollars. He was terrified that chaos would reign. In a piece published on September 28 in Providence's paper, *The United States Chronicle,* under the byline "Tom Thoughtful"—an allusion to "Tom Brainless," the bumbling protagonist of Trumbull's "The Progress of Dulness"—Webster released his pent-up anxiety and rage. "My countrymen," he wrote at the top of this editorial, "the devil is in you"; he then proceeded to use this harsh refrain like a whip. But before doing so, the future lexicographer carefully defined his key term: "the effects ascribed to this prince of evil spirits. . . . I ascribe to the wickedness and ignorance of the human heart. Taking the word 'Devil' in this sense, he is in you and among you in a variety of ways." Webster found evidence of the devil in the farmers' inability to trust Congress, their thirst for swift action and their love of luxury. But the whole country was also at fault. "The weakness of our federal government," he insisted, "is the Devil." As in his *Sketches,* Webster here, too, alluded to the necessity of a "supreme head." For Webster, a stronger union was necessary to give America the exorcism it desperately needed.

After completing his lecture tour in the eastern states, Webster returned to Hartford on October 27. But he was too broke to head directly to Philadelphia as he had hoped. The following day, he bared his financial soul to Franklin: "I labor under some embarrassments which I take the liberty to mention to your Excellency. The profits on the sale of my books, which amount now to £100 per annum, are all appropriated to reimburse the expense I have incurred in prosecuting my designs, so that I cannot with propriety expect any assistance from them for the coming year. My lectures, which have supported me hitherto, are closed; and I have nothing to depend on for subsistence this year but my further exertions in some business."

Webster asked Franklin for help in tracking down some prospects in Philadelphia: "I shall wait here a few days for your Excellency's answer, if an answer will not be too great a trouble; for in my present situation I know not how to act." Though he never received a response from the Doctor, Webster soon summoned up the courage to head south. Not only was he eager to consult with Franklin, who that November was unanimously reappointed president of Pennsylvania, but the forces of history were also tugging at him. Less than two months earlier, the Annapolis Convention had issued a report, then circulating throughout the country, which recommended that Congress meet on the second Monday in May to strengthen the Articles of Confederation. Once again Webster would trust his own resourcefulness. He spent the next few weeks settling his affairs and saying goodbye to family and friends, including Joel Barlow, John Trumbull and Nathan Perkins. He also dashed off a couple of editorials stressing the need for national unity. In an anonymous piece, which ran in the *Courant* on November 20, he cast his opponents as simpletons: "But the anti-federal men think as they have been bred—their education has been rather indifferent. . . . Besides most of them live remote from the best opportunities of information." Three days later, on Thanksgiving Day, Webster left Hartford "to seek a living, perhaps for life."

WEBSTER WOULD ONCE AGAIN travel to Philadelphia by way of New Haven and New York. In New Haven, he gave two more lectures at the state house. In a series of lively dinners and teas, he also discussed the national crisis with Yale President Stiles and his former classmate Meigs, as well as with Roger Sherman, the longtime congressman recently elected the town's first mayor, who, according to Thomas Jefferson, "never said a foolish thing in his life." While his colleagues urged more sympathy for the embattled farmers, Webster held to a hard line. Huddling in his room to avoid the single-digit temperatures and violent snowstorms, he fired off an anonymous editorial, "A Bit of Advice to Connecticut Folks," published in Meigs' *New Haven Gazette* on December 14. Attempting to solve America's economic problems with a statistical sleight of hand, he began, "It is hard times—money is scarce—taxes are high—and private debts push us. What shall we do? Why hear a few facts; stubborn facts,—and then take some advice." Webster's facts consisted of two sets of numbers: Connecticut's "necessary expenses" and its "unnecessary expenses." The big-ticket items in the first category included the salaries of state officials (e.g., the annual hundred pounds for each of its two hundred clergymen), the cost of maintaining its five hundred schools and support of the poor ("very necessary"). In the second category, the once and future attorney placed the eighteen thousand pounds the state spent on lawyers. But by far the biggest waste came from the ninety thousand pounds Connecticut citizens spent on rum. Webster's cure was simple: avoid lawyers' fees and drink. "My countrymen," he concluded, "I am not trifling with you; I am serious. You feel the facts I state." Confident of the wisdom contained in his balance sheets, Webster would reprint this essay a half-dozen times over the next decade.

In New York, Webster ended up giving just one lecture. Attracting much less interest than before, he spoke not at city hall, but at the Queen Street studio of one of the nation's leading dancing masters, John Hulett, with whom Webster would develop close ties. During his next sojourn in New York a year later, Webster would "take a few steps in dancing under Mr. Hulett" and participate in an occasional "heelkicking" at his studio.

On Christmas Day, Webster set off for Philadelphia. He first saw Franklin on the twenty-eighth, and two days later, they dined together. During Webster's ten months in Philadelphia, Franklin would regularly take time out of his busy schedule to meet with him. "The doctor," Webster proudly recalled later, "treated N.W. with much politeness." Though their friendship blossomed—Webster would on occasion accompany "the ladies" to Dr. Franklin's Market Street house—their proposed literary collaboration foundered. Webster soon realized that he didn't see eye to eye with the Doctor, who remained wedded to his old ideas about spelling reform. Speaking in his famous aphoristic style, Franklin told

Webster that "those people spell best who do not know how to spell." What the Doctor meant was that the formal rules of spelling are arbitrary, and that a purely phonetic system would make it easier for most people to read and write. Back in 1768, Franklin had drafted a treatise, *A Scheme for a New Alphabet and a Reformed Mode of Spelling,* in which he proposed substituting the letters—c, j, q, w, x, and y—for six new ones of his own making. The seasoned publisher had also come up with types for printing his new characters. After careful consideration, Webster politely informed Franklin that he wasn't willing to dust off his types in order to create a new alphabet. Reflecting back on this parting of the ways in his memoir, he wrote, "N.W. . . . was then . . . of the opinion that any scheme for introduction of a new alphabet or new characters is and will be impracticable." That account, however, doesn't quite jibe with the facts, for as late as February 23, 1787, Webster was still lecturing about "reforming the English alphabet." A perpetual self-promoter, Webster would not shy away from rewriting history when it suited his purposes.

While sometime during the spring of 1787, Webster lost interest in tinkering with the alphabet, he remained committed to spelling reform. In 1790, he would make the case for a new phonetic system relying on existing letters in a volume entitled *A Collection of Essays and Fugitiv Writings.* Webster's proposals involved, for example, eliminating silent letters such as the "e" in "fugitive" and changing "is" to "iz." Webster took his characteristic strong stand, arguing that "if a gradual reform should not be made in our language, it will proov that we are less under the influence of reezon than our ancestors." But critics found his scheme incoherent, if not absurd. Jeremy Belknap, the Boston pastor who founded the Massachusetts Historical Society, quipped that he objected to "the new mode of spelling recommended and exemplified in the fugitiv Essays ov No-ur Webster eskwier junier, critick and coxcomb general of the United States." In response to such attacks, Webster soon gave up his ambitious plan to revamp the spelling of American English. However, he would never stop pressing for less sweeping changes.

Once Webster settled in at Mrs. Ford's rooming house on Walnut

Street in early January 1787, he had to figure out how to stay afloat financially. He first tried going back to the lectern. On January 3, he met with James Sproat, the pastor at the Second Presbyterian Church at Third and Arch. Sproat was also a trustee at the University of the State of Pennsylvania, and he helped Webster gain access to a room at the university. On January 6, Webster announced in *The Pennsylvania Packet and Daily Advertiser* that he would be giving a series of seven lectures on language, education and government. But subscription sales were anemic. With the Federal Convention slated to come to town in May, Webster's call for national unity, which had generated so much excitement over the past two years, was now old news. Scaling back his plans, he decided to give just two lectures.

But the public was no longer interested in even a small dose of Webster the celebrity speaker. And Webster's social obtuseness compounded the problem. On Tuesday, January 20, the day scheduled for his first lecture, he posted an announcement in *The Pennsylvania Herald and General Advertiser,* in which he further alienated his potential audience by defining it very narrowly: "The public are most respectfully informed that this and another lecture are . . . not designed for *amusement.* . . . They are . . . for people who have leisure and inclination to devote an hour to *serious* study." At the same time, Webster made a feeble attempt to extend his appeal beyond just "thinking men of every denomination," adding, "The first [lecture] is particularly calculated for ladies of sentiment, who are very influential in manners." But his remarks on how fashion had thwarted the purposes of the Revolution didn't endear him to anyone: "This same dress which adorns a miss of fifteen will be frightful on a venerable lady of 70. . . . But the passive disposition of Americans of receiving every mode that is offered them sometimes reduces all ages, shapes and complexions to a level. . . . So long therefore as we look abroad for models, our taste must be entirely subject to the caprice and interest of other nations." Little did Webster realize that Americans were unlikely to embrace his call for independence in sartorial matters.

On the evening of January 20, a hard rain pelted Philadelphia, and with few people showing up, Webster abruptly canceled his first lecture. He tried again a week later, and though the weather was better, he nevertheless drew a small audience. An item in *The New Hampshire Spy* dated January 31—probably written by Webster himself—captured his frustration: "A [Philadelphia] correspondent laments the depraved taste of a number of his fellow citizens, in their neglect of the course of lectures, now delivering by Mr. Webster, from which a useful portion of both instruction and improvement might be derived—whilst the pantomimes . . . appear to be sanctioned by crowded audiences." As Webster would later note in his dictionary, pantomimes (such as "Harlequin in the Moon" playing that month at Philadelphia's South Street Theater) then referred to "a species of musical entertainment." That he was losing potential customers to stage actors—whom he despised— was particularly galling. On February 6, before another disappointing turnout, he recycled the idea from his Connecticut editorial about the pressing need to reduce the number of lawyers. His lecturing days were about over.

Webster was feeling not only angry but bored. Not sure what to do with himself, he whiled away the hours playing whist. The frequent attacks on his integrity in the local press infuriated him still further. In early February, alluding to Webster's "insufferable arrogance," an anonymous writer calling himself "Juvenis" also challenged his business model: "I wish Mr. Webster would publish his observations; . . . I among others cannot afford half a dollar every evening to hear his lectures." On February 17, Webster got into a brawl with a businessman named Mr. Blanchard, in which a chair was broken. Embarrassed by his lack of emotional control, he conceded in his diary, "Folly in little boys is excuseable, but in great boys, it is odious."

In April, a rattled Webster returned to his former line of work, taking a position as an English instructor at the Episcopal Church's Academy for Boys. (The school, founded in 1785, still stands, though it has been transplanted to Devon, a suburb of Philadelphia.) But he was further humiliated when a disgruntled former teacher at the school, identifying himself only as "Seth" in *The Freeman's Journal,* publicized just how far he had fallen: "This learned man . . . is now obliged to accept of two hundred pounds a year of paper money, what at present, allowing for a discount, is scarcely one hundred pounds sterling." Never one to shy away from a verbal smackdown, Webster took to his own defense. Using the alter ego "Adam"—Seth's father in the Book of Genesis—Webster fired back "that the gentleman who is so degraded by his acceptance of a place in the Academy . . . has received as good an education as America can afford and improved it by a personal acquaintance with the greater part of the principal literary gentlemen in the United States." But despite the imprimatur of the literati, Webster now had a grueling day job. On April 30, he observed, "Busy enough with the Boys of the Academy, they have been managed, or rather not managed by poor low Irish masters." This backslide in his professional life might well have led to a crippling depression were it not for an exciting new development in his personal life.

THOUGH IT WASN'T QUITE LOVE at first sight, it took only a couple of weeks for Rebecca Greenleaf to sweep Webster off his feet. Then just twenty, the petite Bostonian with the dark complexion was a head-turner, whose "fine eyes and amiable deportment have made," one contemporary put it, "so much havoc among the beaux." While most schoolteachers wouldn't have had a chance at winning her heart, Webster held out some hope. The twenty-eight-year-old was a nationally known author who was himself dashing; and persistence was his forte.

They met by accident on March 1, 1787, when Webster was escorting Miss Sally Hopkins to visit Pastor James Sproat. During the course of the evening, Webster met Duncan Ingraham, a local importer of European goods, and his family. Rebecca and her brother James were both in town to visit their older sister, Suzanna (Sukey), who had married Ingraham about a decade earlier.

Within a matter of days, Webster was turning his attention away from Miss Hopkins and toward "the agreeable Miss Greenleaf," whom he soon began seeing a couple of times a week. Every minute he spent with "the lovely Becca" was sheer delight. On March 15, Webster had dinner with Dr. Franklin, but discussions about spelling reform suddenly were no longer at the top of his agenda. The highlight of that evening, he noted in his diary, was his visit with "Miss Greenleaf, the black-eyed beauty."

Webster was Rebecca's constant companion at teas and concerts until she left Philadelphia in early summer. A few days before her departure, Webster wrote her a note, in which he enclosed a lock of his hair and revealed his intentions: "Permit me to assure you that your esteem— your friendship is now my only happiness and your happiness the great object of my pursuit. And if I am permitted to indulge a hope of mutual attachment, your inclinations will always be consulted in my future determinations. . . . You must go, and I must be separated from all that is dear to me."

For the first time in his life, Webster was madly in love. He would pursue this object of his affection with the same intensity that he would pour into defeating his political and literary opponents. But with Rebecca, the combative Webster would lay down his arms. Taking on a new persona, he did his utmost to be pleasing and agreeable. "Among other instances of my readiness to obey your wishes," he wrote while courting her, "you may rank the mode of dressing my hair. I have turned it back, and I think I look like a witch. . . . You know I do not dispute against the taste of ladies."

By the summer of 1787, the couple had reached "an understanding" that they would eventually be married. On June 20, 1787, as Rebecca was about to go back to New England, with tears streaming down his cheeks, Webster wrote her, "*Without you* the world is all alike to me; and with you any part will be agreeable." While Rebecca returned Webster's affection, she insisted on delaying the wedding because of his lack of a steady income. The disappointed Webster raised no objections. Though he would continue to socialize with other women, including "the pretty Miss Hopkins," he couldn't stop thinking about his fiancée. As he wrote to Rebecca once she was back in Boston, "I sometimes go to dances and other parties, where I see ladies and good girls, too, they are. But there is not a Becca Greenleaf among them; no such tenderness, such delicacy, such sentiment and unaffected goodness."

Rebecca's appeal went beyond her beauty and kind disposition. Webster was also entranced by the rest of the Greenleafs (derived from the French, "Feuillevert"), a distinguished Huguenot family whose roots in Massachusetts dated back to 1635. As Webster would later advise his daughter Eliza, "When you marry, look out for the stock." Rebecca was the thirteenth of fifteen children of William Greenleaf and Mary Brown, whose ancestor, John Browne, had been a magistrate of Plymouth Colony (and in 1654 had met Webster's forefather, John Webster, at a gathering of key Colonial leaders). Impressed by the Greenleafs' genealogy, that summer Webster first developed what would be a lifelong interest in his own family heritage. Initially he hoped his father might supply some answers, but he soon learned that he would have to do his own digging. "As to the history of our family," Noah Webster, Sr., wrote from Hartford on July 28, 1787, "I have made some inquiry of old people, but cannot be very particular. . . . my desire is you may rise superiour in whatever is excellent and praiseworthy to your ancestors."

Rebecca's father, William Greenleaf, possessed the worldly sophistication that Webster's own father sorely lacked. A tall, slim man, fond of his single-breasted coat and gold cane, Greenleaf was a successful Boston merchant who could easily afford to send his sons to Harvard. An avid Whig, Greenleaf was appointed sheriff of Suffolk by the Colonial governor of Massachusetts on October 31, 1775. The following year, he was at the center of a seminal moment in American history. On July 18, 1776, it fell to Greenleaf to read the Declaration of Independence from the balcony of the old State House on State Street (then called King Street) to the swirling throng below. (But the mild-mannered

Greenleaf was soft-spoken, and upon hearing the insistent cries of "Read louder!," he gave way to Colonel Thomas Crafts, another county sheriff who happened to have a booming voice.) During the war, the British ransacked Greenleaf's elegant Hanover Street home, and the family eventually resettled in Dorchester. As children, Rebecca and her sisters all felt close to their kind-hearted father, whom they would shower with kisses upon his comings and goings. An endless supply of paternal affection would transform the Greenleaf girls into easygoing and devoted wives.

By contrast, Rebecca was wary of her mother, described by family members as "cold" and "haughty." Mary Greenleaf banished several of her infant children to the country, where they were cared for by a wet nurse until they reached three or four. Rebecca's stern mother was the parent to whom Webster would have to prove his dependability as a breadwinner.

Webster was intrigued by the prospect of having so many prominent new relatives. In Philadelphia that summer, he cemented his ties with both the wealthy and savvy Duncan Ingraham and with Rebecca's brother James, then an up-and-coming speculator. Webster would soon become close to the Boston lawyer Thomas Dawes, who had married Rebecca's sister Peggy, and Dr. Nathaniel Appleton, also of Boston, the husband of her sister Sarah. Over the next couple of years, Webster would enlist the help of several members of the extended Greenleaf family in solidifying his finances.

William and Mary Greenleaf, who left behind some eighty-nine grandchildren, would spawn a bevy of distinguished descendants. Their fifteenth child, Nancy, would marry William Cranch—who as a schoolboy, accompanied by his cousin John Quincy Adams, had seen Greenleaf on the balcony of the State House that July afternoon in 1776. Cranch, who became close to Webster, later served as a chief judge of the circuit court of the District of Columbia. One of the Cranches' thirteen children, Abigail Adams Cranch, married William Greenleaf Eliot, the Unitarian clergyman who founded Washington University in St. Louis; among the grandchildren of William and Abigail Eliot was the St. Louis–born Nobel laureate, the poet T. S. Eliot.

ON WEDNESDAY, AUGUST 22, 1787, Webster marched over to the banks of the Schuylkill River to see if the strange invention could, in fact, "walk the waters like a thing of life."

The invention was the steamboat, and its inventor was a tall, thin man with jet black hair and a fiery temper named John Fitch. In the forty-four-year-old Fitch, whom he had first met that winter, Webster found a kindred spirit. A farmboy from Windsor, Connecticut, seven and a half miles north of Hartford, Fitch had stopped attending school not long after his fifth birthday. But Fitch was "nearly crazey after learning" and despite a lack of support from his father, he devoured books such as Thomas Salmon's *Geographical and Astronomical Grammar* in the hope of gathering "information of the whole world." Apprenticed to a clock-maker, Fitch had worked as a brass founder, clock mender and surveyor until 1785 when he could no longer think of anything else but "propelling a conveyance without keeping a horse."

As Webster well understood, inventors faced some of the same challenges as authors. Like Webster, Fitch had recently mounted a copyright campaign to protect the fruits of his labor. By that summer, Pennsylvania, Delaware and New York had passed special laws (analogous to those Webster had requested for his speller) under which Fitch retained exclusive rights to his invention for a period of fourteen years. To gather recommendations from the biggest names in America, Fitch had set up this experimental trial for the "Convention Men." He first invited William Samuel Johnson, a Connecticut delegate, who agreed to ride with him in the boat. And Dr. Johnson—the 1744 Yale graduate and future president of Columbia had received an honorary doctorate from Oxford—had alerted the rest of the delegates. While Webster and a couple of dozen "Convention Men" watched from the shore, about twenty others were on deck for the test run. That afternoon, Fitch's experiment actually took precedence over the nation's business as the delegates adjourned the convention early. "There was very few," Fitch later wrote in his autobiography, "of the convention but called to see it."

Throughout that summer, Webster was spending a lot of time with "Convention Men," particularly those with Connecticut ties. On Independence Day, he had called on Dr. Johnson, as well as on Abraham Baldwin, a Yale tutor during his undergraduate days, who was representing Georgia. In early August, Webster spent an evening with Connecticut's two other delegates, Oliver Ellsworth, his former boss, and Roger Sherman; a few weeks earlier, the pair had fashioned the "Connecticut Compromise," which set up America's dual system of representation in its two houses of Congress. And Webster also socialized with the Virginia delegates, James Madison and John Marshall, at whose house he would spend the evening of August 23.

Some forty-five feet long, the boat was powered by a 12-inch cylinder that sat above a small furnace. A crank over the stern propelled the half-dozen paddles, resembling snow shovels, that lined each side. Though it went just two and a half miles an hour, the vessel completed its journey from the Delaware River to Gray's Ferry in the Schuylkill River without a hitch.

Webster, like the delegates, was impressed. Their unanimous verdict was summed up in a note passed on to the inventor by a servant the following day that began, "Dr. Johnson presents his compliments to Mr. Fitch and assures him that the exhibition yesterday gave the gentlemen present much satisfaction." All of Connecticut would soon be immensely proud of this stunning feat by its ingenious native son. When meeting Ezra Stiles a few days later in New Haven, a beaming Ellsworth, who hailed from Fitch's hometown of Windsor, was as eager to share this exciting news as he was to report on the progress of the convention.

Though the experiment was an unqualified success, Fitch still had lots more work to do. He needed to build a bigger motor and increase the speed. In 1791, he obtained the first federal patent for a steamboat, but he never could raise the funds to proceed any further. Fitch's talents were as an inventor, not a venture capitalist. He soon lapsed into drink and despair, exclaiming, "The day will come when some more powerful man will get fame and riches from MY invention; but nobody will believe that poor John Fitch can do anything worthy of attention." In 1798, he downed a dozen opium pills and died in his sleep. True to Fitch's prophecy, in 1807, Robert Fulton, who had been working as a miniature portrait painter in Philadelphia during the Constitutional Convention, would emerge as "the father of the steamboat" and reap all the financial benefits.

Webster would forever be obsessed with Fitch. A half century later, he wrote to a friend, "A biography of John Fitch is a desideratum yet to be supplied." And in 1842, upon hearing that the writer Eliza Leslie was getting ready to publish her life of the inventor, Webster wrote a long letter to *Graham's Magazine,* the Philadelphia literary journal then edited by a budding writer named Edgar Allan Poe, in which he recalled his first visit aboard Fitch's boat in February 1787. Of Fitch, Webster also noted, "His . . . papers . . . were . . . found to contain a minute account of his perplexities and disappointments. The memoir of such a man . . . cannot help but present the deepest interest." Reflecting back on his own successful literary career, Webster felt that he had narrowly escaped Fitch's tragic fate.

ON MONDAY, SEPTEMBER 17, 1787, in the capacious east room of the Pennsylvania State House on Fifth and Chestnut, which Webster considered "magnificent rather than elegant," the final draft of the Constitution was read aloud. Before the vote, Benjamin Franklin handed Pennsylvania delegate James Wilson a few remarks that he had prepared for the occasion. Reading from Franklin's notes, Wilson stated, "On the whole I can not help expressing a wish that every member of the Convention who may still have objections to it . . . doubt a little of his own infallibility, and to make manifest our unanimity, put his name to the instrument." Franklin's insistence on the pressing need to approve an imperfect document carried the day. Late that afternoon, the Great Convention adjourned. That night, the members dined together for the last time at the City Tavern. Before going to bed, George Washington, who would leave town the next day, wrote in his diary that he "[meditated] on the momentous work which had been executed, after not less than five, and for a large part of the time six and sometimes 7 hours sitting every day . . . for more than four months."

On Tuesday the eighteenth, Webster was in the Pennsylvania State House as President Franklin presented the Speaker of the House of Assembly—Thomas Mifflin—with the plan of the new federal government. Bells then rang throughout the city. Though Americans could now celebrate that a steamy summer of wrangling had resulted in a founding document, another round of fierce debate remained. Before it could become the law of the land, nine states would have to vote for ratification. Recording the historic events that night, Webster noted, "All America waits anxiously for the Plan of Government."

But Webster would be no mere bystander. He would immediately get back to work on behalf of the national unity that he had long desired. And his country urgently needed his pen. On September 15, Thomas Fitzsimmons, a Pennsylvania delegate, had sent a personal note seeking his assistance: "It is already too evident that there are people prepared to oppose it [the Constitution]. . . . From a conviction that your abilities may be eminently useful on the present occasion, I am induced to call your attention to the subject. If as a friend to your country, you can support the act of the convention, I hope you will exert yourself to that purpose." The savvy publicist jumped at the chance to extol what Washington, Franklin, Madison and Hamilton had wrought. Barricading himself in his room for two full days in early October, Webster completed a pamphlet, "An Examination into the Leading Principles of the New Federal Constitution Proposed by the Late Convention Held at Philadelphia," which he dedicated to "his Excellency Benjamin Franklin, Esq." Having been recently vilified in the popular press, Webster signed it "A Citizen of America." This pen name, he felt, was likely to improve his chances of getting a fair hearing.

Published as soon as the ink was dry and excerpted in *The New Hampshire Gazette* later that fall, Webster's essay took Franklin's core argument directly to the American people: "It is absurd for a man to oppose the adoption of the constitution, because he thinks some part of it defective or exceptionable. . . . Perfection is not the lot of humanity." In simple language, Webster explained how America's founding document stacked up against its predecessors created by rulers such as Confucius, Moses and Peter the Great, describing it as "an improvement on the best constitutions the world ever saw." He also emphasized the danger of a reversion to Hobbesian chaos should it not be ratified: "The present situation of our states is very little better than a state of nature."

Though aware of the Constitution's shortcomings, Webster didn't stint in his praise. The future lexicographer found the work of the "Convention Men" eminently clear: "The constitution defines the powers of Congress; and every power not expressly delegated to that body, remains in the several state legislatures. The sovereignty and the republican form of government of each state is guaranteed by the constitution; and the bounds of jurisdiction between the federal and state Governments are marked with precision." His hastily conceived tract, Webster later acknowledged in his memoir, lacked the theoretical sophistication of the Federalist Papers, the series of eighty-five newspaper articles defending the Constitution, which began appearing a couple of weeks later in New York newspapers. As an admiring Webster would put it in 1788, these seminal writings of Hamilton, Jay and Madison passed muster for the same reason as the Constitution itself: "It would be difficult to find a treatise . . . in which the true principles of republican government are unfolded with such precision." Though the Federalist Papers are much better known to history, at the time Webster's pamphlet may well have exerted even more influence, particularly outside New York State. That November, South Carolina's David Ramsay thanked Webster for sending his "ingenious pamphlet," adding that "it is now in brisk circulation among my friends. . . . It will doubtless be of singular significance in recommending the adoption of the new Constitution."

ON OCTOBER 16, 1787, the day before his remarks on the Constitution were published, Webster celebrated his twenty-ninth birthday. "I have been industrious—endeavored to do some good," he confided to his diary, "and hope I shall be able to correct my faults and yet do more good. Put my trunk abroad for New York." His self-esteem was in tatters because, once again, his financial future was up in the air. Two weeks earlier, he had resigned from the Episcopal Academy, and his only source of income was now the trifling three hundred pounds in royalties that he could expect from his books. No longer having any business in Philadelphia, he began making preparations to head north. But where would he go and what would he do to earn the money he needed to be reunited with his beloved Becca?

At the suggestion of Franklin, with whom he spent a couple of evenings before leaving Philadelphia at the end of October, Webster decided to start a new literary magazine. Though the new nation's overall economy was still fragile, this sliver of the publishing industry was booming. Between 1776 and 1800, some forty new magazines would crop up in America, nearly two and a half times as many as had appeared in all the years prior to the Revolution. The reigning king of the genre was Philadelphia's *Columbian Magazine or Monthly Miscellany,* edited by Matthew Carey, which had been modeled on Britain's *Gentleman's Magazine.* With Carey also launching a similar publication, *The American Museum,* in 1787, Webster set his sights on America's second city. As he explained to Benjamin Rush, "The place I have chosen for publishing it is not the seat of literature, but . . . to begin another [in Philadelphia] would be neither generous nor eligible. New York will always be the destination of the packets, and the facility of the intercourse with all parts of America gives it a preference which can never be rivaled." To highlight his continuing interest in shaping his country's identity, Webster resuscitated a title—*The American Magazine*—that had graced the covers of a half-dozen short-lived Colonial periodicals.

After spending a few weeks in Hartford and New Haven visiting family and friends, Webster relocated to New York City on November 29. The following week, he announced his new publication in *The New York Packet*: "This work will . . . will consist principally of original essays in prose and verse upon a variety of subjects. . . . The editor . . . has ever been fond of books, and has leisure to devote most of his time to a publication which, if well conducted, will contribute to the amusement and improvement of his enlightened countrymen." Having learned a lesson from the lukewarm response to his last round of lectures, which were not designed for "amusement," Webster would try, despite himself, to add a touch of levity. In his ad, Webster also solicited contributions from "men of genius."

But with few writers responding to his query, Webster would have to scramble for copy. In the first issue, dated December 1, 1787, but published a month later—at the time, it was common for magazines to appear after the issue date rather than before—he recycled the work of old Yale friends, inserting an excerpt from the Trumbull poem, "The Rare Adventures of Tom Brainless," the first part of "The Progress of Dulness," and the first half of Dwight's valedictory address from July 25, 1776. He would save further installments of both works for future issues. Likewise, Webster reprinted literary efforts by his British heroes, such as "The Fountains," a fairy tale by the recently deceased Samuel Johnson. He also featured the first of what would be fourteen original essays on education, in which he reiterated his pet peeve that American schools had neglected the study of the English language, noting that "the high estimation in which the dead languages have been held, has discouraged a due attention to our own." Finally, that inaugural issue included an editorial on the Bill of Rights, which Webster called "absurd." The reason: "no constitutions in a free government can be unalterable."

To fill up those sixty-four octavo pages each month, Webster also composed numerous lighthearted pieces, which he published under pseudonyms. Writing at a feverish clip, he didn't hesitate to put his own internal preoccupations to paper. Picking up a thread from his nearly empty Philadelphia lectures, "Titus Blunt" railed against the long tails of ladies' gowns as an example of "fashion that besides its inconvenience and the expense it incurs can hardly be reconciled with neatness." Both "Philander" and "Guy Grumbleton" touched on Webster's own anxiety about his upcoming marriage, with the former stating that "all objections to matrimony, arising from an apprehension of the expense, will be removed as soon as a man is heartily in love" and the latter, an unhappy newlywed, carping that "either I was blind or the lady was deceitful." Likewise, in a satiric essay entitled "The Art of Pushing into Business and Making Way in the World" (an eighteenth-century version of *How to Succeed in Business Without Really Trying*), "Peter Pickpenny" gave voice to Webster's frustrations with his chosen vocations. Of law, he quipped, "the success (or profit, which is the same thing) of the *profession* depends much on a free use of words, and a man's sense is measured by the number of unintelligible terms he employs." His advice: "remember that the pence are multiplied with the words in the writing." "Pickpenny" also revealed the magic formula that sparked the staggering sales of Webster's own speller: "the first thing to be attended to is to prepare a blustering advertisement, recommending the work before it appears. People are caught with promises that a work shall be the best that ever was seen altho no one expects it; and who more fit to recommend a publication than the author or compiler?" Webster also turned advice columnist and amateur psychologist. Besieged by those same sexual fantasies that Webster had heretofore confined to his diary, an anxious "Curiosus" wrote to the editor: "I was at a ball a few evenings ago, and my eyes, wandering over a circle of beautiful young ladies, fixed upon a Miss—to whom I am a stranger. Her regular features—fine complexion—persuasive eyes—coral lips—graceful deportment and I know not what attractions, charmed me into admiration and made me commit twenty blunders in dancing." Webster's recommended course of action was simple: "become acquainted with the charming girl." Of Webster's multiple aliases, Ebenezer Hazard, a fellow New York publisher, observed that spring, "NW goes on publishing letters to himself."

Webster's attempts to be entertaining didn't grab too many readers. With sales of the first two issues slow, Webster began flirting with another novel idea, driven by his two major obsessions: American unity and statistics. According to a plan he hatched in early February, ten correspondents scattered across the country would funnel him mountains of descriptive data about America. As he explained to Benjamin Rush, whom he hoped to enlist as his Philadelphia reporter, "I have begun . . . a magazine in this city; but I wish to extend the publication and comprehend all the original and valuable matter in the United States and communicate it to the whole. The business of the proprietors should be to collect [materials on] . . . the state of government, finance, commerce, manufacturers, populations, sciences and every species of arithmetic information and communicate it to the editor." As proprietors, his colleagues would also share in the magazine's profits. Webster was convinced that this "useful intelligence" would both result in a sixfold increase in circulation—then stuck at about five hundred copies a month—and "gradually cement our union." Besides Rush, Webster also reached out to his Yale friends Barlow, Trumbull and Dwight in Connecticut, as well as James Madison in Virginia, and Jeremy Belknap, whom he barely knew, in Boston.

Unfortunately, this new direction for the magazine didn't make sense to anyone but Webster. Typical was the reaction of Belknap, who took four months to write back. Unsure what to make of Webster's interest in "returns of deaths, burials &c., entries at custom-houses, philosophical observations on the weather, the degrees of heat & cold, celestial phenomena, state of civil and ecclesiastical polity, colleges, ancient records & curious anecdotes, &c &c," Belknap decided to consult with his friend Ebenezer Hazard, then America's postmaster general. Though Belknap already had some reservations about Webster the man, whom he nicknamed "the Monarch," he wanted an insider's assessment of the business plan. Hazard recommended that Belknap steer clear of Webster: "I think the Monarch a literary puppy, from what little I have seen of him. He certainly does not want understanding, and yet there is a mixture of self-sufficiency, all-sufficiency and at the same time a degree of insufficiency about him, which is (to me) intolerable." Summing up, Hazard quipped, "The Monarch (I think) ought to reign alone." By late June, when Belknap politely declined Webster's offer, Webster's scheme was already dead. But Webster did manage to sprinkle some data in his pages, which also included his famous description of New York as well as a similar piece about Philadelphia. And without any correspondents supplying him with statistics from New England, he gathered a few from England himself. In the April 1788 issue, he devoted a page to "The London General Bill of Christenings and Burials From Dec 12, 1786 to December 11, 1787." After noting that 8,929 males and 8,579 females were christened and 9,821 males and 9,528 females were buried during this period, he reprinted the causes of all these deaths—a three-column list of diseases followed by a one-column list of casualties (accidents). Under the former were such entries as "Grief, 1" "Headach, 1"; under the latter was a particularly curious entry, "Bit by a mad dog, 0."

The statistical impulses run amok reflected Webster's sadness and loneliness. The months he had spent with Rebecca the previous spring had given him a taste of a whole new way of being in the world, which he sorely missed. As he wrote to her in February, "I sometimes enjoy your company in dreams; a few nights past, I was with you and passt a few happy hours with your smiles and your conversation. Would to heaven every night might be so happy." With Rebecca back in Boston, his courtship had to take place exclusively through the mail. In New York, he did, however, see a lot of her brother James, whom he soon considered a trusted friend. And James Greenleaf was, in turn, grateful to Webster for introducing him to his new business partner, James Watson. The prospect of a future with the Greenleafs kept him from disintegrating. In early 1788, he wrote Rebecca: "You will see by the tenor of this letter that I am in the dumps a little. . . . Well, I wish everybody were as good as James Greenleaf and his sister, Becca. I should then be a much happier man, but as it is, I shall not be unhappy. I am as patient as possible waiting for the sun to disperse the clouds that hang over the head of your cordial friend and admirer." But the wait to marry his beloved Becca would repeatedly try his patience. Over the next year and a half, an overworked and anxious Webster would come close to a nervous breakdown. In the words of Ebenezer Hazard, he was as "unstable as water." And as his magazine faltered, Webster was prepared to do whatever it took to marry Rebecca—even renounce all his literary activities. Summing up his first three decades in 1788, Webster confided to his diary, "I have read much, written much. . . . I will now leave writing & do more lucrative business. . . . But I am a bachelor and want the happiness of a friend whose interest and feelings should be mine."

Marriage and a Turn Away from Words

MARRIAGE, n. The act of uniting a man and woman for life; wedlock; the legal union of a man and woman for life. Marriage is a contract both civil and religious, by which the parties engage to live together in mutual affection and fidelity, till death shall separate them. Marriage was instituted by God himself for the purpose of preventing the promiscuous intercourse of the sexes, for promoting domestic felicity, and for securing the maintenance and education of children.

In the summer of 1788, as Webster worried about whether his marriage with Rebecca Greenleaf would ever take place, there was another union that he could celebrate. On June 25, New Hampshire became the ninth state to ratify the Constitution. Webster's dream of a Federalist United States of America was now a reality. That night, he wrote in his diary, "Great joy at the ninth."

Webster had just returned to New York City after attending the opening of the New York State ratifying convention in its capital, Poughkeepsie. While upstate, he took a brief excursion to see Cohoes Falls, the waterfall on the Mohawk River, where he couldn't resist doing a little quantifying. "I measure," he recorded in his diary, "the banks of the river, 100 feet, the falls more than half that distance." By the time he left Poughkeepsie on June 20, the anti-Federalists, led by Governor George

Clinton of Albany, still outnumbered the Federalists—mostly based in the city—by a margin of more than two to one.

To mark the ratification of the Constitution, New York had hoped to join other cities such as Philadelphia and New Haven that were scheduling parades for July Fourth. But with the state convention still deadlocked, the city put its plans on hold. After a series of postponements, the Revolutionary War hero Colonel Richard Platt, the chairman of the Committee of Arrangements for the New York Procession, settled on Wednesday, July 23. This majestic display of support for America's founding document, Platt figured, could perhaps sway the votes of some upstate delegates.

A fierce advocate of national unity and an arranger extraordinaire, Noah Webster, Jr., quickly became Platt's right-hand man. On July 17, Webster wrote in his diary, "Meet the Committee of Arrangement . . . and order the procession for the 23rd." In the end, Webster would not only organize the parade, he would also become its chief chronicler. Generations of historians have turned to the definitive account, which he "arranged for the public," published under Richard Platt's byline in New York's leading paper, *The Daily Advertiser*. Four decades later, to illustrate the verb "witness" in his dictionary, Webster would note, "I *witnessed* the ceremonies in New York, with which the ratification of the constitution was celebrated, in 1788." But this statement downplays the full extent of his involvement.

Platt recruited Webster because he was the driving force behind the New York Philological Society, an influential coterie of literary scholars, which would be one of roughly seventy trade associations marching in the parade. Besides Webster, who was officially its secretary, this group included the lawyer Josiah Hoffmann, its titular president; the playwright William Dunlap, its treasurer; and the naturalist Samuel Latham Mitchill, then a newly minted doctor. (A future congressman, Mitchill, who shared Webster's obsession with classifying and arranging, was later nicknamed "the Congressional Dictionary" by Thomas Jefferson.) In April, Webster had written the Philological Society's constitution; dedi-

cated "to the investigation upon which language is founded," the organization aimed "to ascertain and improve the American tongue." And to
achieve this goal, as Webster confided to publisher Isaiah Thomas in
June, the society initially planned to produce a dictionary. Though this
massive undertaking never got underway, that spring Webster gave a
series of lectures during the group's Monday night meetings in which
he put his stamp on all its activities. As Ebenezer Hazard observed, "I
do not know all the members of the Philological Society, though I have
understood that they are not numerous. The Monarch reigns supreme . . .
[over] . . . his subjects."

However, Webster's decision to shepherd the Philological Society
wasn't motivated purely by patriotism. He was also looking for more
publicity for his speller. On July Fourth, President Hoffmann wrote an
endorsement on behalf of the society, in which he stated that Webster's
book was "calculated to destroy the various false dialects in the several
states . . . an object very desirable in a federal republic." By establishing
the norms of a new federal language, the group could also, so Webster
hoped, give his textbooks a virtual monopoly in the nation's school systems. That summer, he wrote to his publisher: "When you advertise the
improved editions of the *Institute,* something like the following may be
published. . . . The Philological Society in New York recommend this
work with a view to make it the *federal school book.* The University of
Georgia, preferring this to Dilworth . . . or any other . . . have determined that this alone shall be used in all the schools in that state. The
publishers flatter themselves that the northern states will heartily concur
in the design of a *federal language.*"

Webster thus was counting on the Philological Society to help him
cash in on the passage of the Constitution, which suddenly improved
the commercial prospects for his books.

For the nearly thirty-year-old Webster, the New York procession
represented the triumph of everything he stood for—patriotism, national
unity and order. He felt a sudden surge of optimism, noting in his August piece in *The Daily Advertiser,* "the great object of exultation . . .

was . . . an era in the liberty of man, great glorious and unparalleled, which opens a variety of new sources of happiness and unbounded prospects of national prosperity." In a life filled with anxiety and toil, it would be a rare day of pure exhilaration, which he would share with the rest of a thoroughly delirious and united Manhattan Island.

ON THE MORNING OF JULY 23, Webster, dressed in the black uniform of the Philological Society, left his Maiden Lane residence and walked up to the area then known as "the Fields" (today City Hall Park). He soon joined a throng of some five thousand working men, who had been gathering since eight o'clock. Thousands more started lining up on the spotless streets along the parade route, which had been swept and watered both earlier that morning and the night before. The city's ladies, preferring to avoid the crowds, stationed themselves in doorways and at windowsills.

Just as red, white and blue were the procession's predominant colors, ten and thirteen were its operative numbers. That's because at the beginning of July, Virginia had become the tenth of the thirteen states to approve ratification.

At exactly ten o'clock, thirteen guns from the federal ship *Hamilton*, built especially for the occasion, announced that the procession was to begin. Horsemen with trumpets started down Broadway, along with a company of artillery. Then came Grand Marshal Richard Platt, dressed in a blue coat, red sash and white feather, followed by his thirteen deputy marshals.

Finally, the ten divisions of artisans fell into line, each one led by a man carrying a white banner. The workers, forming a mile-and-a-half retinue, came from all walks of life. In this day of unity, the young, the old, the rich, the poor, the learned and the uneducated were all marching as one.

The first division consisted largely of artisans whose work had something to do with the land or its by-products: farmers, foresters, gardeners, millers, distillers and bakers. As the new United States of America was largely an agrarian nation, this contingent was the longest, containing fourteen subdivisions. Wit and ingenuity were everywhere on display. The bakers featured four masters who carried a ten-foot-long "federal loaf" upon which was emblazoned the names of the ten ratifying states and the initials of the three holdouts: N.Y., N.C. and R.I.

Coopers (makers and repairers of wooden barrels) led the second division. As Webster would later describe their arithmetically appropriate tribute: "Thirteen apprentice boys, 13 years of age, dressed in white shirts, trowsers, and stockings. . . . their hats ornamented with 13 pillars, colored green and white, with ten branches springing from them."

A few hundred yards in front of Webster paraded the chocolate makers, who were grouped with the blacksmiths and instrument makers in the eighth division. Their float captured graphically what he had been writing about for the past half-dozen years. To represent the powerless Congress under the Articles of Confederation, they carried a picture of a naked man, whose thirteen heads were all looking in different directions, upon which was written:

When each head thus directing,
The body naught pursues;
But when in one uniting
Then energy ensues.

Led by Webster, the Philological Society, subdivision 69, marched right behind the "Gentlemen of the Bar" who headed the ninth division. This contingent of the city's intelligentsia also featured subdivisions 70 and 71: students and professors from Columbia, including the college's president, William Samuel Johnson, as well as traders and merchants.

Webster carried a scroll containing the principles of a federal language. Behind him walked President Josiah Hoffmann in a sash of blue and white ribbons, and Treasurer William Dunlap carrying the society's highly intricate coat of arms, which Webster had helped to design two weeks earlier. Its major elements included three tongues, a chevron and an eye over a monument sculpted with Gothic, Hebrew and Greek letters. Its crest, whose symbolism no doubt was understood only by its creators, consisted of a cluster of cohering magnets attracted by a large key, meant to highlight that language was a unifying principle of knowledge. The flag was embellished with the phrase "the Genius of America" and crowned with a wreath of thirteen plumes, ten of them starred. While her right hand pointed to the Philological Society, in her left was a pendant with the word "CONSTITUTION."

After reaching the bottom of Broadway, the procession looped around and headed back north via Queen and Arundel streets. Webster was energized by occasionally glancing over at the ladies, those "fair daughters of Columbia whose animated smiles and satisfaction," he would later write, "contributed not a little to complete the general joy." There was no music and the solemnity of the event precluded cheering: "No noise was heard but the deep rumbling of carriage wheels, with the necessary salutes and signals. A glad serenity enlivened every countenance."

As the marchers arrived at City Alderman Nicholas Bayard's farm, which bordered on the upper reaches of Broadway, they were reviewed by Grand Marshal Richard Platt before dispersing. Leaving their signs on the fields, they headed to dining tables located in the three pavilions built by the architect Pierre L'Enfant (whom Washington would later commission to design the new federal city on the Potomac), in just five days. The banquet area, which was some 600 by 900 feet, featured ten colonnades festooned with wreaths. Under the dome of the middle pavilion—topped by the figure of Fame, carrying a parchment alluding to the three phases of the late war (Independence, Alliance with France, Peace)—sat members of Congress, foreign dignitaries and the city's clergy.

Along with some six thousand other revelers, Webster feasted on roasted mutton and ham and imbibed abundant amounts of beer. At the end of the meal, he raised his glass to thirteen toasts—the last one being

"May the union of the United States be perpetual"—each of which was marked by shots from ten cannons.

In this celebration of unity, no New Yorkers would be left out. Afterward, the same repast was passed on to all the city's prisoners.

At five thirty, the marchers returned to their original stations and were dismissed.

That night, just as Webster was describing the procession in his diary as "very brilliant, but fatiguing," Richard Platt wrote to the Poughkeepsie delegates that "the most remarkable regularity and decorum prevailed during the whole day."

Platt, Webster and their fellow arrangers soon achieved their primary political objective. At nine o'clock on Saturday evening, July 26, as Webster was working away at his newspaper account of the event, he heard shouting in the streets; Poughkeepsie had rendered its final verdict. "News of the Convention's adopting the Constitution received," he wrote in his diary, "& great joy testified."

On August 2, Ebenezer Hazard wrote to the Boston pastor Jeremy Belknap, "I hear the Monarch (not of France) intends to honour this town with a visit."

Webster was indeed heading north to see Rebecca for the first time in more than a year. On Sunday, August 10, along with Hazard and Rhode Island's congressional delegation, he sailed to Providence. Two days later, he waited on "the dear girl" at her home in Dorchester. And on the fourteenth, he officially asked for her hand in marriage. "Ask consent of Mr. Greenleaf," he noted in his diary, "& am happy in receiving it." However, to reassure the Greenleafs of his suitability as a breadwinner, Webster had to promise to give up his literary career and return to law. This decision would soon become a source of constant anguish.

Once back in New York, Webster made plans to dispose of his magazine. In November, he negotiated a deal with both Hazard and another New York publisher, Francis Childs, who planned to revive it the following year under the title *The American Magazine and Universal Register.* Under this proposal, the magazine would be expanded to a hundred pages, and the second half of each issue would feature key documents from American history. "It has been . . . frequently lamented by the lovers of useful license that no particular account of the origin and complete establishment of this rising empire hath yet been given to the world," ran the announcement in New York's *Daily Advertiser.* Webster had hoped to print, for example, John Winthrop's journal, which he had recently discovered at the house of former Connecticut governor Jonathan Trumbull. But nothing came of it. With circulation down to just two hundred, the magazine ceased publication after its one-year run. Rather than adding anything to his coffers, this venture had ended up costing him about two hundred and fifty pounds (five hundred dollars).

That fall, Webster's future in-laws sent him congratulatory notes on his engagement. Writing from Amsterdam, where he had gone to pursue various business opportunities, James Greenleaf assured him, "As you have gained the consent of my parents & friends, if mine is either necessary or acceptable, you have it in the fullest manner." Greenleaf also offered to help Webster financially, though he didn't specify exactly how much money he could provide. In late November, Dr. Nathaniel Appleton of Boston, who had known Rebecca for a decade, observed, "If you make this girl your partner for life, you will have acquired the most amiable and all accomplished lady for a man of sentiment and taste for domestic life, which this metropolis affords. You cannot prize her too highly." With Webster deciding to move to Boston, Appleton found him temporary lodgings: the best room at Mrs. Archibald's, the Court Street residence where he had lived the summer before, for twenty-four pence a week. Webster was looking forward to living near all the Greenleafs.

On December 20, Webster was "happy to quit New York." He spent Christmas with his parents in the West Division. On New Year's Eve, Webster arrived in Boston, where he soon enjoyed frequent visits with his "agreeable new friends." On those evenings when he wasn't having dinner with Rebecca or other members of the extended family, he was socializing with the city's elite. On January 28, 1789, he met the incoming vice president, John Adams, at the home of former governor James Bowdoin.

Building a legal practice, he soon realized, would take at least a few years. On February 1, in a letter to James Greenleaf, then still in Amsterdam, Webster highlighted his precarious finances: "I have done with making books. I shall enter upon the pursuit of law immediately and practise either in Hartford or this town. . . . I am as happy as the heart of the loveliest of her sex and the kindness and esteem of all your connections can make me. . . . I shall try to make it convenient to marry in the course of the year, but it depends partly on your assistance and partly on the events that are not altogether in my power."

Two weeks later, Webster received his first letter from Greenleaf in months, in which he learned that his future brother-in-law had married a Dutch woman, Antonia von Scholten. Webster wrote back the next day, once again stressing his need for a handout: "I perceive by your letter . . . that you have engaged some provision for Becca at her marriage. This will furnish a house genteelly. . . . As a person interested in your favors to your sister, I feel grateful and number you among my benefactors as well." As Webster also explained to Greenleaf, he now planned to move back to Hartford where he had more contacts in the legal community.

That winter in Boston, Webster superintended the publication of what he thought would be his final book, *Dissertations of the English Language*, the four-hundred-page tome that featured the language lectures from his two-year book tour. Published in May, it fell on deaf ears. On account of the printing costs, Webster was out four hundred dollars. His only consolation was praise from Benjamin Franklin, to whom he had dedicated it. At the close of 1789, just a few months before his death, the Doctor would write Webster a long letter about this "excellent work . . . [which] will be useful in turning the thoughts of our country men to correct writing."

In May, Webster moved back into the Hartford residence of his longtime friend John Trumbull, where he would be paying tenpence a week. Upon his return to his hometown, his former boss Oliver Ellsworth wrote him a welcoming note from New York, where he was serving in the U.S. Senate: "I congratulate you and the city of Hartford on your settlement there in the practice of law." Ellsworth also offered Webster the option of moving back into his home—now vacant—where he had lived a few years earlier. (Two years later, Webster and his wife would wind up there.) Webster was once again circulating among the town's beau monde. That summer, he dined with Colonel Jeremiah Wadsworth, the influential merchant then serving in the House of Representatives; Dr. Lemuel Hopkins, the well-known poet; Nathan Perkins, the West Division pastor; as well as his Yale classmates Oliver Wolcott and Uriah Tracy.

Though he enjoyed reconnecting with his Hartford friends, Webster was feeling frustrated. His new profession was turning out to be no more lucrative than his old one. Legal work was hard to come by. And for the first time in years, he had no new literary project to fall back on. In addition, that summer, due to a hand injury, he could barely manage to keep up with his correspondence. Bored, he didn't know what to do with himself. On June 17, he wrote in his diary, "Begin to bathe in the morning." The following day, he added, "Repeat it with benefit." "Ditto" was his wrap-up of the nineteenth.

In late August, Webster's spirits revived when he heard from Greenleaf for the first time since April. "I cannot refuse," his soon-to-be brother-in-law wrote, "to join my approbation to that of my family that your marriage may take place as soon as you think prudent." To express his affection for the young couple, Greenleaf advanced them a thousand dollars. Webster promptly rented a comfortable house in the center of town from Colonel Wadsworth for a hundred dollars a month. Throughout the first week of September, as he recorded in his diary, he was "still employed in getting furniture." Starting a new life with Rebecca was now his top priority. For the time being, he would do without words.

———————

ON SATURDAY, OCTOBER 24, 1789, at about two o'clock in the afternoon, President George Washington made his entrance into Boston. Washington, who had taken the oath of office on April 30 on the steps of Federal Hall in New York City, was touring New England for the first time as president. The previous week, he had visited Hartford, where he had spent a day in the company of Webster's social circle, meeting with both Wadsworth and Ellsworth. Upon crossing the Charles River from Cambridge, Washington was whisked to the balcony of the state house. There he was serenaded by an ode that began:

> Great Washington the Hero's come!
> Each heart exulting
> Thousands to their deliverer throng
> And shout him welcome all around!

Washington reviewed a procession of Boston's artisans, tradesmen and manufacturers that took place on the street below. That evening, the city's main public houses (such as the Coffee House on State Street) were illuminated, and there was also a fireworks display. The roughly twenty-five thousand spectators who saw the president behaved with "good order and regularity," according to *The Boston Gazette*.

"All the world is collected to see [Washington]," Webster wrote in his diary. One of the few people then in Boston not in attendance was Webster himself; he was incapacitated by nausea.

Webster had been a nervous wreck for weeks. Financial concerns were gnawing at him. On October 12, he wrote James Greenleaf from Hartford:

> The progress of young lawyers is nearly ascertained in this town. . . .
> [After four years, they] . . . make a little money & after that, they
> have generally pretty full practice. . . . I have as good a prospect as

my neighbors; better I cannot expect. Still I am anxious. The dear girl who has given me her heart and who has made a sacrifice of all her natural connections for a union with me has a claim, not merely to kindness, but to peculiar attention. She has sensibility and must be very particularly unhappy in any misfortunes that should befall us. I feel already a thousand anxieties on her behalf.

Five days later, on October 17, 1789, the day after turning thirty-one, Webster headed to Boston for his wedding. In his diary, he couldn't quite face this fact head-on, alluding instead to "an important errand" (a word he would define in 1828 as "a mandate" or "order"). Though Webster had longed for this day for years, he was suddenly filled with dread.

Webster contracted the flu on Wednesday, October 21. For the next four days, he could barely move. On the night of Washington's visit, he was reduced to using the third person to describe his symptoms. "The head appears," he wrote in his diary, "to be fastened with chains, and the disorder is attended with a cough. The best remedy is hot liquors to produce perspiration. . . . But if the stomach is disordered & refuses diet, a puke is necessary."

On Sunday, October 25, Webster was still confined to his room: "My disorder has come to its crisis." Crisis was then primarily a medical term referring to a change in a disease state—toward either recovery or death. Fortunately, for Webster, it would mean the former.

The following day, Webster felt well enough to assume his role as bridegroom. Presiding over the ceremony at the Greenleafs' Dorchester home was Pastor Peter Thatcher of Boston's exclusive Brattle Street Church. (George Washington himself had visited Thatcher's congregation the day before.) The wedding proceeded, he noted in his diary, without incident: "Much better. This day I became a husband. I have lived a long time a bachelor, something more than 31 years. But I had no person to form a plan for me in early life & direct me to a profession. . . . I am united to an amiable woman, & if I am not happy, shall be much disappointed." As Webster the expert definer well knew, he hadn't really been a "bachelor"—a term reserved exclusively for adults—for three decades, but that's how he felt. Unlike Rebecca, he hadn't experienced a deep sense of connection with either of his parents as a child. Remarkably, despite his outsize expectations, Rebecca would never let him down. For the next half century, she would provide the emotional anchor that he so desperately needed. Patient and self-controlled, Rebecca, whom her brother Daniel called "an angel," would nurture her husband with the same dedication as she would the couple's seven children. Once described by a family member as "neatness and order itself," she was the perfect match.

On November 7, Webster and his bride moved into Colonel Wadsworth's house in Hartford. Accompanying the newlyweds was Rebecca's older sister Priscilla, who would stay for a few months.

The fifth of the fifteen Greenleaf children, "Sister Priscy," as Webster called her, was as attractive as her seven sisters, but more discriminating about prospective suitors. According to a joke then circulating in Boston, after young clergymen got their license, they typically proposed to Prissy Greenleaf. Before marrying at nearly forty in 1794, she would receive thirty proposals, twenty-three from pastors.

That first month in Hartford was nerve-wracking. The day after their move, Rebecca was stricken with the flu, and Priscilla the next day. On Sunday the fifteenth, Webster had to stay home from church to tend to them. The following Sunday, he went with Priscilla because Rebecca hadn't yet recovered. Rebecca soon improved, and despite violent storms, Webster and the two Greenleaf sisters managed to travel back and forth to his parents' home for a Thanksgiving meal on Thursday, November 26 (the first federal celebration). As Rebecca put it in a letter to her brother John, Webster enjoyed "demolishing" the eleven pumpkin puddings she baked. Webster's mother was initially standoffish with his new bride; the farmer's wife didn't know what to make of the sophisticated city girl's elegant outfits, such as her green brocade featuring pink and red roses. But as Mercy Webster taught her new daughter-in-law how to knit, the two women began to warm up to each other.

Rebecca missed the familiar surroundings of Boston. On December 4, she wrote to her brother John, "Yesterday, I was terrible homesick, and did nothing but bawl the whole day . . . & husband was out almost the whole time. Today the sun shines clear and the world wears a different appearance." While Rebecca continued to have occasional bouts of gloominess, Webster was in a state of wedded bliss. "[Your sister Becca] is all that is kind and amiable," he observed to her brother James on Christmas Day, "and you may rest assured that I now realize all my former ideas of her worth. I may safely say that our happiness is not exceeded in the world; for so far as our hearts are concerned, our happiness is without alloy." However, Webster was still dogged by financial anxiety. In that Christmas letter, he also asked James for another infusion of money. According to his account, the newlyweds were experiencing a sudden two-hundred-dollar shortfall because Rebecca had insisted on buying some extravagances such as chintz furniture: "The deficiency however was to me wholly unexpected, till a short time before our union, and when I informed your sister, she cried as if to break her little heart." Webster may well have been embellishing (or creating) the drama to plead his case; Rebecca's version of this incident doesn't exist.

Webster's Yale mentor John Trumbull offers a more plausible explanation for the source of his money troubles. In a letter that December to Webster's classmate Oliver Wolcott, then Connecticut's comptroller, Trumbull observed, "Webster has returned, and brought with him a very pretty wife. I wish him success; but I doubt, in the present decay of business in our profession [law], whether his profits will enable him to keep up the style he sets out with. I fear he will breakfast upon Institutes, dine upon Dissertations and go to bed supperless." While Webster's descendants have long denied that his law practice in Hartford in the early 1790s was anything but lucrative, he would indeed struggle to provide for his new wife. As he acknowledged in his memoir, "[NW] began housekeeping with very unfavorable prospects." In the end, he would never be able to make a living as a lawyer.

In addition to financial stress, Webster also was experiencing a surge in existential angst. Though Webster had assured the Greenleafs that he would stop writing, just a few weeks after his wedding he realized that he couldn't keep this pledge. After all, literary activity was what made him feel most alive. For the next few years, Webster the lawyer and family man would be in constant conflict with Webster the scribe. But he typically kept this tension to himself. In a letter to George Washington written less than a year after his marriage, he noted: "I have written much more than any other man of my age in favor of the Revolution and my country. . . . [However], I wish now to attend solely to my profession and to be unknown in any other sphere of life." While Webster would stop drawing attention to himself as a writer, he wouldn't stop writing. To resolve his dilemma, he ceased putting his own name on his new literary projects.

IN LATE 1789, Webster joined a legal club whose members included such friends as Trumbull, Wadsworth, Chauncey Goodrich, later a U.S. senator, and Peter Colt, the state treasurer. At weekly dinners, the group would discuss the pressing policy issues of the day. In a December meeting at Trumbull's house, the question was whether the state's excise tax on the retail sale or use of imported goods was consistent with the Constitution. As in the 1784 debate over taxes, while the state's agrarian elements supported the excise tax, its shopkeepers were up in arms. With neighboring states levying no such tax, Connecticut's consumers had an incentive to shop elsewhere. The area's leading merchants such as Wadsworth soon petitioned Webster to take up his pen to articulate their concerns.

A week after the dinner at Trumbull's, Webster spent two nights working on an eighteen-page pamphlet, "Attention! Or New Thoughts on a Serious Subject: Being an Inquiry into the Excise Laws of Connecticut," which he published in late December under the pseudonym "A Private Citizen." Addressed to "the Freemen of Connecticut," Webster's

anonymous article also circulated widely in Connecticut and Massachusetts newspapers over the next few months.

The future lexicographer was in full view. At the heart of the matter
was the interpretation of a single sentence in the tenth section of Article
I of the Constitution, which stated that "No state shall, without the
consent of Congress, lay any imposts or duties on imports or exports,
except what may be absolutely necessary for executing its inspecting
laws." The bulk of Webster's essay focused on defining these key terms.
To frame the debate, he began by alluding to "the best compilers of
dictionaries" who "explain impost to be any tax, toll or tribute." Webster
noted that Malachi Postlethwaite (author of the mid-eighteenth-century
British classic *Universal Dictionary of Trade and Commerce*) "defines *impost* to be 'a tax or duty laid by the sovereign authority.' . . . It does not
appear by this definition that a particular mode of levying and collecting
a tax is necessary to constitute it as an *impost*." He then elaborated on
the true meaning of the words "imports" and "exports." For example, he
asked hypothetical questions about when exactly goods shipped from
abroad lose the name of "imports": "Is it when they are landed? When
they are opened? Or when they are sold to the retailer?" Webster continued to split such hairs for another ten pages before concluding that
Connecticut's excise tax was inconsistent with both the letter and the
spirit of the Constitution. As in the 1784 impost debate, Webster again
identified himself with the cause of national unity. This tax, he contended, ran the risk of "defeating the commerce of America, and per-
petuates the life of the monster with thirteen heads." Thanks to Webster's
fierce advocacy, the state legislature repealed this statute by a nearly
unanimous vote in late May.

As 1790 began, Webster's mood remained upbeat. He published an
anonymous New Year's poem, in which he celebrated the dawn of a new
era in America, but he issued the following proviso:

But all must first their station fix,
Nor craze their skulls with politics;

His proper calling each pursue,
And thus his worth and wisdom show.

According to Webster, what America now needed was to get organized. While astronomers, he wrote, had to churn out their almanacs, pedagogues had to teach and parsons had to preach. But Webster didn't yet have his own niche. While he took on occasional legal assignments, such as drafting writs for clients, his new profession was hardly keeping him busy. "Little business done," his summary of May 14, was a typical journal entry. Better than expected sales from his books were keeping him afloat. His initial predictions for the arc of his legal career had been overly optimistic. As he reported to James Greenleaf, "The business of lawyers is at a lower ebb than was ever known before . . . some who have been in business ten years scarcely maintain their families." Webster hoped to get by on his royalties and to wait it out until "we can push off some of the old lawyers."

That spring and summer, Webster managed to find a variety of new outlets for his compulsive energy. Shortly after Benjamin Franklin's death on April 17, 1790, he returned to the cause of spelling reform, authoring a series of fourteen editorials for *The American Mercury* (six initialed and the other eight anonymous). These front-page pieces, entitled "Remarks on the English Language," also alluded to those fine distinctions so dear to Webster's heart. "One half of the world," he griped in his second installment, "use words without annexing cleer [*sic*] ideas to them." Here he distinguished between "genius" ("the power of invention") and "great capacity" ("a power of receiving the ideas communicated by others"). In June, he also published his *Collection of Essays and Fugitiv Writings,* a volume of his old articles, in which he fleshed out his ill-fated scheme to revamp spelling. And at the same time, he took on another concern dear to Franklin—street paving. Back in 1757, concerned about the dirt and mud on Philadelphia's Market Street, Franklin had backed an elaborate bill to bring order to the entire city. Completed in early May, Webster's plan for covering Hartford's streets with hard stone would prove, as he proudly noted in his diary, "pleasing to many." For the next few years, a local tax of fourpence on the pound supported Webster's measure.

And once the warm weather came, Webster also enjoyed tilling the soil. As he noted in a short article, published that June, "The Farmer's Catechism," he considered farming "the most necessary, the most healthy, the most innocent and the most agreeable employment of men." In the garden behind his kitchen, he planted potatoes, beets, carrots, parsnips and cucumbers. Webster loved classifying and arranging potatoes as much as words. On June 25, he performed the following experiment: "Lay 3 square yards of mellow earth with seed potatoes about 8 inches apart, cover them with half rotten hay and straw, cover 1 yard with shoots broken off from the potatoes." Webster's passion for the potato would work its way into his dictionary, where he defined it as "one of the cheapest and most nourishing species of vegetable food. . . . In the British dominions and in the United States, it has proved one of the greatest blessings bestowed on man by the Creator."

On Saturday, July 24, 1790, William and Mary Greenleaf arrived in Hartford. The reason for this visit, as Rebecca's brother Daniel explained to Webster, was their hope of "being present at a grand *launching* on Monday [the 26th] . . . which day completes nine months since your marriage." The Websters' first child was indeed on its way, but the baby arrived slightly behind schedule. On Monday, August 2, Rebecca became ill and for the next two days, was incapacitated by crippling pain. Finally, at half past four on the fourth, as Webster noted in his diary, his daughter came into the world. The difficult birth would force him to hire a nurse for the month that Rebecca remained bedridden. The Websters called the baby Emily Scholten (adding the middle name in homage to the Dutch wife of James Greenleaf). The following Monday, "Papa and Mama," as Webster referred to the Greenleafs in his diary, went back to Boston. By the middle of 1790, Webster was feeling closer to his in-laws than to his own parents, who were undergoing a new round of misfortunes. In April, they were forced to sell the West Division farm and move into a house in Hartford with Webster's sister Mercy and her husband, John Belding. Though occasionally sending his father money, Webster was as financially strapped as ever. In late August, he was reduced to borrowing eighty-five dollars from a friend, Benjamin West, to cover living expenses.

While Webster wasn't a successful attorney, he was a prominent one. On Friday, October 22, 1790, the U.S. Supreme Court came to Hartford—for its first century, its justices would "ride circuit"—and a few days later, in a ceremony presided over by Chief Justice John Jay, Webster was one of about ten local attorneys admitted to practice in the district court. Webster and Jay were destined to become lifelong friends. That Sunday, Webster also enjoyed socializing with Associate Justice William Cushing (known in history books as the last American jurist to wear a wig).

On Tuesday, October 26, Webster celebrated his first wedding anniversary: "One year past, and no quarelling." This domestic peace would endure, but Rebecca would usually be the one doing the compromising. As one of the couple's children would later note in a memoir, "I never knew my mother [to] argue a point with my father. She would express an opinion and defer to him as the best judge of matters."

In December, Webster began a new writing project, which he kept secret from his family and friends. In a series of twenty anonymous essays, published weekly in *The Connecticut Courant,* he would address the frustrations of everyday life. Like a stage prompter who helps actors remember their lines, Webster was hoping to "prompt the numerous actors upon the great theater of life." As he asserted in the introduction to the book version, *The Prompter; or A Commentary on Common Sayings and Subjects,* released in October of 1791, "He [the writer] cast about to find the method of writing calculated to do the most general good. He wanted to whip vice and folly out of the country." Patterning himself after Benjamin Franklin's Poor Richard, Webster eschewed "a pompous elegance of diction." This anonymous alter ego bore little relation to Webster's everyday personality; in one essay, he even mocked "learned word-mongers." He would talk directly to the common man. "Vulgar sayings and proverbs, so much despised by the literary epicures are . . . the pith and marrow of science." With his speller teaching America's children how to read, and his *Prompter* its uneducated masses how to live, few Americans could now escape Webster's pedagogical influence.

The Prompter was motivated by the same internal pressures that would drive all his literary efforts. This lover of order relished the challenge of organizing information in a clear and useful way. Noting that "there is nothing new in the field of knowledge" and that everything has been said before, the expert compiler and arranger dispensed homespun advice by making "common things appear new." While in his various books on language he aimed to fix the wrongs of previous lexicographers and grammarians, here he sought to set all of humanity aright, choosing as his epigraph a verse from Pope's *Essay on Man*: "To see all others' faults and feel our own."

Claiming to be an objective purveyor of truth, Webster concluded his anonymous introduction by assuring his readers that "there is not in this book one personal reflection." But this volume was actually overflowing with his own feelings and experiences. Consider "Prompter No. II," published on December 13, 1790, and called "The Fidgets." The chronically nervous Webster embodied the concept, which he would define in 1828 as a "vulgar" term for restlessness. In this uncharacteristically amusing essay, Webster argued that the disorder was not uncommon: "A man who is fairly hyp'd and a histericky woman are remarkable for fidgets. . . . But those who think these are the only people who have the fidgets think wide of the truth." Webster went on to identify its various subspecies: domestic fidgets, political fidgets and the purse fidgets, which he called "the most laughable." He noted that lawyers often manifested symptoms of this particular malady when they shouted out "adjournment—continuance—false—my client is wronged—I'll have a new trial." This comic aside reflected his concerns about whether his day job would ever pay his bills.

Despite the pressing need to unburden himself of his own obsessions, in *The Prompter,* as in the speller and, later, in the dictionary, Webster still connected with the reader. Americans liked his mixture of satire and practical advice. Though a razor-sharp analytic thinker, Webster also had a common touch. No uppity aristocrat, this pugnacious Federalist had a knack for distilling human experience. In the article "When a Man is going down hill, everyone gives him a kick," Webster captured the anxiety felt by legions of Americans: "While a man is *doing very well,* that is, while his credit is good, every one helps him—the moment he is pressed for money, however honest and able he may be, he gets kicks from all quarters." In January 1796, Webster finally revealed himself as the author. Several months later, the Harvard-educated journalist Joseph Dennie, later dubbed the "father of American Belles-Lettres" by Timothy Dwight, sent him a copy of his own influential collection of essays, *The Lay Preacher,* enclosing the tribute, "I have been amused by *The Prompter.* The simplicity and ease of style of that little volume taught me the value of the Franklin Style. . . . consider the author as your debtor." Two years later, a British edition appeared with the following editor's note: "Americanisms have been retained, as it would have been uncandid to cover American ground with English leaves." Of its success across the pond, Webster was particularly proud. "In an English notice of the little book," he wrote in his memoir, "it was said to be a very good shilling-worth publication." Webster's book would remain popular for decades; by the mid-nineteenth century, millions of readers would devour a total of one hundred editions.

> Will be happy to receive from gentlemen in other states any orders
> for business, either in his professional or business capacity, and will
> execute them with fidelity and promptitude.

SO RAN THE AD that Noah Webster, Jr., attorney and counselor at law, placed a couple of times in *The New York Daily Advertiser* in August 1791. With his Hartford shingle not drawing in enough clients, Webster felt compelled to cast a wider net. And a month earlier, he had personally

met with Connecticut's Governor Samuel Huntington in Norwich, who
had helped him add "notary public" to his titles. But despite his tena-
cious efforts, business would not pick up. Fantasizing about a magical
solution to his financial woes, Webster would continue to buy the occasional lottery ticket.

He also took recourse in a source of comfort that he had first discovered as a preadolescent, pouring out his frustrations in letters to the
editor. In September 1791, one of his alter egos dashed off a jeremiad
to *The New York Daily Advertiser,* which was reprinted in various New
England papers later that fall. Purporting to be from New York, "P.Q."
addressed a series of unrelated pet peeves that had cropped up during
his recent travels in three "sister states"—Rhode Island, Massachusetts
and Connecticut (Webster himself had hopped around New England
that summer). While Newport irked him because "the houses are falling
to pieces and deserted," he was surprised that Bay State residents were
allowed to sue one another in any county: "How the wise state of Massachusetts can indulge such laws, I leave others to conjecture." But
"P.Q." reserved his harshest words for Connecticut's chief justice, Colonel Eliphalet Dyer (whom Webster knew socially): "He had such confusion of ideas or of language that I thought no mortal could understand
him; and I found the by-standers were all as much puzzled to understand
him as myself." For Webster, the realization that having a way with words
wouldn't necessarily help him rise in his new profession was devastating.
"P.Q." also expressed frustration with other aspects of Connecticut life:
the pews in its churches tended to be just four feet long, requiring ten
people to crowd on top of one another. "All must sit like statues," he
complained. Likewise, writing as "Peter Puzzle" in the *Courant* a few
months later, Webster unleashed his fury on other parts of the nation
besides New England. He attacked the Senate as "an aristocratic junto,"
Southerners for their "microscopic minds" and Washington's would-be
successors, predicting that "nine tenths of our future Presidents will be
clear devils."

But this latest string of disappointments might not have led to so much anger had his own future looked brighter. Webster, who had hardly enjoyed a moment of financial stability since his abrupt exit from his father's farmhouse, was feeling despondent. He confided his troubles to James Greenleaf, who responded the following January from Amsterdam: "I am sorry to observe in your last something that borders on a depression of spirits. . . . If you are not so rich as you wish to be or even as you are conscious of deserving, you have on the other hand such domestic happiness as falls to the lot of but few." Unable to find much gainful employment for himself, Webster turned his attention to the welfare of others. On January 2, 1792, the *Courant* published Webster's "New Year's Gift"—the first of a new series of eight weekly essays called "The Patriot" and subtitled "On the means of improving the natural advantages of Connecticut and promoting the prosperity of its inhabitants." Webster addressed a wide range of pressing economic issues including trade, transportation and global warming, a subject he would come back to in a treatise a half-dozen years later. And in a front-page column on January 23, Webster highlighted the need for his hometown to have its own bank: "For want of specie, articles in market must be bartered—and barter is a public and private calamity." Webster's thesis was well taken; after all, the cash-strapped lawyer was himself prone to rely on "this instrument of knavery." (Several years earlier, when Hartford's First Episcopal Church was raising capital, Webster had contributed three pounds in the form of seven dozen of his spellers.) Soon after publishing this influential article on the utility of banks, Webster—along with John Trumbull and Chauncey Goodrich—drafted the petition to establish the Hartford Bank, which was approved by the state legislature in May.

Webster's increasing civic commitment manifested itself in other ways as well. In late March, he was elected to be a member of Hartford's governing body, its Common Council. He also began to take a keen interest in the plight of the city's underclass. "But there are in every town, more especially in Hartford, great numbers of mechanics and other laborers . . . who . . . have no means of subsistence but their daily earnings," he wrote in an anonymous piece published in December 1791 in the *Courant,* in which he proposed establishing a Charitable Society of Hartford. Webster would devote considerable energy to realizing this vision. The following year, he helped draft the group's constitution and became its secretary. By 1793, the Charitable Society, which relied on small contributions—a dollar or more—from employers for each worker, was up and running. Thanks to Webster, his hometown established a social insurance system for the poor, sick and disabled some hundred and forty years before Roosevelt's New Deal.

Webster also took up the cause of another segment of the downtrodden—slaves. In May 1791, he became a charter member of Connecticut's abolitionist society. On May 9, 1793, he gave the third annual address at the state's Society for the Promotion of Freedom, which he expanded into a fifty-page treatise, *Effects of Slavery on Morals and Industry,* published later that year. As he noted in his preface, Webster had wanted to put together his thoughts on slavery for years. As befit his sensibility, Webster's critique hinged on a utilitarian argument: "The exercise of uncontrolled power, always gives a peculiar complexion to the manners, passion and conversation both of the oppressor and the oppressed." As a result, this "barbarous and wicked" institution, he asserted, was bound to exert pernicious effects not only on "the blacks in the United States," but also on the nation as a whole. To buttress his claim that slavery's stupefying influence can be traced back to the far reaches of history, Webster put forth a philological analysis: "It is remarkable that the word *lazzi,* which among our Saxon ancestors was the denomination or the lowest order of bondmen or servants, is the origin of our English word lazy. . . . If slavery had this effect upon our own ancestors . . . surely modern philosophers need not resort to an original difference of race for the cause of that . . . want of mental vigor. . . . in the enslaved. . . ." According to Webster, etymology cast "a flood of light" not only on language but also on history. Yet Webster's etymological investigations, to which he would later devote an entire decade of his life, would be the weakest link in his oeuvre. The rigorous definer had a penchant for making wild guesses about the roots of words; in fact, there is no such word as "lazzi" in Anglo-Saxon, a language which has no "z's."* Nevertheless, the supremely self-confident Webster was convinced that his linguistic backtracking supplied definitive proof of his sociological assumptions.

Despite his abhorrence of slavery, Webster feared "total sudden abolition." To make his case, Webster went back to the demographic data that he had first gathered during his trans-American odyssey. He looked at how the nation's seven hundred thousand slaves—out of a population of four million—were sprinkled across the country. While the ratio of slaves to free inhabitants in New England was 1 to 190, in the six southern states it was 1 to 2.5. "An attempt to eradicate it [slavery]," Webster concluded, "at a single blow would expose the political body to dissolution." Decades later, a more conservative Webster would express nothing but contempt for New England's Abolitionists. In 1837, he wrote to one of his children, "They are absolutely deranged. . . . slavery is a great sin and a great calamity, but it is not our sin."

As Webster was polishing up his antislavery treatise, his legal career was falling apart. As he later recalled, "In 1793, N. W. found that his professional business, with small emoluments of his office of Notary Public was not adequate to the support of his family. . . . He then began to contemplate a change of business." Now the thirty-four-year-old father of two—his second daughter, Frances Juliana, was born in February 1793—Webster became frantic; he was willing to consider anything. He thought about running a farm. He was also open to the suggestion, raised by his brother-in-law Dr. Nathaniel Appleton, of taking over the Boston Book Store. On June 24, 1793, he wrote James Greenleaf, who had recently returned from Amsterdam, of his internal deliberations: "All I ask (or ever wished) is business, and whether on a large or small

---

* Likewise, in an article written about the same time, Webster made the preposterous argument that Americans should use the phrase "them heavens" because it is closer to the original German, "in dem Himmel." This etymological howler reveals that he then also lacked a knowledge of basic German; by the time he wrote his complete dictionary, his command of both Anglo-Saxon and German was somewhat better, but still not stellar.

scale I will be satisfied with it. To renounce all my literary pursuits, which are now very congenial with my habits, would not be altogether agreeable; but it would not make me unhappy." Four years into his marriage, Webster was still willing to give up his beloved words for his wife.

Webster kept Greenleaf abreast of his possible career moves because he figured he could count on his brother-in-law for further financial help. And with good reason. Like a contemporary hedge-fund manager, Greenleaf had vast sums of money under his control. Though Webster wasn't privy to the details, between 1789 and 1792, the speculator (along with his business partner Watson, then also a director at the new Bank of the United States) had secured from Dutch investors a series of twelve loans totaling $1.3 million—equivalent to roughly $400 million today. And that March, Greenleaf had also been appointed U.S. Consul to Amsterdam. Approaching thirty, Rebecca's older brother, who would soon abandon his Dutch wife and children, was emerging as an internationally renowned business leader. The five-foot-seven, hundred-forty-pounder with the ruddy complexion cut a dashing figure with his gray eyes and powdered wig. In 1795, the same year that Gilbert Stuart painted Greenleaf's portrait, Abigail Adams observed, "The girls here, I believe, wish his wife dead. He is sufficiently a favorite wherever he goes."

As with previous benefactors, Webster was open about the dire nature of his financial situation. In a letter to his brother-in-law dated July 8, 1793, Webster noted that his debts came to a total of $1,815 (roughly $545,000 in today's dollars). As Webster explained, about half that amount "grew out of the expenses of my education (which contributed to involve my father & finally to ruin him) out of the expenses of my Southern Tour in 1785—& out of the expenses incurred by publishing my Dissertations in 1789." Another five hundred dollars (which was then a typical annual salary for a lawyer) was owed to other Greenleafs— Rebecca's father and her older brother Daniel. But the actual amount of Webster's indebtedness was far greater, since he no longer included in his calculations James Greenleaf's many loans, which he had initially prom-

The twelfth child of William and Mary Greenleaf, James Greenleaf (1765–1843) was a year older than Webster's wife, Rebecca. Without the financial assistance of the well-heeled "brother James," Webster could not have married and started a family.

ised to repay at a hefty interest rate. As an embarrassed Webster concluded, "This is a short statement of my affairs, & nearly correct as I can make it. . . . It is bad enough in all conscience; it is a situation that has made me very unhappy." While Webster was owed $680 and held a valuable asset—the New York copyright of his speller—he was despondent about getting out of debt anytime soon.

Throughout what he called "the hottest summer ever known," Webster kept thinking about how he could make more money. On July 24, he noted in his diary, "We have squashes from our garden and watermelons in market."

But a national crisis would again knock Webster out of his doldrums. Edmond Genet, the French ambassador to the United States, was stepping up his efforts to drag America into another war with England. To keep America at peace, George Washington would once again turn to his trusted protégé. And Webster would soon be able to earn a good living by writing a torrent of words on behalf of his country. Nothing could have pleased him more.

7

Editor of New York City's
First Daily

NEWSPAPER, n. A sheet of paper printed and distributed
for conveying news; a public print that circulates news,
advertisements, proceedings of legislative bodies, public
documents and the like.

E dmond Genet was very much on Webster's mind even before
the Washington administration came calling.

Since his arrival in April, "Citizen Genet," as he called himself, had waged a vigorous public relations campaign on behalf of
France's bellicose revolutionary government. Through his fiery speeches,
which were widely covered in the press, the ambassador was gaining
considerable support among Democratic-Republicans, the party led by
Secretary of State Thomas Jefferson. Fearing that another war could
cripple America economically, Washington had issued a Proclamation of
Neutrality. But Genet remained undeterred. He began outfitting French
privateers in American ports. France's ambitions were vast: It hoped to
receive American assistance in wresting Canada from Britain and both
Louisiana and Florida from Spain.

In late July 1793, Webster enlisted his colleagues in Hartford's Common Council to draft a resolution in support of Washington's stance of
neutrality. The letter, which was published in the *Courant* and sent to the
president himself, concluded with a personal touch, "we still retain . . .

that just gratitude for your services and respectful attachment to your person." Washington, whom the Republican press had vilified for standing up to Genet—Philip Freneau of Philadelphia's *National Gazette* kept denouncing him as a "king"—was deeply moved. The president replied immediately, "The address . . . affords a new proof of that characteristic love of order and peace, of that virtuous and enlightened zeal for the publick good, which distinguishes the inhabitants of Connecticut."

On August 8, a few days after finishing this missive to the president, Webster headed to New York City on a business trip. Though no longer the capital—Philadelphia had housed the federal government since 1790—New York, with a population of some thirty-five thousand, was now America's biggest city. Having saturated the New England market for his textbooks, Webster was hoping to boost his sales in western states such as New York. But he would soon stumble upon an entirely new publishing venture.

SINCE HE WAS LEAVING his family behind, Webster chose to travel by land rather than water. While fares were inexpensive, stagecoaches, which typically transported about a dozen passengers sprinkled across three seats, were still no place for women and children; on the rocky and muddy roads, the ride was rarely smooth. To prevent them from toppling over, the cigar-smoking drivers had to yell every now and then, "Now, gentleman, to the right!" and "Now, gentleman, to the left!"

After stopping off at Durham, New Haven and Norwalk, Webster reached Kingsbridge—located in the northern tip of what is today the Bronx—on Sunday the eleventh. The following morning, his coach arrived in New York's South Street terminal. As Webster walked up toward his lodgings on Maiden Lane—a few houses from where he had stayed shortly after the war—he became rattled by a deafening din. The steamy streets were packed, and rows upon rows of pedestrians were clamoring.

"*Vive La France*," some intoned. "Down with King Washington," shouted others. Others were singing the French national anthem, "La

Marseillaise," *"Allons enfants de la patrie. . . ."* And a chorus continued to cry, "*Vive* Ge-net, *Vive* Ge-net, *Vive* Ge-net."

As Webster couldn't help but notice, Genet was now also in Manhattan.

Genet had recently sent Washington an angry letter insisting that the president call for a special session of Congress to consider whether to side with the French. In early August, Washington responded by urging the French government to recall Genet.

On August 7, the ambassador sailed from Philadelphia to New York where he hoped to whip up some fervor for the French cause. To combat Washington's rebuff, he vowed to "appeal directly to the [American] people." As Webster would later recall, he was then beginning to wonder whether it was Genet—not Washington—who ruled America.

Upon his arrival in the Battery on the eighth, Genet received a warm welcome. An editorial in a leading Republican newspaper observed, "Americans are ready to mingle their most precious blood with yours." On Genet's first day in town, some thousand New Yorkers—including Governor George Clinton—joined him as he strode up Broadway toward Wall Street.

Day after day, the crowds came out for Genet.

As Webster reached his Maiden Lane destination—Mr. Bradley's Inn—on the afternoon of the twelfth, he breathed a sign of relief. He couldn't stand shouting mobs—and shouting mobs of pro-French Republicans he liked even less.

After he unpacked his bags, Webster heard more animated voices coming from the direction of the inn's barroom. As he opened the door, he heard several people yelling, "Americans love you." Webster then did a double-take. Right in front of him was none other than Edmond Genet himself, surrounded by a circle of admirers. As Webster soon realized, his temporary way station was also Genet's home for the night.

The thirty-year-old Genet was a handsome man with an oval face and a long, thin nose. Curious about the identity of the new guest, Genet asked Webster the reason for his visit to New York. Webster explained that he was an author who was supervising the printing of New York editions of his textbooks. Genet then invited Webster to join him for dinner that evening.

Sitting around Genet's reserved table a few hours later were a couple of American businessmen, Timothy Phelps from New Haven and a Mr. Haxhall of Petersburgh, as well as Genet's extensive retinue, including his personal secretary, Monsieur Pascal, and the military leader Captain Jean-Baptiste Bompard. A week earlier, Bompard's 44-gun *Embuscade* had defeated the British frigate *Boston* in a bloody and closely watched battle off the coast of New Jersey. Though diminutive and elderly, Bompard was a key figure in France's military offensive in America, which called for taking over British ships in neutral territory.

After dinner, Webster told Genet, "I just heard a report from Boston that the Governor of Massachusetts has taken measures to secure a prize or two which had been sent into that port by a proscribed French privateer."

Immediately, Monsieur Pascal mumbled, *"Monsieur Washington fait guerre à la nation française"* [Mr. Washington makes war with France]. Pascal thought that he was just talking to Genet and Bompard, who both nodded their assent, and he was surprised that Webster's French was good enough to pick up what he was saying.

Webster then asked Genet what he was thinking.

"The Executive of the United States," Genet responded, "is under the influence of British gold."

An outraged Webster stated, "It would be impossible to subject the independent freemen of the United States to any foreign power. The Executive Officers, President Washington, Mr. Jefferson and Mr. Hamilton are no fools."

Genet, too, became irate, retorting, "Mr. Jefferson is no fool."*

The two men then began shouting at each other. Losing his cool, Webster called his adversary "a madman" as well as a host of other epi-

---

* The secretary of state was the only member of Washington's cabinet who was sympathetic to Genet.

thets. As he later confided to his Yale classmate Oliver Wolcott, then an official in the department of treasury, "I cannot with propriety state all I said myself on that occasion."

The dinner was over, and the men retired to their rooms for the night. Though that would be Webster's last personal encounter with Genet, verbal sparring with the French ambassador would soon become his day job.

Over the next two weeks, Webster would meet with several key Federalists, including Chief Justice John Jay, New York senator Rufus King and James Watson, then James Greenleaf's business partner and later also a New York senator. As Webster learned, Washington hoped to loosen Genet's grip on the American public by starting a Federalist newspaper in New York City. At a dinner at Watson's home on August 21— the James Watson House still stands at 7 State Street—Webster was offered the job of editor. He told Watson that he was eager to take this position, but that he lacked start-up capital. Watson soon arranged for a group of a dozen influential Federalists, including Treasury Secretary Alexander Hamilton, to each furnish a hundred and fifty dollars. This five-year loan of eighteen hundred dollars would be interest-free.

The new editor of New York's first daily newspaper would never work as a lawyer again.

ON AUGUST 30, the day after Webster arrived back home in Hartford, he finalized an agreement with George Bunce of 37 Wall Street to begin printing his newspaper by the end of the year. Four days later, he sold off his law library for $300. Needing every cent he could lay his hands on, he also put a couple of ads in the *Courant* for his chaise (a two-wheeled carriage), for which he hoped to receive as much as a hundred and thirty dollars. But there were no takers, and it would go with him to New York.

On October 9, Webster heard from Greenleaf, who had completed all the preparations for the move. "I have just returned from the south-

ward," wrote his brother-in-law from New York on October 7, "my first
object since my return has been to look out for a home for you, & I have
happily succeeded. Our Dear Becca . . . will be lodged like a little
queen. . . . I shall have a good deal of my own furniture put into it."
Missing the joke, Webster assumed that Greenleaf had neglected to
mention where the house was located. But Greenleaf's largesse, he soon
learned, would enable his family to live in style in a large rented house
at 168 Queen Street.

In a postscript to his letter, Greenleaf asked Webster to insert in
Connecticut newspapers an announcement that the city of Washington
was looking to hire mechanics and brickmakers "on a large scale." This
remark related to Greenleaf's own new venture. While traveling down
South in September, the speculator clinched the biggest real estate deal
in the history of the young country. His charge: to build from scratch
America's new federal city. On September 18, Greenleaf joined a crowd
of thousands that witnessed the Masonic ceremony at which George
Washington laid the cornerstone of the U.S. Capitol. During the day-
long festivities, which culminated in the consumption of a five-hundred-
pound ox, the city's commissioners offered for sale lots for America's
newest city. But though President Washington himself bought a few to
spur interest, most went unsold. The enterprising Greenleaf immediately
sprang into action. Five days later, he bought three thousand lots for a
pittance—a mere $66.50 each (the going rate had recently been as high
as three hundred dollars). As part of the deal, Greenleaf was supposed
to build ten brick houses a year and loan the commissioners $2,660 a
month. Washington had high expectations. On September 25, the president wrote Tobias Lear, his former secretary (who had taken on the
tutoring job declined by Webster a decade earlier), "You will learn from
Mr. Greenleaf that he has dipped deeply, in the concerns of the Federal
City. I think he has done so on very advantageous terms for himself, and
I am pleased with it notwithstanding on public ground; as it may give
facility to the operations at that place." Two months later, Greenleaf
formed a partnership with the Philadelphia businessmen Robert Morris

(then America's richest man) and John Nicholson, and managed to wrest away another three thousand lots from the city's commissioners at a bargain-basement price. Greenleaf now controlled about half of the government's salable land in the new capital.

On October 31, Webster, his wife and two young daughters, along with the black maid who had lived with them in Hartford, set out for Middletown to wait for the sailing vessel. Though travel by water was more comfortable than by coach, it could take much longer. Due to unfavorable wind conditions, the family didn't arrive in New York Harbor until November 13. The delay upset eight-month-old Frances, and Webster was frequently called upon to calm the crying baby.

The Websters spent their first two nights at the home of James Watson, now Greenleaf's former business partner, as the two men had just dissolved their firm. On November 15, the Websters settled into their new quarters on Queen Street (renamed Pearl Street the following year, as New York attempted to shed its remaining British trappings). Four days later, Greenleaf and his friend Charles Lagarenne, a Royalist exile from France, moved into the Webster household, which would soon also include a nurse and manservant. America's "first capitalist" would be using Webster's home as a base of operations while he traveled around the country meeting potential investors.

On December 9, 1793, Webster published the first issue of *American Minerva,* which he subtitled "Patroness of Peace, Commerce and the Liberal Arts." The four-page paper would come out every day but Sunday, at four in the afternoon. An annual subscription cost six dollars. Webster envisioned that the city's first daily—Alexander Hamilton's *New York Post* would not begin its run until nearly a decade later—could be instrumental in exporting American democracy to the rest of the world. In his editor's note in that first issue, he wrote, "It is the singular felicity of Americans and a circumstance that distinguishes this country from all others that the means of information are accessible to all descriptions of people." An informed citizenry, Webster believed, could help Americans tackle all the political and economic challenges that they faced.

Minerva is the Roman name for Athena, the Greek goddess of wisdom, wit and war. As was common in the early Republic, Webster often looked to ancient Rome for inspiration.

Webster's Federalist organ quickly made a mark. A few weeks after its launch, Vice President John Adams wrote from Philadelphia to his wife, Abigail, of New York's new publishing phenomenon, "Mr. Noah Webster who is lately removed from Hartford to that city . . . is said to conduct his gazette with judgment and spirit upon good principles."

One of Webster's first tasks was to bring down his old nemesis, Genet, whose fortunes were already tumbling. On December 5, when Washington attacked Genet on the floor of Congress, most congressmen sided with the president. Webster kept up the pressure. In an editorial addressed to Genet a few weeks later, he insisted that the American people were too savvy to fall for his duplicity: "Had you passed a few weeks only in acquiring a slight knowledge of the American yeomanry, you would have discovered real people, as little known to Europeans as the fabled Amazons of antiquity. A people in short who are not found in any other region of the globe, a people who know their rights and will neither suffer you or any other man to invade them." Genet soon also lost the support of his own countrymen. The following month, the new Jacobin government issued an arrest notice, demanding his return to France. Fearing the guillotine, Genet immediately appealed for political asylum, which Washington approved. In a strange twist, Genet married Cordelia Clinton, the daughter of New York's governor, in November 1794, and the newlyweds settled on a Long Island farm.

WEDNESDAY, DECEMBER 25, 1793, was a normal business day for Webster. He went ahead with the publication of his paper that afternoon. The Christmas edition featured an article on Genet; some death statistics from Philadelphia, recently hit by an outbreak of yellow fever; and a rental ad for the front room of his Queen Street home (which he figured could be used as a hardware store). Webster also stuck in an item praising his *Prompter,* which claimed that "many householders deem it so useful as to purchase a copy for every adult in their families." Webster wasn't celebrating Christmas—then dismissed as "a popish holiday" by Congregationalists; he was thinking about how to define America.

Webster put his musings in a letter to his friend Jedidiah Morse, who was seeking help with a geographical dictionary that would include a "description of all the places in America." A few years earlier, Webster had contributed a twenty-page review of U.S. history after the Revolution to Morse's *American Geography,* a textbook for schoolchildren. (Nearly as successful as Webster's speller, this frequently reprinted book later earned Morse the sobriquet "Father of American Geography.") A recent Yale graduate (whose first child, Samuel, the inventor of the telegraph, would later paint a celebrated portrait of Webster), Jedidiah Morse was then serving as pastor in Charlestown, Massachusetts. Webster was eager to pitch in. After all, Morse's project bore a close resemblance to the elaborate fantasy that he had hatched five years earlier, in which proprietors scattered across the nation would funnel information about America back to him. However, one obstacle remained. "Indeed it appears to me," Webster had written Morse on September 20, "very difficult to ascertain what I have to do or what will be the portion of labor each of us must bestow. This is my great objection to undertaking such a work with others."

Having settled in New York, Webster was now ready to address the thorny matter of exactly how they might collaborate. In his Christmas Day letter, he suggested the following protocol: "My idea is that each of us take a state—give the best account of each town, river, &c in that state that we can; each place on a *detached sheet of paper*—all which papers may be easily stitched together. When I have finished that state, I will forward the MSS to you—and you may supply all you know, in addition to my account and & so vice versa. . . . After the description of each place is completed, the separate sheets can be arranged alphabetically and numbered."

Morse eagerly embraced Webster's ideas. In fact, in his response in early January, he insisted on adding a few more touches to the already elaborate protocol. The two men, Morse wrote, should also be sure to fold the paper in quarto so that the margins could be a quarter of an inch all around. In addition, they might also put the first letters of the place described on a given sheet in the top left corner—say, BOS for Boston. Though Webster couldn't wait to get started on this massive task of compiling and arranging, his newspaper work intruded. Three years later, he would concede defeat, writing Morse, "My own labors require all the nerves I have." While Morse went on to complete the book by himself, *The American Gazetteer,* published in 1797, showed signs of Webster's influence. To describe Lower Manhattan, Morse recycled Webster's "Description of New York"—an essay that ended up serving as a model for Morse's own entries, many of which included precise house counts.

Webster's first three years as editor were trying. Unable to afford an assistant, he had to do everything himself, including correcting proofs and paying the bills. He would later recall, "My labors in writing and editing and translating from the French papers were very severe." His body started to register the stress almost immediately. On two occasions that first winter, Webster was terrified to discover that his pulse was barely perceptible. Once again, financial aid from James Greenleaf (and the promise of more if needed) proved life-saving. In a letter dated Sunday, March 2, 1794, Webster wrote to Greenleaf, who was away on business, "My resources are exhausted. . . . I hope to receive more money from some gentlemen in this city, but I am not certain of it. . . . Becca & myself have sometimes hard struggles to keep our spirits up, but we have dismissed one servant & we endeavor to retrench every unnecessary expense." Time also became a precious commodity. On April 23, he noted in his diary, "It is too much trouble to make particular remarks every day."

During his first six months at the helm of his paper, Webster provided constant coverage of the major international story of the day: the emergence of the "Reign of Terror" in France. Besides posting extracts from the French papers, Webster wrote a series of editorials which he republished that spring as the pamphlet "The Revolution in France Considered in Respect to Its Progress and Effects." As in his slavery essay, here, too, Webster showed little patience for abstract theorizing. Results were all that counted. Though he was supportive of the ideals of the Revolution, he was horrified by the attendant chaos. To capture his sentiments, for the only time in his life the future lexicographer felt compelled to coin a neologism: "All wars have, if I may use a new, but emphatic word, a *demoralizing* tendency; but the revolution in France, in addition to the usual influence of war, is attended with a total change in the minds of the people." Webster was convinced that the rejection of religion promoted violence and lawlessness. With Jeffersonian Democrats continuing to look to France for guidance, Webster was concerned that the mayhem might spill over into America. On April 20, 1794, he sent a copy to President Washington: "The enclosed is intended to aid the cause of government and peace. . . . Be pleased to accept it as a proof of my attachment to you and the Constitution of the United States." On May 9, 1794, the president issued a warm response, noting that "your motives in writing it are highly laudable, and I sincerely wish they may meet the reward which is due to them."

In June, with the *Minerva* down to just 250 subscribers—half the number needed to remain viable—Webster was despondent. Though he was enraged with his partner, the printer George Bunce, whom he considered incompetent, he wasn't about to give up. He started a semi-weekly offshoot called *The Herald: A Gazette for the Country*. He tailored this paper, also a four-pager and consisting entirely of previously published *Minerva* articles, to readers outside of New York. He would exclude the advertising to save on the hefty postage costs and cut the price in half. On launch day, June 4, 1794, Webster promised his readers, "The compiler will spare no pains to render it respectable in regard to the purity, authenticity, variety and value of its materials." As a newspaper man, Webster considered himself less an editor than a compiler, which he would define in 1828 as "one who forms . . . a composition from various authors or separate papers." Organizing information would be central to most of his literary labors.

Despite his frantic efforts, Webster wasn't able to improve the balance sheets of his papers right away. In December 1794, he complained to Hudson and Goodwin, the Hartford publisher of his speller, with his characteristic hyperbole, "I have endured more drudgery and suffered more anxiety on account of the bad execution of the paper, than perhaps ever fell to the lot of man in the same time; partly from the difficulties attending a new business . . . and partly from the inability of Bunce." But Webster's persistence eventually paid off. By 1796, he was earning "handsome profits" and was able to hire an assistant editor and clerk. The following year, when *American Minerva* was renamed *The Commercial Advertiser,* circulation was up to seventeen hundred subscribers, some five hundred more than its nearest competitor. His net profit, Webster estimated, was the considerable sum of five thousand dollars a year.

Back in 1794, when his papers were still in the red, Webster was also coping with a series of personal losses. As the "mortuary notice" in the *Courant* on October 13, 1794, put it, "Died at West-Hartford, the 5th instant, the wife of Noah Webster, Esq. aged 67." Webster was caught off guard because his mother had been in robust health; the cause was a sudden attack of dysentery. A harried Webster didn't attend the funeral. As he had grown closer to Rebecca's family, he had grown further and further apart from his own parents. Webster would continue to have only occasional contact with his father, who in 1806, at the age of eighty-four, moved into the West Division farm of a new bride, Sarah Hopkins. Squire Webster, despite his prominent social status, would still have to beseech his son for an occasional twenty-dollar bill until his death in 1813.

That October, Webster's intimate friendship with James Greenleaf, who had repeatedly provided a financial lifeline, also drew to an abrupt close. A few months earlier, Webster had gotten his first inkling that Greenleaf might not be quite the man he professed to be. On July 26, 1794, Nathaniel Appleton wrote from Washington, where he was help-

ing out with the real estate transactions, "[Brother James] makes large &
bold speculations hitherto they have proved successful. . . . I frequently
wish however for his sake, as well as my own, that his concerns were not
so extensive." In his visits back to the Queen Street house, Greenleaf,
who no longer seemed interested in reuniting with his Dutch wife, would
raise a ruckus with his drinking companions. Webster was aghast, and
on October 11, he put his foot down, writing in a note to Greenleaf,
"When you are at home, the house work is greatly increased, & Becca is
compelled to become servant herself. . . . the perpetual run of company,
often thrown upon her without notice . . . wounds her pride. . . . You
cannot conceive how unhappy you make her." Greenleaf soon moved
out of both Webster's house and his life. Of the man who had bankrolled
him during the first few years of his marriage, Webster would tell Rebecca's brother Daniel in 1797, "I knew his baseness years ago, and
thanks to my good fortune, I quarreled myself out of his clutches."

By 1797, James Greenleaf also was persona non grata with the rest
of the family because of his shady business dealings. In 1795, Greenleaf
and his two well-heeled partners, Nicholson and Morris, formed the
North American Land Company, which expanded their speculative ventures across the South. But Greenleaf proved dishonest, and the following year, both partners wanted nothing more to do with him. Greenleaf
was soon besieged by angry creditors. In July 1796, Greenleaf wrote to
Alexander Hamilton, offering a fifth of his net worth—then a staggering
$5 million—if the prominent attorney would lend his "name, responsibil-
ity and talents in the liquidation of my concerns and payment of my
obligations." Hamilton turned him down. Two years later, a penniless
Greenleaf was whisked off to Philadelphia's Prune Street Debtors'
Prison. In April 1798, the *New London Bee* identified Webster as one of
the prominent Federalist editors whom this disgraced "bankrupt specu-
lating nabob" had once bankrolled.

As 1794 wound down, Webster was turning his attention from
France to its neighbor across the Channel. In November, President
Washington's special envoy, John Jay, negotiated a commercial treaty

with England, which addressed several nagging conflicts dating back to the Revolution. At the time, the British still maintained a strong presence in the Northwest Territories and routinely seized American ships bound for France (along with their cargo, which included slaves). Under the terms of the agreement, the British promised a gradual pull-out from the Northwest, but little else. Though Jay's Treaty would manage to avert another war with England, it was not popular even among some of Washington's staunchest supporters. Sensitive to the fervent opposition, which would deepen the divide between the Federalists and Republicans, Washington delayed passing it on to the Senate for six months.

The *Minerva* immediately rallied to Washington's defense. Soon after hammering out the treaty, Jay, who was by now Webster's close friend, began forwarding exclusive materials from London for publication. In July 1795, Webster followed up by writing the first of ten pro-treaty editorials. Using the pen name "Curtius," Webster was responding to a writer posing as "Decius," who was attacking the Washington administration in the *Argus,* a competing New York paper. Webster's position was pragmatic. To his Yale classmate Oliver Wolcott, who had recently replaced Hamilton as secretary of the treasury, he acknowledged that while "the Treaty, as modified by the Senate, makes no sacrifices which are dishonorable to us as a nation . . . my own hopes are in some measure disappointed." After reading the first installment, Thomas Jefferson, who, like many readers, assumed that "Curtius" was Alexander Hamilton, realized that the Republicans were facing a formidable opponent. To his fellow Virginian James Madison, Jefferson wrote, "Hamilton is really a Colossus to the anti-republican party. . . . In truth, when he ["Curtius"] comes forward, there is nobody but yourself who can meet him." In fact, Hamilton himself would soon enter into the debate, writing three dozen essays in support of Washington's second administration under the pseudonym "Camillus." But Webster would succeed, as he proudly noted in his memoir, in out-Hamiltoning Hamilton. After the treaty was funded in April 1796, Webster overheard Senator Rufus King telling Jay, then New York's governor, that "Webster's writings had done more to quiet the public mind and reconcile people to the treaty than the writings of Mr. Hamilton . . . [due to his] style and manner of treating the subject." Webster, who would have a dramatic falling-out with Hamilton in 1800, was delighted by the idea that posterity might consider him the more articulate Federalist scribe.

In the wake of the Jay Treaty, Webster's papers became required reading for the nation's elite. He was now at the pinnacle of American journalism. On February 9, 1795, his brother-in-law Thomas Dawes reported from Boston, "I am highly gratified by the success of your paper. It is my duty to tell you that I hear it spoken of in the most flattering terms in all companies. I suppose, tho' you can tell the best, it has the greatest currency of any composition of the kind on the Continent." On February 13, a proud Webster reported to his Hartford friend Josiah Blakely, who had undertaken new business ventures in the Caribbean, "My family are generally well—my business not ill and growing better. . . . Our country enjoys peace and unexampled [sic] prosperity."

But his calm didn't last long. By the end of July, New York City came face-to-face with one of the most serious public health crises in its history. Yellow fever—so called because its victims looked as "yellow as gold"—was back. The viral disease, which had literally decimated New York in 1702, was now working its way across the entire eastern seaboard. For the next four months, the specter of imminent death would hang over every New Yorker.

Two years earlier, when Webster first heard of the "raging malady" in Philadelphia, he was deeply shaken. On September 26, 1793, he wrote Oliver Wolcott, then still working under Hamilton at Treasury, "The melancholy accounts received from you and others of the progress of a fatal disease . . . excite commiseration in every breast. An alarm is spread over the country." In fact, that fall, President Washington was whisked away from the capital, and the entire U.S. government was nearly shut down.

While other cities remained largely unaffected, Webster immediately became interested in the many scientific questions surrounding what the Philadelphia College of Physicians initially termed "the plague." He was eager to classify the menace as quickly as possible. On October 10, 1793, as he was preparing to leave Hartford, he wrote Wolcott, "I am not acquainted with diseases of this kind; but I have an idea that the plague of the Levant, the yellow fever of the West Indies and the malignant fevers of our country are all diseases of the same genus." He also tried to keep track of the body count. "Fever in Philadelphia carries off 159 in a day," ran the entry the following day in his diary. Though by November the disorder in Philadelphia abated, it had felled five thousand city residents in just a few months.

In the spring of 1795, upon hearing reports of a new outbreak of yellow fever in the West Indies, New York City health officials issued an edict requiring ships originating from that destination to be anchored at least a quarter mile from the city's shores. New York's first casualty was a man named Thomas Foster, who initially sought medical help from Dr. Malachi Treat, the health officer to the city's port, on July 6, 1795. According to the account of Dr. Treat's assistant, Dr. Valentine Seaman, Foster's bright yellow skin was "covered with purple spots, his mind deranged, his tongue covered with a dry black sordes, with hemorrhages from his gums and nose, and a discharge of black and very offensive matter from his stomach and bowels." Foster died on July 9. Two weeks later, Dr. Treat himself was stricken, and by the end of the month, he, too, was gone. In mid-August, as two New Yorkers a day were dying, the city's physicians were ordered to quarantine all afflicted patients at Bellevue Hospital.

Soon Webster, like the rest of his fellow New Yorkers, could think of little else. On the evening of September 16, the young doctor Elihu Hubbard Smith, upon returning home from a visit to Webster's home, wrote in his diary, "This whole city is in a violent state of alarm on account of the fever. It is the subject of every conversation, at every hour, and in

every company; and each circumstance of terror acquires redoubled horror, from every new relation. In reality there is reason to be alarmed. I am
told that 24 persons died yesterday."

Even more frightening, the epidemic was no longer confined to
the harbor. As Dr. Seaman would also report, "For in every . . . situation, favoring the accumulation of filth and stagnation of putrefactive
materials, there it [the fever] was no stranger." And with few sanitation
measures yet in place, Manhattan was a virtual garbage dump. Rotten
cabbage along with dead rats and pigs could be found in the middle of
just about every street, alley and bylane. Elegant Pearl Street, where
Elihu Smith (who had learned music from Webster as a Connecticut
schoolboy) also lived in a rented room, was no exception. In fact, its
stench, as Webster reported in the *Minerva,* was so overpowering that he
often felt a need to keep the windows closed—even on hot days—to
avoid vomiting. Webster feared that the sink right in front of his house,
which contained the kitchen refuse and yard wash of the surrounding
lots, was a breeding ground for the deadly disease. By mid-October,
New York was already mourning its five hundredth casualty.

On October 27, the day after returning to New York from a brief
trip to Philadelphia, the Websters hosted Smith and a couple of other
guests for tea. While Webster fulminated about the treachery of Edmond Randolph, who had recently resigned as secretary of state when
Washington learned of his secret negotiations with the French, politics
weren't the primary focus of the evening. "Much talk about the fever,"
noted Smith.

Once again, high anxiety pushed Webster to new creative heights.
Feeling compelled to do something, he took the only kind of decisive
action of which he was capable—he began compiling and arranging the
facts of the epidemic.

In the October 31 edition of his paper, Webster printed a circular
addressed to the physicians of Philadelphia, New York, Baltimore, Norfolk and New Haven, the cities hardest hit over the past three years. "To
decide on the nature and origin of the yellow fever," he asserted, "we

want the evidence of facts; and it is not improbable that facts have occurred in the U. States, sufficient in number and clearness to furnish . . .
universal conviction, shall those facts [be] . . . ordered to the public in
a mass." Webster asked the physicians to pass on whatever information
they had gathered from their own practice. This questionnaire, which
he designed in an attempt to restore "happiness" and "prosperity" to
his country, was the world's first scientific survey; it also helped give
birth to modern medical research. Inspired by Webster, Elihu Smith
released a similar circular a year later, in which he solicited research on
the fever from physicians across the country. Smith soon found a home
for these articles by starting *The Medical Repository,* America's first medical journal.

   Despite the gravity of this crisis, Webster's Republican counterparts
could not resist the temptation to pounce on him. On November 6, Dr.
Franklin's grandson, the editor Benjamin Franklin Bache, mocked "Noah
Webster, Esq., Author and Physician General of the United States" in a
letter published in his Philadelphia paper, the *Aurora.* Accusing Webster
of venturing into an arena he knew nothing about, Bache stated, "It is
to be deplored, sapient sir. . . . that not a physician, no not one can be
found to investigate its origin. . . . To the author of the *Institutes,* the
Editor of the *Minerva* . . . is reserved the honor and the glory to triumph
over a malady." (In a cruel irony, a few years later, the disease would level
Bache at the age of twenty-nine.) But Webster was undeterred. After the
fever dissipated in late November—New York's final death toll was 730
people, the equivalent of about two hundred thousand today—he kept
up his furious correspondence with the numerous physicians who responded to his query.

   In mid-1796, Webster published these reports in his book *A Collection of Papers on the Subject of Bilious Fevers, prevalent in the United
States for a Few Years Past.* Webster's 250-page volume consisted of ten
chapters, the first eight of which contained contributions by leading
physicians such as his New York neighbors, Elihu Smith and Samuel
Mitchill. Their accounts were short on hard data. For example, noting

that poor immigrants constituted a significant percentage of the dead, Smith postulated that "the sudden intermingling of people of various and discordant habits [was] a circumstance favoring the production of disease." Smith also agreed with the conventional wisdom, first articulated by Philadelphia's Benjamin Rush, that blood-letting was the most effective form of treatment. In the last two chapters, Webster—who repeatedly referred to himself as the "compiler"—presented his own observations and conclusions. While Webster was unable to prove his hypothesis, which posited that the fever's spread had something to do with the city's grime, he nevertheless saw this scourge as a vindication of the virtues he lived by. In the book's last lines, he implored his fellow countrymen "to pay a double regard to the duties of order, temperance and cleanliness. The most fatal effects follow from neglect in these particulars."

Webster soon became a fierce advocate for tidying up America. Over the next year, in frequent editorials in his paper, Webster put pressure on city officials to step up efforts to water and sweep New York's streets. In the fall of 1797, Webster followed up with a series of twenty-five letters to the Philadelphia physician William Currie, challenging his view that the disease was of foreign origin. As Webster argued, since "plagues are children of cities, camps and unwholesome places," America was what needed to be fixed. For Webster, eliminating this public health menace required changing the "structure and arrangement" of all cities across the nation. In Webster's utopian vision, urban planners would unite "the utility of the town with the salubrious air of the country." "All populous towns in the United States," he predicted in his last letter to Currie, published on December 20, 1797, "will hereafter be afflicted with malignant fevers and plague, unless a speedy and effectual stop should be put to 30 feet streets, 20 feet lots and contiguous homes." While Webster's letters to Currie received plaudits from many eminent medical men, including Benjamin Rush, his doomsday scenario didn't spur anyone to action.

Though Webster couldn't reorder America, he could change his own place of residence. In the first half of 1796, he moved his family into Corlear's Hook, a section a mile north of downtown—near Grand Street today—which came close to his urban paradise. His detached villa, which jutted out into the East River, featured an elegant garden. The Connecticut farmboy could once again keep a horse, and he enjoyed commuting to his office at 40 Pine Street on horseback. Webster's spacious home also became a haven for numerous stray cats that had been displaced by the pestilence. On April 6, 1797, about a year after the move, Webster's third child, a daughter named Harriet, was born there. Elihu Smith provided medical care to the three Webster girls, and also frequently walked up from downtown for tea and lively conversation. In his diary, Smith described Webster's "country house" as "a pleasant place."

Smith, who remained Webster's closest New York friend, shared both his thirst for knowledge and some of his eccentricities. The doctor's copious diaries include "Tables of Industry," in which he tallied up the number (and size) of the pages he read and wrote each month. Smith was the founder of a conversation society called the Friendly Club, a successor to Webster's own Philological Society. Though not a member himself, Webster fraternized with the major figures, who included William Dunlap and Samuel Mitchill, both active in his earlier group; the lawyer James Kent; Charles Adams, the dissolute son of President John Adams; and Charles Brockden Brown, later dubbed "the father of the American novel." The British artist James Sharples, who painted the last sitting portrait of Washington in 1796, also hovered around these literati and created pastels of most of them.

Once he moved to Corlear's Hook, Webster's daily life was much less harried. Though his pen still churned out copy at a furious pace—the equivalent of about five octavo volumes of prose a year, according to his own estimate—with the help of his small staff, he could often return home by late afternoon. Nevertheless, the numbness of his first few years in New York gave way to a gnawing unhappiness. The intense partisan wrangling was proving too much even for the perpetually argumentative Webster. William Cobbett, the editor of the Philadelphia

Artist James Sharples charged fifteen dollars for a profile and
twenty dollars for a portrait. Webster chose the more expensive
option, which required two hours of sitting.

newspaper *Porcupine's Gazette,* repeatedly heaped abuse on him, flinging
around epithets such as "a most gross calumniator, a great fool and a
barefaced liar." Moreover, Webster's heart just wasn't in the newspaper
business any longer. He missed more probing scholarly investigations.

Though editing kept him immersed in words, he was "growing weary
of the drudgery," using the term that his idol Samuel Johnson had famously applied to lexicography. For Johnson, the writer of dictionaries
was "an unhappy mortal" who toiled "at the lower employments of life."
Not so for Webster. What had once been a chore for Johnson remained

Webster's overriding fantasy, his dream job. A decade earlier, after he had completed his tripartite *Grammatical Institute,* the Reverend Elizur Goodrich of Durham, a friend and Yale trustee, had suggested that Webster round out his pedagogical legacy by compiling a dictionary. Other friends and colleagues also planted this seed, such as the Maine writer Daniel George, who, after reading two of Webster's books on language, wrote in 1790, "But, Sir, we must . . . have a Dictionary, and to YOU we must look for this necessary work." Webster heartily agreed with such sentiments, but as long as he was struggling financially, he was forced to dismiss this massive project as impractical. In late 1796, he confided his frustration to fellow author Joseph Dennie: "I once intended to have devoted my life to literary pursuits. The cold hand of poverty *chilled* my hopes, but has not wholly *blasted* them. The necessity of attending to business to procure a living for my little family *retards* my projects, but they are not *abandoned.* My plan of education is barely begun. When I shall complete it is uncertain." His true talent, Webster felt, was "buried."

But not for much longer. Two years later, buoyed by a steady stream of income from his papers and books, Webster plotted his return to the literary obsessions that gave meaning to his existence. In the spring of 1798, the thirty-nine-year-old father of three handed off the management of his Pine Street office to George Hopkins, the publisher who had replaced Bunce, and moved to New Haven. Of his newspapers, he "would have no care . . . farther than to give them their political complexion." Now free to spend his days compiling and organizing words, Webster would suddenly come smack up against a more intimidating adversary than polemical journalists: his own inner demons.

PART THREE

Lexicographer

LANGUAGE, n. 1. Human speech; the expression of ideas by words or significant articulate sounds, for the communication of thoughts. *Language* consists in the oral utterance of sounds, which usage has made the representatives of ideas. When two or more persons customarily annex the same sounds to the same ideas, the expression of these sounds by one person communicates his ideas to another. This is the primary sense of *language*, the use of which is to communicate the thoughts of one person to another through the organs of hearing. Articulate sounds are represented by letters, marks or characters which form words. . . . 5. The inarticulate sounds by which irrational animals express their feelings and wants. Each species of animals has peculiar sounds, which are uttered instinctively, and are understood by its own species, and its own species only.

Setting His Sights on
Johnson and Johnson Jr.

RIVAL, n. 1. One who is in pursuit of the same object as
another; one striving to reach or obtain something which
another is attempting to obtain, and which one only can
possess; a competitor; as rival in love; rivals for a crown. Love
will not patiently bear a *rival*. 2. One striving to equal or exceed
another in excellence; as two *rivals* in eloquence. 3. An
antagonist; a competitor in any pursuit or strife.

I t was a house that defined grandeur.

Back in 1771, its original owner built the mansion to make a
statement. The two pillars on either side of the front door were meant
to demonstrate that someone important lived there. So, too, were the
other trappings—the white picket fence, the louvered windows, the mahogany paneling and the second outhouse. The West Indian trader, who
had recently amassed a fortune, was eager to gain entrance into the upper
echelons of New Haven society.

The one-acre, eighteen-perch (rod) estate at 155 Water Street, overlooking Long Island Sound where the merchant's three ships were docked,
would eventually become the most famous piece of real estate in New
Haven. But not entirely for the reasons that the man—Benedict Arnold—
had hoped. His infamy also helped to create its legend.

In 1782, shortly after Arnold was discovered to have "joined the
enemies of the United States," the State of Connecticut confiscated the

property and sold it to the Revolutionary War hero Captain John Prout Sloan. After Sloan died in 1786, his widow, Mary, stayed on.

That was, until April 1, 1798, when the Websters moved in. The price: $2,066.66, which Webster paid in full to Mrs. Sloan a month and a half later.

For Webster, as opposed to Arnold, the two-story Georgian house represented not his entrance into society but his retreat from it. Escaping New York, Webster sought insulation from "the bustl of commerce & the taste of people perpetually inquiring for news and making bargains." As he also noted in his diary, he was taking refuge in the familiar: "the State of Connecticut, my acquaintances, [and] my [literary] habits." The site of his college triumphs did indeed prove welcoming to Webster, who would become a local celebrity. As one neighbor later put it, Noah and Rebecca Webster "were the most noticeable people who walked the streets [of New Haven] both for their beauty of face and elegance of carriage."

Webster relished what stood behind the house—the stable (he would never again live without a horse) and the garden. Webster was proud of his peach and cherry trees, as well as his neatly arranged flower beds. And his neighbors in what one contemporary writer called "the Eden of the Union" were of a like mind. "The neatness of [New Haven's] houses," wrote Timothy Dwight, who had succeeded Ezra Stiles as Yale's president in 1795, "is extended to everything around them. Little that is old or unrepaired meets the eye. The courts, and garden, which exist almost everywhere are prettily enclosed. Fruit trees, and ornamental trees and shrubs, abound every where."

Over the next decade and a half, Webster would raise his rapidly expanding family in this "lovely home," as his fifth daughter, Eliza, born there in 1803, later observed. A stickler for symmetry, Webster had hoped for ten children. "Let units be tens," he would blurt out at the family dinner table. But he had to settle for seven. The other additions were Mary, born in 1799; William, his sole male heir, born two years later; and his last child, Louisa, who would be saddled with an unidenti-

The Benedict Arnold House, as Webster himself referred to the first home he ever owned, was shrouded in mystery until the day it was torn down in 1917. The large attic, which was used as a children's playroom, contained an old scabbard said to have once covered one of Arnold's swords. To head up the wooden stairs to play with their dolls, the Webster girls had to turn a big key, which, according to rumor, once opened a jail cell. Likewise, legend had it that Arnold built the basement vaults as a hideaway either for himself or for goods "that had not paid an entrance fee to the country."

fied mental handicap, born in 1808. Another son, Henry, born in 1806, lived just nine weeks.

The second-floor study—right over the east parlor (which served as the family dining room)—with its big window seat was Webster's sanctum sanctorum, where he found the peace he urgently sought. By the time he arrived in New Haven, Webster had difficulty coping with the stresses of daily life; and nothing was more unsettling to him than having to relate to other people. "Either from the structure of my mind or from my modes of investigation," he would acknowledge a few years later, "I am led very often to differ in opinion from many of my respectable fellow citizens. . . . it [is] necessary for me to withdraw myself from every public concern and confine my attention to private affairs and the education of my children."

Twenty years after finishing Yale, Webster was no longer an adventurous youth, but a chronically anxious middle-aged man who felt, as he wrote to Benjamin Rush in 1801, a need to "husband my health with the utmost care." From his second-floor cocoon, Webster would attempt to preserve his mental equilibrium by taking on a series of scholarly projects, which all involved organizing vast amounts of information.

AFTER CAPTAIN JOHN MILES' BOAT dropped the family off in New Haven, Webster first spent a week and a half arranging the furniture in the Arnold House; then, on April 10, 1798, as he noted in his diary, he dug in: "Begin to write my History of Epidemic Diseases, from materials which I have been three months collecting."

In late 1797, just as he was finishing up the last of his twenty-five letters to Dr. Currie, Webster had started to write the definitive work on epidemics. Eager to uncover the root causes of yellow fever, Webster felt it necessary to "trace back the history of such diseases as far as the records of history extend." In early 1798, he scoured the new nation's major research libraries in New York, Boston, Philadelphia and New Haven. On March 17, as he was preparing to leave New York, he issued a circular in his paper seeking subscribers for his new book. "The facts collected," Webster insisted, "will enable me to demonstrate that many of the common ideas respecting pestilential epidemics are unfounded or extremely incorrect." With few readers willing to shell out the two dollars he requested, Webster wasn't able to publish the volume that summer as originally intended. But though the public balked, Webster did continue to receive encouragement from fellow scholars. In late April, Benjamin Rush wrote from Philadelphia, "Go on—go on with your inquiries. Cause physicians to blush, and instruct mankind to throw off their allegiance to them. Posterity will do you justice. The man who . . . persuades the world to conform to it [the truth], will deserve more of the human race than all the heroes, or statesmen that ever lived." The challenge appealed to Webster's grandiosity. This die-hard contrarian relished the chance to contradict—if not demolish—the authorities behind the conventional wisdom.

That spring, Webster also started compiling facts of another kind. Delighted to be back in his home state, he suddenly felt a compelling need to do a complete inventory. On May 7, 1798, he drafted yet another circular, which he addressed to the state's clergymen: "Gentlemen . . . I have some leisure and great inclination to be instrumental in bringing forward a correct view of the civil and domestic economy of this state, and if you will furnish me with the materials, I will arrange and publish them in a form that will . . . supply the present defect of such a work." Webster was seeking factoids that he had monitored before, such as house and church counts as well as death statistics. His questionnaire also asked about "mode of cultivation, as to order of crops; species of manure used; produce of crops by the acre." To prepare for this undertaking, Webster himself began tallying various bits of statistical information about Connecticut—its number of oxen, horses, coaches, chaises and the like.

But few of the clergymen seemed to share Webster's passion for number-crunching. Only Reverend Frederick William Hotchkiss of Saybrook responded, and his remarks were often imprecise. Next to climate, for example, Reverend Hotchkiss wrote "good." A frustrated Webster had no choice but to give up. But, as he later noted on his copy of this 1798 questionnaire, "This project was never carried into effect, but it may have had an influence in exciting other gentlemen to form the Connecticut Academy." In fact, in 1799, Timothy Dwight became the founding president of the Connecticut Academy of Arts and Sciences, a literary and scientific group. And in early 1800, with the help of its corresponding secretary, Noah Webster, Jr., the CAAS sent off its own thirty-item questionnaire, a reworking of Webster's 1798 version, to all of Connecticut's 107 towns. The so-called statistical account project resulted in several detailed town histories—replete with statistics— such as a hundred-page one by Dwight on New Haven, published in 1811.

ON JULY 4, 1798, Webster was the featured speaker of New Haven's Independence Day celebration at the Brick Meeting House. This honor bestowed by the town's elders signified that Webster had arrived. The following year, Webster would become a member of New Haven's Common Council; and within a few years, he was also serving both as a justice of the peace and as a representative in the Connecticut state legislature.

However, it was not Webster's official Independence Day oration but rather his second set of remarks that afternoon, a short impromptu speech given on top of a banquet table, that had the bigger impact on his new neighbors.

On the morning of the Fourth, all New Havenites were roused out of bed at precisely 4 a.m., when bells were rung and cannon balls discharged. But the break in the heat wave made getting up less of a chore; for the first time in days, the thermometer wouldn't reach the mid-90s. At nine, Webster joined a long and well-choreographed procession that moved from the "new township" (near today's Wooster Square) up Chapel Street, before snaking its way over to the Green, which, like the Yale chapel, was draped in red, white and blue. At the head marched the Governor's Guard and several artillery companies. Webster paraded near the front along with Timothy Dwight. Right behind the two speakers trailed the state's judges and New Haven's mayor.

After a military review, Webster and the other marchers walked into Center Church. Soon New Haven's inhabitants filed in; while men found spots on the ground floor, the ladies, wearing cockades in their hats, headed to the galleries. In the pews of the 75-by-55-foot church, filled to its capacity of nine hundred, were also seated both clergymen and residents from neighboring towns.

Dwight gave his sermon first. He began by reading from the sixteenth chapter of the Book of Revelation ("Behold, I come as a thief. Blessed is he that watcheth, and keepeth his garments, lest he walk naked, and they see his shame.") and then advised his fellow citizens to avoid France's slide into atheism. Noting that "Sin is the nakedness and shame of the scriptures and righteousness the garment which covers it," Dwight moved many to tears. As the reporter for *The New York Gazette* put it, Dwight's sentiments merited "being written in letters of gold and affixed to every conspicuous place."

After Dwight finished leading a series of prayers, Webster stepped toward the pulpit at the west side of the church. In his prepared remarks, Webster, too, would focus on the most pressing political issue of the day—the growing tension between America and France, then close to the boiling point. Since the passage of the Jay Treaty, which had strengthened America's bond with England, the French had cast a wary eye across the Atlantic. Routinely seizing American trading ships, the French refused to seat the American ambassador. The "XYZ Affair," revealed by President John Adams a few months earlier, in which French agents had demanded a substantial bribe in return for resuming negotiations, was just the latest in a long string of overtly hostile acts toward America.

While most Americans shared Webster's frustration with French perfidy—in fact, just three days later Congress would officially rescind existing treaties and gird the nation for war—Webster's sense of outrage knew no bounds. He launched into an assault on all things French, including those very ideas that had helped launch the American Revolution. "Such are the inevitable consequences," Webster asserted, "of that false philosophy which has been preached by Rousseau, Condorcet, Godwin and other visionaries who sit down in their closets to frame systems of government, which are as unfit for practice, as a vessel of paper for the transportation of men on the troubled ocean."

But Webster didn't stop there. Included in his rebuke were all Americans who expressed opposition to Federalist policies, and no one more so than their ringleader, Jefferson, whom he compared unfavorably to the subject of his current book project—the yellow fever. As he stated, "In all ages of the world, a political projector or system-monger of popular talents has been a greater scourge to society than a pestilence." Webster refused to let go of his outdated concept of American unity, which saw political parties as inherently dangerous. Equating open debate with chaos, Webster preached obedience to authority: "Let us never forget that the cornerstone of all republican governments is that the will of every citizen is controlled by the laws or the supreme will of the state." Like Dwight, within just two decades this veteran of the Battle of Saratoga had gone from revolutionary to counterrevolutionary.

After Webster concluded, the procession regrouped and headed next door to the state house. In the open hall on the third floor, Webster was among the three hundred and fifty gentlemen who feasted on a sumptuous dinner. The President of the Day, Isaac Beers the bookseller, led a total of sixteen toasts, beginning with "the United States" and ending with "the Day." The town's ladies congregated separately for tea under a bower in the New Gardens, where the men joined them later that afternoon.

The whole crowd sang "Hail, Columbia," America's unofficial national anthem, whose lyrics Joseph Hopkinson had penned earlier that year. Then suddenly Webster's former classmate Josiah Meigs, who had recently returned to Yale as a professor of mathematics and natural philosophy, jumped up on a table. A firm supporter of the French Revolution, Meigs was outside of the political mainstream in Federalist Connecticut. His words silenced the crowd: "In 1793, the bones of multitudes of our fellow citizens lay unburied on Long Island exposed to the summer's sun. I insisted that they ought to be buried." By harking back to British atrocities committed during the Revolution, Meigs was underlining the distastefulness of allying with Britain against France. Beers then remarked as to how the social mirth of the day had been interrupted.

Seizing the opportunity, Webster himself leaped up onto the table and passed by Meigs. "True it is," he shouted, "many of our fellow citizens perished in the revolution and their bones might have been exposed. No man regrets or honors the brave men more than I. But I pledge my

word to lay my own bones with them sooner than surrender the independence of my country to the French!" A thunderous applause rang
out, along with calls for Webster to drop his hat. Removing the flowers
that hung on their breasts, the ladies created a garland, which they
placed around Webster's hat. The "Presidente" [*sic*] of the ladies, Mary
Clap Wooster, the wife of the Revolutionary War hero Major General
David Wooster, then had the great pleasure to crown Webster. After
proposing a toast to General Wooster, Webster led the crowd in another
chorus of "Hail, Columbia":

> Firm, united let us be,
> Rallying round our liberty,
> As a band of brothers joined,
> Peace and safety we shall find.

Though not typically exuberant, on this occasion Webster had filled
the hearts of those around him with joy. "The spirits of the company
which had been damped by the first intrusion were," *The New York Gazette* reported, "re-animated and the evening passed off with great mirth
and social glee."

THE HEAT WAVE resumed shortly after Independence Day and lasted
through the end of September. One day in August, when Webster stuck
his trusted thermometer (which he used to make daily calculations of
the temperature in his garden) into the sand on the highway near his
house, it registered a sweltering 118 degrees.

Just as Webster returned to his research on yellow fever, the fever
itself came back with a vengeance. "The disease assumes," Webster
wrote in his diary, "this year, in Philadelphia and New York more of the
characteristics of the plague, is contagious and fatal beyond what has
been known in America for a century." By September, Webster's paper
reported, New York was losing nearly sixty people a day. In his diary,

Webster kept close track of the epidemic, which ended abruptly with the arrival of a severe frost and some snow in early November:

> Number of deaths in Phil.— 3436
> d° [ditto] in N York—about 2000
> d° in Boston 200
> d° in Wilmington 252
> d° in New London 80

Included in those disturbing totals were some familiar faces, such as his former New York neighbor, Dr. Elihu Smith, who died in late September. Webster feared that he, too, might be reduced to a statistic. On August 20, as he was finishing up a short stay in New York, during which he saw Smith for the last time, Webster himself was struck down with the same bilious fever that ended up killing several other Connecticut visitors. The cause, he assumed, was breathing poison from the New York air. Miraculously, in Webster's case, the symptoms were not severe, and by November, he was fully cured. Still, this close call left him shaken. Webster later recorded in his memoir, "From this he recovered; but he had two or three relapses in which the disease took the form of a regular tertian [parasite]. These left him in terrible health, which continued several months. This was the only instance of his being affected with severe disease, after the age of twenty years." Though physically he was drained, Webster's mind remained as sharp as ever. On September 26, he published a notice in *The Connecticut Journal* expressing dissatisfaction with the responses to his query about disease statistics: "But I am sorry to say that the communications do not answer to my views, for want of more precision. The statements will be useless to me unless they specify the year when a particular epidemic prevailed."

By the end of 1798, Webster finished his *Brief History of Epidemic and Pestilential Diseases with the Principal Phenomena of the Physical World Which Precede Them and Accompany Them and Observations Deduced From the Facts Stated*. The title was a misnomer—his two-volume treatise ran to more than seven hundred pages. Due to lackluster interest, Webster delayed publication until the following December. And despite much critical praise in the literary and scientific community, the book never did gain a following among the general public. It sold just a fraction of the thousand copies, leaving Webster out nearly eight hundred dollars.

The first volume traced epidemics throughout history, moving from biblical accounts (namely, chapter five of the Book of Exodus) to medical reports, beginning with the Greeks and going up to the late eighteenth century. In the second volume, Webster provided analysis. Its first chapter, composed entirely of charts, featured bills of mortality for a half-dozen cities (London, Augsburg, Dresden, Paris, Boston and Dublin) over the previous two centuries. After covering this historical turf, Webster tried to explain why his fellow Americans had been dying at such an alarming rate. However, he wasn't able to refine his thinking beyond the vague environmental causes—dirt, pollution and the like—that he had identified in his earlier book on the subject. Wedded to the empirical method, Webster was forced to acknowledge the tentative nature of his findings: "More materials are necessary to enable us to erect a theory of epidemics which shall deserve full confidence."

Not sure exactly how to combat this frightening public health menace—he opposed quarantines—Webster looked for a silver lining in the idea that disaster is a necessary tonic, writing, "The natural evils that surround us . . . lay the foundation for the finest feelings of the human heart, compassion and benevolence." In the long and mostly positive review in his literary journal, *The Monthly Review,* Charles Brockden Brown found this fatalistic turn puzzling: "The work is concluded with certain moral reflections which are indeed of an equivocal and hazardous kind. . . . The tendencies of the universe and the motives of its maker are to this observer extremely evident." Webster, Brown felt, was being a bit presumptuous when he concluded that God was using the plague to send a message.

While Webster didn't pinpoint the cause of the disease, he did help fill a gaping hole in the scholarly literature. Few writers, he aptly noted, had ever attempted systematic studies of medical conditions such as the fever: "In respect to useful history . . . modern compilers appear to have written for fame or money. . . . These observations have arisen out of my enquiries, relative to pestilential diseases. I have discovered that many of the histories or rather abridgements and compilations . . . are very incomplete." In the final analysis, Webster managed to put public health on a scientific footing. The Johns Hopkins professor Dr. William Osler, a giant of late nineteenth-century medicine, later described Webster's book as "the most important medical work written in this country by a layman."

Like most of America's city dwellers, for the next few years Webster would live in constant fear of another outbreak. "We are well; although we have had slight indispositions, especially of the throat," he reported to his brother-in-law Daniel Greenleaf a few months after publishing his treatise. "Five or six cases of fever have occurred in New Haven with anomalous symptoms and in August, would be called *yellow*. But if you read my books, you will see that I am not surprised at this—Don't say from this that yellow fever is in New Haven. Names are terrible things." The fever did return intermittently throughout the nineteenth century, but never again with the same intensity as in 1798. Nearly a century later, scientists finally solved the puzzle; the disease was transmitted by mosquitoes.

JUST AS WEBSTER RELEASED his *History of Pestilence* (the abbreviated title mentioned in newspaper advertisements), he was leveled by some disturbing news out of Virginia. "On the 14th of December 1799," he recorded in his diary, "died the Great and Good Washington in the 68th year of his age, of a cynanche tonsillaris, after 24 hours illness. All America mourns." Since his retirement two years earlier, "the Hero of the Age" had been enjoying robust health; his sudden death left Webster, like the rest of America, nearly speechless with grief. As Webster's *Commercial Advertiser* lamented on December 20, "When WASHINGTON

IS NO MORE . . . let not the voice of eulogy be heard, lest the weakness of talents, and the deficiency of language do injustice to the lustre and fame of the deceased." But before too long, Webster sought to become Washington's biographer. Three months later, he wrote to his longtime friend Timothy Pickering, then secretary of state, for help in currying favor with Judge Bushrod Washington, the late president's nephew, who held the family papers. "If I had the materials," Webster stated, "it would be my great pleasure to make the best use of them that my abilities would permit." In the end, Judge Washington chose John Marshall, the future chief justice, then a member of the U.S. House of Representatives.

After Washington's death, Webster's attitude toward national politics changed markedly. For Webster, the chance to serve Washington, his surrogate father whom he never stopped idealizing, had been a unique pleasure. He didn't feel the same level of commitment to other Federalists. While Webster was a steadfast supporter of John Adams, he was not in awe of the second president. In the fall of 1800, as Adams faced a tough reelection battle against his vice president, Thomas Jefferson, Webster praised the president for his "pure morals," "firm attachment to republican government" and "inflexible integrity and patriotism." He also called Adams "the best read statesman that the late Revolution called into notice." Family connections played a role in Webster's emergence as an "Adamite"; after all, his brother-in-law William Cranch was Adams' nephew, and Webster would spend time in Adams' hometown of Quincy when visiting the Greenleafs in Massachusetts. But Webster could also acknowledge Adams' faults, such as his "occasional ill humour at unreasonable opposition and hasty expressions of his opinion."

Webster's support for Adams' reelection put him at loggerheads with his former ally, Alexander Hamilton, who throughout the 1790s penned editorials in Webster's paper. By the election of 1800—which ran from April until October as states held separate votes—Hamilton, who had recently resigned from his post as a major general in the army, had grown disgruntled with Adams. That fall, Hamilton published a fifty-four-page pamphlet that attacked Adams' character and conduct. While Hamilton recalled with fondness the president's service during the early stages of the Revolution and offered a lukewarm endorsement of his candidacy, the tone was harsh. After airing his personal grievances (such as the president's reluctance to name him commander of the army after Washington's sudden death), Hamilton went on the attack. Alluding to Adams' "disgusting egotism" and "eccentric tendencies," the general painted the sitting president as emotionally unstable: "It is a fact that he is often liable to paroxysms of anger which deprive him of self-command and produce very outrageous behavior."

Not surprisingly, Hamilton's tirade about Adams' peevishness enraged Webster, who feared, as did other Federalists, that Hamilton had just handed Jefferson the presidency. Under the pen name "Aristides," Webster published a letter to Hamilton that addressed the general's pamphlet about Adams. Webster stressed the personal over the political: "It avails little that you accuse the President of vanity. . . . were it an issue between Mr. Adams and yourself which has the most, you could not rely on an unanimous verdict in your favor. The same remark is applicable to the charge of self-sufficiency." "Vanity" and "self-sufficiency" were epithets often hurled at Webster, and the fact was that the two men shared the same combustible temperament. And once they began heaping insults upon each other, their relationship was beyond repair. Saving his biggest dart for last, Webster added that if Adams were to lose the election, "your conduct will be deemed little short of insanity."

The following year, after Jefferson succeeded Adams as president, the conflict between Webster and Hamilton reached new heights. No longer able to use Webster's newspaper as his personal mouthpiece, Hamilton decided to start his own. In the spring of 1801, Hamilton met with a group of influential New York Federalists at the "country house" of Scottish merchant Archibald Gracie—today the official residence of New York City's mayor—to plan this rival paper, which he would call the *New York Evening Post*. Now known simply as the *New York*

Post, Rupert Murdoch's tabloid, America's longest-running daily has its roots in Hamilton's falling-out with Noah Webster, Jr., a little more than two centuries ago.

Just as he heard of Hamilton's intention to launch the *Evening Post,* Webster embarked on another scholarly fact-finding mission. Having attempted an inventory of his state, he now moved on to one of his livelihood, the newspaper business. Webster first got interested in the history of American journalism when John Eliot, a Boston pastor, contacted him in 1799 for assistance with an article for the Massachusetts Historical Society on the emergence of New England newspapers. As Eliot noted in his acknowledgments, Webster provided "a very accurate list of Connecticut newspapers to the present time." "To collect authentic facts respecting the origin and progress of the public prints in the United States," Webster drafted another survey, which in mid-June he sent out to newspaper editors in every state except Connecticut. For a given town, his questionnaire included such items as the year the first paper was established, the number of papers and the frequency of their publication. Over the next six months, Webster received only about a dozen replies, and he was forced to abandon this project, too. However, Webster's efforts were not entirely in vain. Two years later, in a thousand-page tome covering worldwide advances in science and culture, curiously entitled *A Brief Retrospect of the Eighteenth Century,* the Reverend Samuel Miller did come up with an official tally—America had two hundred different newspapers (seventeen of which were dailies), approximately thirteen million copies circulated annually—and he appears to have relied at least in part on statistical information supplied by Webster.

By the fall of 1801, Webster turned his full attention to Hamilton's machinations. In a letter dated September 11, 1801, a nervous Webster confided his fears to Benjamin Rush: "At this time I have more than usual calls on me to counteract the designs of my Federal friends, who are establishing two papers precisely on the principles of mine and calculated to interfere with both in a manner that carries with it strong evidence of a design to ruin mine." (Hamilton was also planning a second weekly paper, which he called *The New York Herald*, the original name of Webster's weekly.) In early October, Webster trekked off to New York to find out for himself exactly what was going on. The journey carried some risk, as the yellow fever was back. Though the outbreak wasn't as serious as in 1798, some residents living near the East River had to be evacuated from their homes. After speaking with his contacts in Manhattan, Webster learned that "a secret enmity to me for the part I took in the controversy between Mr. Adams and General Hamilton" was indeed the reason that Hamilton had appointed William Coleman, an erudite lawyer from Greenfield, Massachusetts, as editor of the *Evening Post*. Upon returning to New Haven on October 13, Webster wrote Oliver Wolcott that he wouldn't back down from a battle with Hamilton, whom he considered ungrateful: "No man in America has labored so incessantly to oppose anarchy as I have done from the peace of 1783 to this hour. I can show more columns written for this purpose than any twenty men in the United States. I have spent the best portion of my life and with little pecuniary reward, and an attempt to deprive me and my family of subsistence at this period of life, too late to renew my profession, is a proof of an unfeeling heart in any man who can deliberately make the attempt."

Webster had indeed been America's most prolific journalist, but Hamilton didn't owe him anything. The general, too, had a right to publish a paper. This was an ideological battle rather than a purely personal one. But still traumatized by his father's abandonment twenty-five years earlier, Webster viewed Hamilton as another rejecting authority figure who failed to recognize his self-worth. Webster and his dreaded foe, Jefferson, would end up sharing one common belief—both considered Hamilton "the evil genius of his country."

Over the next couple of months, Webster kept deliberating about what to do. He initially thought about luring Coleman away from Hamilton—either by hiring him as his editor or selling him his papers outright. But this scheme didn't pan out, and Coleman would serve as Hamilton's amanuensis until Aaron Burr's pistol ended the general's life in 1804. Coleman never much liked Webster; he once wrote of his wish to give "that pedant . . . Webster . . . a rousing box on the ears. . . . I can never forgive this man for his infamous and unprincipled attack on the great and good Hamilton." To combat Coleman, Webster hired as his new associate editor Samuel Bayard, a young lawyer from a prominent New York family. Bayard (who later helped found the New-York Historical Society) would work directly with Ebenezer Belden, the son of Webster's older sister, Mercy, who had replaced George Hopkins as publisher in 1799. After learning of Webster's appointment of Bayard, another New York paper observed, "It appears that Mr. Coleman's intended *Evening Post* has given Mr. Webster a little uneasiness. . . . he trembles for its fate." On November 13, 1801, just three days before the *Evening Post* began its legendary run, Webster published a brief announcement about his new colleague, which began: "The proprietor . . . having by a long course of intense application and sedentary life enfeebled his constitution so as to render some relaxation a duty to himself and those who depend on him for support, has associated himself in the superintendence of his papers a gentleman of known talents and respectability who will by his daily attention contribute to preserve their reputation and acknowledged usefulness."

But Webster was confusing cause with effect. In truth, his sedentary life hadn't produced his nervous condition, but was his refuge from it.

Hamilton and Webster now engaged in a vicious circulation war; the first source of contention was which Federalist could lay claim to being the fiercest critic of Jefferson, the new president whom they both detested. Alleging that he wished to give Jefferson a fair hearing, Webster waited five months into the new administration before rendering his predictably harsh verdict. In the fall of 1801, Webster published a series of eighteen anonymous letters in his paper; Hamilton would follow with his own eighteen-article series in the winter. Webster's first piece, which ran on September 26, 1801, analyzed Jefferson's inaugural: "Yet after a few sentences, you tell us that 'every difference of opinion is not a difference of principle; that we are all Republicans—all Federalists.' It follows from these declarations that in your opinion, the parties have contended not for *principles,* but for *unimportant opinions.* . . . But this concession criminates you and your friends; for unimportant concerns can never justify men in violent and animated exertions to change an administration."

Webster still equated the opposition of Jefferson and other Democratic-Republicans to the Federalist administration of John Adams with disloyalty to America. Much to Webster's surprise, the president himself never responded directly to this "candid estimation" of his job performance. But in a letter to Secretary of State James Madison, Jefferson did reveal what he was thinking: "I view Webster as a mere pedagogue of very limited understanding and very strong prejudices and party passions." The obtuse Webster, however, never did figure out that Jefferson didn't want anything to do with him. When his first dictionary came out several years later, he sent the president a copy, asking him to "give it such encouragement as you may think it deserves." Jefferson left that letter unanswered, too.

As Webster ceded more and more editorial control to Bayard, he fought less and less with his two archenemies, Jefferson and Hamilton. But this longtime partisan scribe was not just losing his stomach for heated political debate; he was also losing his feeling for his fellow man. Isolated in the relative tranquility of the Arnold House, Webster turned increasingly antidemocratic. Teetering on paranoia, he saw opponents everywhere. As he wrote to Benjamin Rush, "As to mankind, I believe the mass of them to be 'copax [*sic*] rationis.' They are ignorant, or what is worse governed by authority & the authority of men who flatter them instead of boldly telling them the truth." This harsh view of human nature led Webster to endorse wildly reactionary ideas. "It would be better for the people," the middle-aged writer continued in this jeremiad to Rush, "they would be more free and more happy, if all were deprived of the right of suffrage until they were 45 years of age, and if no man was eligible to an important government office until he is 50, that is, if all powers of government were vested in our old men." Apparently, Webster didn't see anything paradoxical in both inveighing against blind obedience to authority and asking his fellow Americans to place all their trust in their elders. But soon he would give up his fantasy of restoring order to America through political change; he would increasingly focus on organizing words rather than people.

By the second half of 1803, Webster began preparing to unload his papers. The following year, the initial fourteen-year federal copyright for his speller was due to expire, and he sensed that reissuing the book could be a financial bonanza. (He turned out to be right. *The American Spelling Book* would sell a staggering two hundred thousand copies a year—one for every thirty Americans—netting Webster, who earned a penny a copy, an annual revenue stream of two thousand dollars.) Webster could now afford to exit the newspaper business. On October 15, 1803, he published his last article as a newspaper editor, an angry epistle to William Coleman, in which he charged the *Evening Post* editor with twisting the core ideas of his work on the plague. Webster's sign-off was dramatic: "With a gentleman of candour and fairness, discussion might be attended with pleasure and productive of mutual benefit. With you, sir, I disdain to pursue the controversy." Two weeks later, Webster and his nephew sold the business to Zachariah Lewis. New York's first daily paper would live on in various incarnations until 1923, when as *The Globe*, it was folded into *The Sun*.

In the same issue of *The Commercial Advertiser* in which Webster penned that farewell letter to Coleman, he wrote a long article under the pen name "Rusticus"—the Latin word for country-dweller—on a totally different subject, literary history. "It has been a subject of controversy whether *intense application* [italics mine] of mind," began Webster, repeating the same phrase he had earlier used to describe the putative cause of his enfeebled constitution, "tends to shorten life. Opinions on this point are various; and perhaps we may throw light on it by an appeal to the facts." This controversy was, of course, largely of interest to

"Rusticus" himself; it was the obsession that consumed his mind, not those of his readers. For Webster, understanding the health effects of a sedentary life was a pressing concern, as he was then deciding whether to throw himself into the dictionary.

To arrive at a definitive answer, Webster gathered four sets of data, which he presented in chart form. Each one was a bill of mortality for a famous group of writers—those from ancient Greece, ancient Rome, modern Europe and England. For the Greek and Roman authors, Webster mentioned the age and year of death. While the Greek list featured the great philosophers and scribes of the age—Plato, Socrates, Thales, Euripides and the like—it also included some obscure names such as Xenophilius, who was placed at the top because he supposedly had lived to the age of 169.

For modern writers, Webster's charts also contained the year of birth. Here are a few of the English writers he selected—all personal heroes since his undergraduate days—listed in the same order as in the newspaper:

	Born	Died	Age
Newton	1643	1727	84
Hobbes	1588	1679	91
Johnson, Samuel	1709	1784	75
Bacon, Francis	1560	1626	66
Pope	1688	1744	56

Webster didn't perform any elaborate statistical analysis. For each of the four groups, he just tallied up how many writers died after ninety, eighty, seventy and sixty. (In the case of the English list, which at thirty-one names was the longest, those figures came out to three, eleven, seventeen and twenty-seven, respectively.) Satisfied that this far-from-scientific survey showed a link between literary greatness and longevity, Webster offered these tentative conclusions: "It is probable . . . that the unusual proportion of learned men who live to a great age may be in part ascribed to their temperate habits of life—and to an original firmness of constitution." Webster was now convinced that he had the right stuff to rank up there with his icons. And in the hope of one day being at the top of a new list—that of American literary immortals—he became a full-time lexicographer.

By 1803, WEBSTER had already cemented his reputation as an obsessive definer. In an 1802 satiric play, *Federalism Triumphant* by Leonard Chester, a character based on his friend John Trumbull thus mocks him, "If he [brother Noah] should get angry, he'll oppose my favorite scheme of augmenting the number of judges of the superior court and come into the house and spend three days on the word augmentation, as he did on shews."

After finishing his book on epidemics, Webster had purchased the eighth edition of Samuel Johnson's 1755 masterpiece, published in London in 1799, and began combing through these two quarto volumes, line by line. (Webster's copy, complete with all his marginalia, has been preserved in the rare-book room of the New York Public Library.) Curiously, in his memoir, Webster was vague about this bit of personal history: "At what particular time, N.W. began to think seriously of attempting the compilation of a complete dictionary of the English language, is not known. But it appears that soon after leaving New York in 1798, he began to enter particular works and authorities on the margin of *Johnson's Dictionary*, to be used, if occasion should offer." This lapse in memory is surprising, given the precision with which Webster recorded so many other key events in his literary career. Regardless of the exact date he began thinking about his magnum opus, by early 1800 Samuel Johnson, the idol whom Webster had worshipped since adolescence, became the father figure whom he sought to slay. It was high time, Webster believed, for Americans to entrust defining to one of their own.

But Webster didn't get started in time to become America's first lexicographer. Another Connecticut Federalist—who just happened to have the perfect name for an up-and-coming lexicographer, Samuel Johnson, Jr.—had already beaten him to the punch. No relation to the Dr. Johnson of Lichfield, England, this Samuel Johnson, born a year before Webster, was a teacher in nearby Guilford. In 1798, Johnson Jr. published *A School Dictionary,* which offered "an easy and concise method of teaching children the true meaning and pronunciation of the most useful words in the English language." In contrast to Webster, the Connecticut Johnson hadn't attended college and lacked lofty ambitions. He sought to Americanize not the comprehensive work by his British namesake, but rather *The Royal Standard English Dictionary* by William Perry, a Scottish schoolteacher. Johnson's two-hundred-page text was largely an abridgement of Perry's pronouncing dictionary, originally published in London in 1775 and in America a decade later. Most of Johnson's four thousand entries were lifted directly from Perry's thirty thousand, but this new American product had one twist; in contrast to Perry, Johnson divided up words according to the principles laid out in Webster's *Grammatical Institute.* In fact, in his introduction, Johnson Jr. fawned over the pedagogical trilogy by "the ingenious Mr. Webster." Webster was thus a big supporter, and he was one of a half-dozen subscribers listed in the *Connecticut Journal* ads.

Johnson Jr.'s 1798 dictionary sold out within several months, and by the middle of 1799, he resolved to put out a revised version. This time, Johnson enlisted a collaborator, Yale-educated John Elliott, the pastor in neighboring East Guilford (now Madison). In May 1800, Elliott—the reverend was listed as first author—and Johnson published *A Selected Pronouncing and Accented Dictionary.* Webster, who had seen a draft a year earlier, supplied the following endorsement, "I have not time to examine every sheet . . . but have read many sheets in different parts of it; your general plan and execution I approve of." Also designed for schools, this volume aimed to help students keep up with a changing world: "Custom is daily introducing new words into our language, many of which are frequently used, and their signification important to be known." Containing about five thousand more words than its predecessor, this dictionary was the first to include Americanisms such as "President," "federal," "Capitol" and "freshet." Elliott and Johnson also added American-Indian words ("tomahawk" and "wampum") and recently coined scientific terms such as "telegraph."

Under the stewardship of the devout Reverend Elliott, whom one parishioner described as "a man of upright constancy," this school dictionary also attempted to purify the English language. "To inspire youth with sentiments of modesty and decency," the authors wrote in the preface, "is one of the principal objects of early instruction; and this object is totally defeated by the indiscriminate use of vulgar and indecent words." While the new volume removed "tosspot" (a synonym for drunkard) and "whore," it also overreached; such supposedly saucy entries as "diabetes" (defined in 1798 as "involuntary discharge of urine") and "obstetric" were also axed. It also toned down some definitions; for example, "rouge" evolved from "red paint used on the face of prostitutes" to "red paint used on the face," and "voluptuous" no longer had anything to do with the sensual, but now was defined simply as "extravagant." Curiously, despite all these moves in the direction of chastity, the authors left in the French F-word, "foutra"—defined as "a scoff, insult or gibe"— which had appeared in both Johnson's 1755 and Johnson Jr.'s 1798 volumes. Calling this expression "unprintable," an irate writer in the *American Review and Literary Journal* noted in 1801, "we cannot soil our page with the transcription of it; it is to be found under the letter *F* and is called *French,* but we are sure no French dictionary would admit a word so shockingly indecent and vulgar."

On Wednesday, June 4, 1800, just a few weeks after the publication of Elliott and Johnson's school dictionary, Webster announced his ambitions in *The Connecticut Journal*:

> Mr. Webster of this city, we understand, is engaged in completing the system for the instruction of youth, which he began in the year 1783. He has in hand a Dictionary of the American Language, a work long since projected, but which other occupations have delayed till

this time. The plan contemplated extends to a small Dictionary for schools, one for the counting-house, and a large one for men of science. The first is nearly ready for the press—the second and third will require the labor of years.

But Webster soon abandoned this school dictionary. The precise reason is unclear. In his memoir, he offered an incomplete explanation: "the plan not pleasing him, he [N.W.] destroyed the manuscript." In contrast to his two Connecticut neighbors, Webster would focus solely on the adult marketplace and go far beyond just incorporating Americanisms. As he also noted in this initial press release, "A work of this kind is absolutely necessary, on account of differences between the American and English language. New circumstances, new modes of life, new laws, new ideas of various kinds give rise to new words. . . . The differences in the languages of the two countries will continue to multiply and render it necessary that we should have Dictionaries of the American Language." Though a political reactionary, Webster was a linguistic revolutionary. He proposed to create an entirely new language, an American version of English. His dictionary would thus make obsolete the work of both Johnson and Johnson Jr.

The revelation that one of America's foremost men of letters had officially entered the lexicography business was national news. However, the swift verdict rendered on Webster's new vocation, which was nearly unanimous, was: ridiculous. Both Federalists and Republicans responded with contempt. Just three days later, a columnist in *The Gazette,* one of Philadelphia's leading Federalist papers, advised Webster "to turn his mind from language-making to something really useful. . . . there is nothing I am more desirous to avoid than God's curse in a confusion of tongues." A generation after the Revolution, most Americans, including Webster's Federalist allies, saw the linguistic status quo as sacred. In an article, "On the Scheme of an American Language," published in his journal, *The Monthly Magazine and American Review,* that summer, Charles Brockden Brown traced this mainstream view back to the Hebrew scriptures, which had taught that "diversity of language" was an "evil." As Brown argued, Webster was heading in the wrong direction: "This evil, like other evils inflicted by heaven, we are permitted to repair and diminish in some degree." After all, in the preface to his dictionary, Samuel Johnson had also railed against the "caprices of innovation" in language. The lexicographer's job, as Johnson defined it, was to create order out of chaos, and Webster, according to his critics, proposed to do just the opposite.

Likewise, on June 12, Joseph Dennie—the editor of Philadelphia's other prominent Federalist paper, *The Gazette of the United States,* who four years earlier had written Webster a fan letter about *The Prompter*— also lambasted him. Dennie's weapon of choice was a half page of missives from faux readers exemplifying the chaos that might ensue should Webster's new publishing venture succeed. The following letters illustrate two potentially new forms of debased English:

> To Mr. noab Wabstur
>
> Sur,
>
> by rading all ovur the nusspaper I find you are after meaking
> a nue Merrykin Dikshunary; your rite, Sir; for ofter looking all over
> the anglish Books, you wont find a bit Shillaly big enuf to beat a
> dog wid. so I hope you'll take a hint, a put enuff of rem in yours,
> for Och 'tis a nate little bit of furniture for any Man's house
> so it 'tis.
>
> > Pat O'Dogerty

> Brother noab
>
> Instead of *I keant keatch the keow,* an English man or *a town bred
> american* would say, *I cannot Catch the Cow,* but you being a brother
> Yankey will be sure to spell right in your new Yankey dictionary
>
> > yours, &c.
> >
> > *Brother Jonathan*
> > N.B. *mind and give us a true deffinition of bundling.*

Describing himself as "An Enemy to Innovation," Dennie also added to the barrage: "If as Mr Webster asserts, it is true that many new words have already crept into the language of the United States, he would be much better employed in rooting out the noxious weed than in mingling them with the flowers. Should he, however, persist in his attempt to erect a revolution in our language, I trust that a system fraught with such pernicious consequences will meet with the contempt it deserves from all the friends of literature."

Twenty-five years after Lexington and Concord, Webster's plan to replace the King's English had few takers; his linguistic revolution would be a lonely one.

The equally fierce Republican opposition was actually the more surprising. Though Republican editors had been vilifying Webster's political views for nearly a decade, they might have been expected to embrace his "bottom-up" approach to lexicography. After all, Webster the wordsmith was a compiler, not a prescriber; in the dictionary, as in the speller, he championed the words of the common man—language as it was, not as it ought to be. But that June, Benjamin Franklin Bache, the editor of Philadelphia's Republican paper, the *Aurora*, smeared Webster, calling him "this oddity of literature." For Bache, in contrast to the Federalist editors, Webster's whole career—not just his recent turn to lexicography—was an embarrassment:

> After involving the question of the yellow fever in deeper obscurity, and producing nothing but the profit by the sale of the work, he now appears as a legislator and municipal magistrate of Connecticut; writes nonsense pseudo-political and pseudo-philosophical for his newspapers at New York, and proposes to give to the American world no less than three dictionaries! . . . The plain truth is . . . that he means to make money by a scheme which ought to be and will be discountenanced by every man who admires the classic English writers.

But Bache was just heaping abuse on Webster. In reality, Webster had already made his money. For Webster, as opposed to his idol, Samuel Johnson, dictionary-making was not a means, but an end in itself.

Even Connecticut Federalists had nothing kind to say. In the fall of 1801, Warren Dutton—dubbed "a pupil of the Connecticut pope" because he had studied divinity under Timothy Dwight at Yale—repeatedly attacked Webster in his "Restorator" columns in the *New England Palladium,* a new Federalist paper out of Boston. On October 2, Dutton, who worked as assistant editor under Webster's longtime friend Jedidiah Morse, mocked "the great lexicographer" for planning to add a bunch of silly words to the English language. Dutton didn't think much of the locally grown "happify" (which Webster had used in his recent editions of his speller), "lengthy" or "belittle." According to Dutton, Webster would be creating not an American dictionary but rather one solely of "the vulgar tongue in New England." Noting that the explorer Sebastian Cabot had first discovered the eastern states, Dutton wondered, "Would it not be better to prefix to it [the dictionary] the epithet Cabotian?" In his November 2 column, "the Restorator" published an inflammatory letter by "Aristarchus" (the pen name of the Boston pastor John Gardiner). Concerned that Webster had not yet been "subdued," Gardiner hoped to prevent the Connecticut lexicographer from injecting "barbarisms . . . into books." "But if he will persist," Gardiner lamented, "in spite of common sense, to furnish us with a dictionary which we do not want, in return for his generosity, I will furnish him with a title for it. Let, then, the projected volume of foul and unclean things bear his own Christian name and be called NOAH's ARK."

Webster felt betrayed. On November 10, he fired back with a letter to the *Palladium* in which he accused Dutton of attempting "to vilify a fellow citizen . . . whose whole life has been devoted to . . . the honor and . . . the rights of his country." Webster replied that it was reasonable to add many well-established words to English lexicons; all that mattered was that the new definitions were "correct." To put Dutton in his place,

Webster clarified the meaning of his pseudonym: "As the word Restorator is the least known in this country, I might take the liberty of defining it according to the sense it bears in the gentleman's own writings, *viz, a man who . . . retails ordinary fare.*"

One of the few sympathetic voices was William Rind, editor of the *Washington Federalist,* who expressed his hope that Webster, "heedless of the sarcasms of those who are fond of *belittling* every thing American. . . . will bestow on his mediated undertaking all that attention and investigation which have marked his former writings." But even without any encouragement, Webster was prepared to go on. This loner was used to fighting against the rest of the world. Though nothing could stop him now, completing his two planned dictionaries would prove much more difficult than he ever imagined.

9

Paterfamilias

FAMILY, n. The collective body of persons who live in one
house and under one head or manager; a household, including
parents, children and servants, and as the case may be, lodgers
or boarders.

W hen will Squire Webster be returning home?"
            That's what Rebecca Webster, eight months pregnant
            with the couple's sixth child (who would turn out to be
Eliza), kept hearing from her Water Street neighbors throughout December
1803. Though she wasn't sure herself, Rebecca would answer, "At
Christmas."

But Webster wouldn't be back until after the beginning of the New
Year.

Shortly before Thanksgiving, Webster headed to Philadelphia to
procure types for the revised version of his spelling book. During his
two-month hiatus, New Haven was not quite the same. Without its
leader, the choir at the Brick Meeting House ceased singing.

During his travels, Webster stayed in touch by mail. The letters from
his two eldest daughters, Emily, then thirteen, and Julia, then ten, provide a unique glimpse into how the Webster children related to their
paterfamilias.

Feeling put upon by all the activity in his bustling household, the
socially awkward scholar demanded not only submission to parental au-

thority but also cheerfulness. He was a topsy-turvy parent, tending to
look to his children for affection and support rather than the other way
around. His manner was intimidating, and his preferred mode of communication was the lecture. When writing from upstate New York that
summer, he tried to turn his itinerary into a pedagogical exercise: "Such
is my progress my dear girls and you must take your maps and trace it
out. . . . It will help you to remember the geography of this country."
Quick to anger, Webster could get highly animated about matters of
principle. And jokes with double entendres or coarse references of any
sort could set off a tirade. While he mostly directed his outrage toward
other adults (rather than family members), his children often felt fear in
his presence. After witnessing a harsh rebuke toward a particular "cul-
prit," one of the girls once blurted out, "Papa makes me siver [shiver] like
a top." Webster also had a punitive streak. While on a trip years later,
he wrote to Eliza, "If my name is a terror to *evil doers* at home, I hope
there will be little occasion to use it. Tell Louisa there must be no *evil
doings* at home & if I do not learn that she is a good girl, I shall not bring
her pretty things when I return."

In their letters that winter, both Emily and Julia tried their best to
win their father's favor. Unfortunately, this tack meant internalizing his
critical temperament and burdening themselves with feelings of inade-
quacy. On November 24, 1803, an apologetic Emily had a hard time
putting pen to paper, writing from her father's study, "However, as it
[this letter] is intended for my father's perusal, and he well knows what
an ignoramus his Emily is—I will scribble just what pops into my head
first." Identifying with Webster, Emily, too, lapsed into the third person
to talk about herself; likewise, just as he often complained about family
intrusions into his dictionary-making, the teenager expressed annoyance
with her rambunctious younger siblings—namely, her sisters Harriet
and Mary, and the two-year-old William: "Pardon, Dear Pappa, the many
mistakes and blots I have made occasioned by frequent interruptions
and the noise of the children in the next room."

A couple of weeks later, Rebecca, Emily and Julia all passed on their thoughts in a joint update to Webster. Keenly missing her husband, Rebecca was upset that a time had not yet been set for his return: "It is now three *long* weeks since you left us." She also complained of ill health, stressing, "Yet I am as well as I can *reasonably* expect to be." In contrast, Emily's tone was more lighthearted; she reported on how she and her siblings, no doubt patterning themselves after the eminent wordsmith, made fun of the baby's pronunciation errors: "William grows fat and very funny. . . . Some times we speak a hard word on purpose to hear his little blunders for he repeats every word we say." Up next, Julia hoped to impress her father with her industriousness and attention to detail, writing, "I go to school very steadily & pass 8 or 9 hours there every day, there are 68 scholars. . . . I have began [*sic*] ciphering [arithmetic] and have got to multiplication. & I have almost finished a little cap—for somebody." After finishing her remarks, Julia signed off with "your most dutiful daughter," omitting her name.

The day after Christmas, Emily shared some joyful news with her father: "The dear babe is plump and weighs 8 pounds; we wait for your consent to call it Elizabeth." In that letter, Emily also added a poignant plea for his love: "We have just received your kind letter, but I am half angry to think that papa would say William needed beauty when he is so much handsomer than any of us so that is as much as to say we all [*sic*] ugly as witches, but it is a truth I always knew and tho wanting in beauty I hope I am not wanting in affection to my dear papa."

"HAVE YOU COMPLETED your dictionary?" So asked Webster's uncle, Eliphalet Steele, in a letter dated May 20, 1801, at which time the forty-two-year-old retired newspaper editor had hardly begun.

Webster would face this query time and time again over the next twenty-seven years, and he eventually gave up trying to respond. As he would write his brother-in-law Thomas Dawes several years later, "I am often asked what progress I have made in the compilation of my proposed dictionary; and when in all probability it will be completed. To these questions I am not able to give precise answers, as the field of inquiry enlarges with every step I take."

On June 6, 1804, Webster placed an anonymous article in *The Connecticut Courant,* in which he updated the public about his literary activity. After announcing that his new *American Spelling Book*—about to become the valuable annuity that would support his family for the rest of his life—was to be published in a few weeks, he described the status of the next project on his assembly line:

> In compliance with repeated solicitations from the friends of American literature in various parts of the country, who urge the utility of a complete system of books for the instruction of youth in our language by a *single hand,* the same author has prepared a *Compendious Dictionary* of our language, upon the latest edition of Entick improved—correcting the more palpable mistakes, and adding three or four thousand words with which the vast improvements in chemistry, natural science, have within half a century supplied the language.

Webster, an inveterate self-promoter, here attempted to gloss over the widespread abuse heaped on his initial announcement four years earlier. In fact, few people were clamoring for his name to appear on yet another pedagogical text; the impetus for his first dictionary came largely from within. A warm-up exercise to his complete dictionary, Webster's *Compendious Dictionary*—compendious means concise—was a rewriting of the *New Spelling Dictionary of the English Language* by John Entick, which had been reissued numerous times since its initial publication in 1764. "This work," Webster declared, "will be put to press in a short time, and an elegant edition may be expected in the course of the summer." But Webster's first foray into lexicography wouldn't actually appear for another two years. Writing a dictionary, Webster would learn, typically takes longer than expected.

One reason for the delay was that Webster was also engaged in compiling another massive reference work, *Elements of Useful Knowledge,* an encyclopedia for children. The first two volumes, which concerned the history and geography of the United States, appeared in 1802 and 1804, respectively; the third volume, on Europe, Asia and Africa, came out in 1806; and the fourth volume, on animal history and classification, in 1812. He relished documenting the inherent order in the universe. "Nature, in all her works," he wrote in the preface to volume 1, "proceeds according to established laws, and it is by following her order, distribution and arrangement, that the human mind is led to understand her laws, with their principles and connection." Thus, at the same time as Webster was defining words for adults, he was also defining places, people and animals for children. According to his master plan, he would become the pedagogue for all Americans: "My views comprehend a whole system of education—from a spelling book through geography and various other subjects—to a complete dictionary—beginning with children and ending with men."

Webster's encyclopedia read like a dictionary. The text consisted of short paragraphs, given numbers in the last two volumes, each of which clarified a particular term. (He hoped that this format would enable children to commit his words to memory, but this fantasy was never realized.) Though Webster believed he was transmitting only hard facts, his personal prejudices were much in evidence. Consider, for example, paragraph 224 in volume 3, describing the "character and morals" of his least favorite nation, France: "Ancient authors all agree that the Gauls were a fickle, perfidious people, prompt to action, but impatient of toil, and ever studious of change. The present French are remarkable for their vivacity, gayety and politeness; fond of show and pleasure, but not cleanly in their houses. The sanguinary scenes of the late revolution manifested a ferociousness of character, rarely found among civilized men, and impress the mind with horror."

The reclusive scholar was now obsessed with categorizing and describing everything in the external world, which he no longer had much interest in exploring in the flesh. He preferred to live among the thoughts percolating inside his own mind. Though teachers in Connecticut ordered this text, it didn't have much of a market outside his home state.

After selling his papers, Webster stopped commenting on national politics. In occasional freelance articles, he explored his various avocations, such as tending to his fruit trees and making cider. In October 1804, he wrote a couple of columns for the *Courant* devoted to "the diffusion of agricultural knowledge"—the ultimate utilitarian, Webster never could do anything entirely for the fun of it. He prefaced both "Farmer's Repository" pieces with an epigraph from Jonathan Swift that conveyed his disgust with the Jefferson administration: "Whoever can make two ears of corn, or two blades of grass grow upon a spot of ground where only one grew before, deserves better of mankind and does more essential service than the whole race of politicians put together." In the first one, dated October 24, he began by describing himself as a member of a small breed of "philosophical agriculturalists": "I possess not a farm on which to indulge my inclination for experiments, my experience is limited to a small garden; but even this experience may have offered a few useful truths, to spread the knowledge of which this is the sole motive for this communication." Webster went on to dispense some advice for coping with insects that preyed on Connecticut homes during winter: "I make it a practice to scrape off these lodgers to expose them to bad weather and destroy as many as possible."

Another of Webster's favorite pastimes was monitoring the weather with a mathematical precision. He tracked these observations in his diary, which, after his move to New Haven, contained information about little else. The odd meteorological patterns in the first half of 1805 piqued his intellectual curiosity. "The snow in January of 1805," he wrote in his "diary of the weather"—to cite a phrase he himself embedded within the definition of "diary" in his 1828 dictionary—"was about 3 feet deep. This was the severest winter since 1780. But the snow left the earth in March in good season & spring was early. I cut asparagus on the 14th of April, 9 days earlier than last year." That spring, in an article, "Meteorological," published in *The Connecticut Herald,* Webster tried to "throw together a few facts" to put this stretch of turbulent weather in historical context. After rank-ordering the most severe winters in America's two-hundred-year history, he offered a head-to-head comparison between 1805 and the record-breaking 1780: "The present winter did not begin so early as that of 1780 by three weeks—nor has the cold been so intense and continued. In January and February 1780, the mercury fell below 0 twelve days; and seven days to seven degrees under 0. . . . But in the present year, it has fallen only once to 16 degrees in the same place; and one other time to 9 degrees." Noting that "winters of the utmost severity . . . do not exceed three, four or five in a century," Webster encouraged his fellow citizens not to despair.

The harsh winter of 1805 also led Webster to expand his talk, "On the Supposed Change in the Temperature of Winter," initially given before the Connecticut Academy of Arts and Sciences in 1799. Webster had first taken a systematic look at climate change while researching his book on plagues. Ever since the Revolution, numerous writers had taken the position that American winters were becoming milder. These advocates for the eighteenth-century version of "global warming" included Thomas Jefferson, who had addressed the question in his *Notes on Virginia*; Benjamin Rush; and Samuel Williams, a Harvard historian. The man-made cause was allegedly the rapid deforestation of states such as Vermont. Webster challenged his predecessors on the basis of their lack of evidence. Noting Jefferson's reliance on personal testimony rather than hard data, Webster wrote disparagingly, "Mr. Jefferson seems to have no authority for his opinions but the observations of elderly and middle-aged people." Though Williams, in contrast, did engage in some statistical analysis, Webster convincingly argued that he had misconstrued the facts at hand. While Webster acknowledged that winter conditions had become more variable, he maintained that America's climate had essentially remained stable: "there is, in modern times,

[no] . . . actual diminution of the aggregate amount of cold in winter." Webster completed this additional section in 1806, and he would eventually publish both papers, which one modern-day geographer has called "a tour de force," in the Connecticut Academy's flagship journal in 1810.

ABOUT TWO WEEKS before the publication of his *Compendious Dictionary,* Webster launched his own publicity campaign. On January 21, 1806, under the pen name "Americus," Webster placed a front-page essay, "American Literature," in *The Connecticut Herald.* To garner enthusiasm for his idea that America was ready for a language of its own, Webster challenged the conventional wisdom that harped on "the inferiority of the writings of our citizens." Though America, he acknowledged, had yet to produce writers of the stature of Milton, Johnson and Pope, Britain, he stressed, had benefited from a four-century head start: "The comparison, to be just, should be instituted between the great body of respectable writers in the two countries; and in such a comparison, the writings of American citizens will not appear to a disadvantage." Looking back over the last thirty years, Webster concluded that Americans in every genre—from political theory to poetry—matched up well against their British counterparts. Webster lauded a number of American writers such as his Connecticut chums Dwight, Trumbull and Barlow, as well as Jeremy Belknap of the Massachusetts Historical Society. He also wrote favorably of Alexander Hamilton; now that his bitter rival was dead, Webster didn't mind praising the "style, argument, arrangement and accurate knowledge" of the author of *The Federalist.* Webster did, however, acknowledge one major roadblock to American literary greatness: the existence of "only three or four tolerable libraries." The net result, he asserted, was that "no American undertakes . . . any work of great magnitude. We shall never have authors of great celebrity in the literary world, till our citizens execute works on a large scale, which will be interesting to foreign literati."

Webster would be the exception. Having just finished what he called his "compend," his "convenient manual," he was now dedicating his life to his complete dictionary, which would indeed force foreigners to stop and take notice of American literary achievement.

On February 11, 1806, Americans first learned about "Webster's Dictionary."

The now-familiar phrase appeared as the headline of the advertisement that Webster placed in *The Connecticut Herald* on publication day. *The Compendious Dictionary*, with its 432 large duodecimo pages, cost a dollar fifty. The book contained roughly forty thousand words. While Webster added five thousand new scientific terms from diverse fields including chemistry, mineralogy and botany, he eliminated many vulgar words found in Johnson (and Johnson Jr.) such as the irksome "foutra." The text resembled a contemporary thesaurus because most entries consisted of just one or two quick definitions. For example, he defined "author" as "one who makes or causes, a writer." As this announcement mentioned, in the back of the book Webster appended seventeen tables "for the merchant, the seaman, the classical student and the traveler." While Entick's *Spelling Dictionary* had featured a few addenda such as alphabetical lists of "Heathen Gods and Goddesses," "Heroes and Heroines" and the most common Christian names of men and women, this hefty supplement was largely a Websterian touch. The tables covered such diverse topics as currencies, weights and measures, demographic data, the location of post offices, historical events and inventions. The statistician, the census taker and the encyclopedist were thus all merged into the lexicographer. "These tables," Webster noted proudly, "are all new, and compiled with great labor and minute attention to correctness."

In his twenty-four-page, single-spaced preface, which went way over the head of most readers, Webster explained his method for revising "our present dictionaries" to arrive at "a correct knowledge of the language." Since Webster had already begun planning the sequel, this conceptual overview actually referred as much to the massive book he was about to write as to the small book he had just written. The future of the English language, Webster insisted, was to be found in its past; a generation

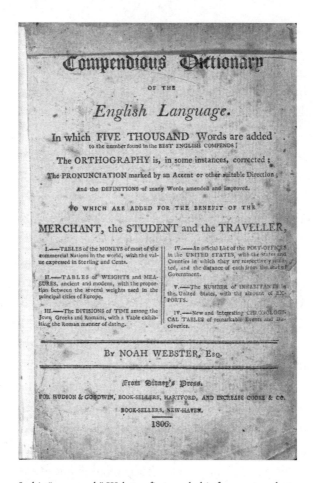

In his "compend," Webster first made his famous tweaks to
British English. "In omitting *u* in *honor* and a few words of
that class," he wrote in the introduction, "I have pursued
a common practice in this country, authorized by the
principle of uniformity and by etymology."

after the Revolution, he was talking up a different version of American linguistic identity. Americans, he now believed, should be at least
as British as the British—if not more so. For this reason, Webster argued, all Americans should start sounding like New Englanders: "It
is . . . to be remarked that the common unadulterated pronunciation of
the New England gentlemen [*sic*] is uniformly the pronunciation which

prevailed in England anterior to Sheridan's time* and which I am assured by English gentlemen is still the pronunciation of the body of the English nation." Likewise, for spelling, Webster insisted that Americans should go still further back in time—to Anglo-Saxon (a language of which Johnson had known little). Thus Webster turned the charge of "innovation" upon its head; according to his new analysis, he was rescuing his fellow Americans from the corruptions wrought by Johnson and his contemporaries.

Webster was quite right to pounce on Johnson for ignoring the history of words. In contrast to Webster, Johnson had little patience for etymology, which he considered the path not to the truth, but to the ludicrous. But Webster's own grasp of Anglo-Saxon was shaky. Though he began studying it after returning to New Haven, he never proceeded very far. (In contrast, Thomas Jefferson, then residing in the White House, who had first encountered Anglo-Saxon as a teenage law student in 1762, happened to be the country's reigning expert.) As one scholar who examined the marginalia of Webster's Anglo-Saxon book collection a half century ago concluded, "to assume that Webster was more than a mediocre student of Anglo-Saxon is to accept his professions too credulously." In the preface to his "compend," Webster noted that anyone with "the smallest acquaintance" of Anglo-Saxon could track down Johnson's errors; and the sum total of his knowledge may not have been much greater than that.

Despite the deficiencies in Webster's Anglo-Saxon, the new course he charted for orthography was, with a few notable exceptions, eminently reasonable. He advocated a middle ground between extremes. While he described English spelling as "extremely irregular," he now critiqued the development of a new phonetic alphabet—the position that he had taken in 1790—as "impractical" and "not at all necessary." But Webster also opposed no reform at all, arguing that "gradual changes to accommodate

---

* Thomas Sheridan (1719–1788) was an Irish actor and educator who published a widely read book on elocution in 1762. A lifelong foe of the theater, Webster was eager to diminish its influence on the English language.

the written to the spoken language when they occasion none of these evils, and especially when they purify words from corruptions . . . illustrate etymology [and] are not only proper, but indispensable." This was the theoretical justification for Webster's most famous tweaks to British English such as eliminating the "u" in "favour" and the "k" in "musick." "The practice," he wrote, "in . . . [Johnson's] time of closing all words with k after c . . . was a Norman innovation," thus suggesting that he was also liberating Americans from the unscrupulous practices of the French. Grounding all his changes in such historical investigations, Webster also identified a few other classes "of outlaws in orthography," including, for example, words ending in "re" ("theatre" thus became "theater") and those ending in "ce" ("defence" thus became "defense").

But the study of Anglo-Saxon also led Webster to make the case for other spellings that we now consider eccentric. He repeatedly removed the final "e" in words such as "doctrine," "determine" and "discipline." His other idiosyncratic preferences included "tung" ("tongue"), "wimmen" ("women"), "ake" ("ache") and "wether" ("weather"). In these instances, where he knew that he would be facing fierce opposition, he listed what he considered the etymologically correct spelling merely as an alternative. He eventually gave in to the majority opinion, albeit grudgingly. In his 1828 dictionary, under the definition "women," he still felt compelled to add, "But it is supposed the word we pronounce is from Sax . . . and therefore should be written wimen [sic]."

Webster concluded the preface by stepping up his attacks on Johnson. While praising his predecessor as "one of the brightest luminaries of English literature," Webster stressed that "no original work of high reputation in our language . . . contains so many errors and imperfections." He then launched into an aside on biography: "To assign the causes of these defects is by no means difficult. We are told in the accounts given of Johnson's life that he was almost always depressed by disease and poverty; that he was naturally indolent and seldom wrote until he was urged by want. . . . Hence it happened, that he often received the money for his writings before his manuscripts were prepared. Then, when called upon for copy, he was compelled to prepare his manuscripts in haste."

Webster was keenly aware of how he stacked up against his rival. As he aptly noted, he was the more methodical and industrious, a difference in temperament which was indeed an asset. However, Webster's allusion to Johnson's book advances was gratuitous. Johnson's manic intensity was an essential part of his character; it was not dependent on the timing of his payments. Webster was teeming with envy because he had no patron, not even an unappreciative Lord Chesterfield. In contrast to Johnson, he would have to bear most of the financial risk himself. As Webster knew, in his case, the dictionary could well mean not an escape from but a descent into poverty.

The reaction to the publication of Webster's first dictionary was mostly indifference. No review appeared for three months; and the first one, published in May 1806, in the *Panoplist,* a new Christian periodical founded by his friend Jedidiah Morse, was brief and not particularly glowing. Expressing concern about some "errors in the execution," the *Panoplist* offered only a tepid endorsement: "On the whole, we are highly gratified in seeing a literary work which bears such strong marks of deep research. . . . we wish it may find a place not only on the toilette [then a synonym for cloth covering], but in the printing office and counting house. We hope also it will be introduced into our schools."

But sales of the seven thousand copies never did take off. A year later, Webster printed only four thousand copies of a school dictionary, for which he reduced the price to a dollar. At the last minute, he tried to expand the market for this abridgement to the yeomanry as well as to students by removing the scientific terms. As the ads stated, "It contains a selection of more than thirty thousand words, comprehending all which are necessary or useful for farmers and mechanics." But while his school dictionary, unlike his "compend," would eventually go into a second printing, this wouldn't happen until 1817.

"Darkness at Noon!"

"The Great Eclipse of the Sun!"

So exclaimed the headlines of America's leading newspapers in the weeks leading up to Monday, June 16, 1806.

Webster the amateur meteorologist was caught up in the national excitement about this once-in-a-lifetime event. He began giving daily lectures to his wife and children about the meaning of this remarkable phenomenon, thoughts which later worked their way into his 1828 definition of eclipse: "Literally, a defect or failure; hence in *astronomy,* an interception or obscuration of the light of the sun, moon or other luminous body."

On the morning of the sixteenth, Webster equipped each of his three girls—Julia, Harriet and Mary—with a piece of smoked glass as they headed off to school. (Emily, the eldest, then sixteen, had completed her education and was visiting her uncle Thomas Dawes in Boston.) He wanted to make sure that they could keep peering into the sky as the moon began to cover the sun that afternoon.

Webster's girls attended the Union School on Crown Street, which their father had been instrumental in launching in 1801. Pedagogy was Webster's passion, and when he found out that New Haven lacked an adequate school for ladies, he organized the town's parents. Within just a couple of years, nearly seventy girls had signed up. At the Union School, the girls learned the three Rs as well as sewing. As chairman of the trustees, Webster himself signed the hundred shares that had been sold to raise money for its founding.

As noon approached, Webster's daughters were eager with anticipation. But suddenly, much to their surprise and consternation, their teacher, Miss Eunice Hall, took away their optical safeguards. Picking up a piece of smoked glass, she held it to her eye and declared, "Oh, I would not have you see it for the world." Wedded to superstition, Miss Hall had no interest in science instruction. Closing the windows and shutters, the teacher transformed the classroom into a den of darkness. Though study was nearly impossible, Miss Hall did not dismiss the students early. By the time Webster's daughters arrived back at the Arnold House, it was too late to see even a glimpse of what one paper called "one of the most sublime spectacles this age has produced." During the eclipse, the particular cast of light shrouded America in a deathlike gloom.

Until that day, Eunice Hall had been highly regarded in and around New Haven. A month earlier, the *Connecticut Journal* praised her "genius and industry" during the school's two-day annual exhibition held in the assembly room of the state house. Rebecca, who had attended to watch her girls, was also impressed by Miss Hall's pedagogical skills. As a result of the teacher's direction, Rebecca reported to a traveling Webster, "The young ladies performed extremely well."

But Webster was aghast by Miss Hall's actions on the afternoon of the sixteenth. "A teacher who shows herself so ignorant and tyrannical," he told his family, "is not fit to instruct children."

Webster's second eldest, Julia, the school's reigning wit, was equally outraged. Indulging her taste for doggerel, she wrote a poem about a cauldron of comestibles to which each student contributed something. The last line featured the person who had ruined her day:

Julia Webster, put in a lobster,
Eunice Hall, ate it all.

According to the family's account contained in the biography by his granddaughter, Webster immediately withdrew his daughters from the school. But in fact, it was Miss Hall who ended up having to change venues. A month later, the teacher put the following notice in the *Connecticut Journal*, "Miss Hall . . . shall discontinue keeping the Union School for young ladies and misses. . . . she intends opening a similar school in New Haven on her own account, where she hopes by an assiduous attention to her school, to merit the approbation of the public and her employers."

But Miss Hall soon left Connecticut and opened a school and boarding house in Elizabethtown, New Jersey. A disgruntled Webster, her onetime employer, had run her out of town.

LATER THAT SUMMER, the "compend" finally got some of the attention Webster had been craving. But nearly all the feedback was negative. The coverage in the popular press was brutal, and even some family members expressed uneasiness. Webster's brother-in-law Thomas Dawes, though reluctant to make a judgment in a field outside his expertise, quipped, "I ain't quite ripe for your orthography."

In July, Webster's foe, William Coleman, wrote a series of six vicious articles in *The New York Evening Post*. Noting that the English nation "felt an interest and a pride" upon the publication of Johnson's dictionary, Coleman gleefully reported, "Webster's Dictionary has now been several months in print . . . excepting a meager article in the *Panoplist*, none of our numerous writers have condescended to bestow a word upon it."

In his comprehensive review, Coleman lashed out at Webster from every possible angle. Chief among his complaints was that Webster had unfairly slammed Johnson: "The appearance of attempting to depreciate the labours of others to exalt our own ought always to be shunned as most invidious." But Webster had been taking heat from Coleman ever since the birth of the *Evening Post*, and he wasn't expecting anything enlightened. On July 30, he aired his reaction to his friend Jedidiah Morse, "You will see his [Coleman's] criticisms are . . . misrepresentations from beginning to end . . . indeed it requires the exercise of great charity to believe him *honest* in his statements."

Webster tried to take his case to the public by submitting a long letter to the *Evening Post*. Though Coleman printed Webster's response, he made sure that he got the last word; throughout Webster's prose, the editor interspersed his own running commentary, which he set in a larger type. Webster stressed that Coleman's aim was "to destroy the reputation of the book." Despite Coleman's protestations to the contrary ("I certainly believe that I have dealt very gently by him"), Webster was correct in asserting that he had not gotten a fair hearing.

That month, a writer identified only as "C" published another negative review in the *Albany Centinel*. Webster found his piece more troubling than Coleman's because he had more respect for the source, telling Morse in that same July 30 letter, "The *Albany Centinel* is a paper better written than Coleman's." "C" rehashed the argument that his dictionary would cause linguistic chaos. While acknowledging Webster's "rare erudition," "C" wished his book would simply disappear: "Such is Mr. Webster's disposition to revolutionize and disorganize the English language . . . that sober and judicious men who are disposed to . . . preserve the uniformity and stability of the English tongue will lament that learning and talents so respectable should be the auxiliaries of a taste so false and a judgement so perverse. Is it not madness to endeavour to establish . . . an American or United States dialect . . . ?"

In his response to "C," published in the *Connecticut Herald* in August, Webster countered that the growth of the English language was inevitable: "But the question is whether new words, and new application of words, introduced by new ideas, arising from objects natural and moral, which are peculiar and appropriate to our country and state of society, shall all be condemned and proscribed as 'corruptions and perversions' of the language." On the future course of the English language, Webster would repeatedly demonstrate remarkable prescience.

The attacks on his "compend" kept pouring in. In November 1806, the second president's son, John Quincy Adams, a newly appointed U.S. senator from Massachusetts, issued a polite but pointed rebuke. Adams was a family friend—Dawes had personally passed on a copy—who served as a trustee at Harvard. Siding with the reviewer in the *Albany Centinel*, Adams wrote to Webster: "Where we have invented new words or adopted new senses to old words, it appears but reasonable that our dictionaries should contain them. Yet there are always a multitude of words current within particular neighborhoods, or during short periods of time, which ought never to be admitted into the legitimate vocabulary of a language. A very large proportion of words of American origin are of this description, and I prefer to see them systematically excluded." Adams added that he suspected that Harvard's president, Samuel Webber, was unlikely to support "your system of spelling, pronunciation or of departure from the English language."

Undaunted, Webster hatched a new plan to drum up support for his dictionary. In February 1807, he drafted a circular asking for financial contributors, which he addressed to "the Friends of Literature in the United States." To counteract the rejection from Harvard, he appended recommendations by academics at several of America's other leading colleges, including Yale, the College of New Jersey, Dartmouth, Williams and Middlebury. But he ended up enlisting only a dozen donors, most of whom were old friends such as Timothy Dwight and Oliver Wolcott. His net proceeds were about a thousand dollars, and he was hoping to raise a full third of the fifteen thousand he estimated the book would cost (the actual figure turned out to be twice that amount). In August of 1807, he sent around a second circular asking for just ten dollars per subscriber, but that didn't generate much of a response, either. Armed with a specimen of his dictionary, Webster then traveled to New York, Philadelphia, Newburyport, Boston and Salem in the hope of soliciting a large number of ten-dollar contributions in person. This direct appeal also failed. That summer, he met with more frustration when David Ramsay of South Carolina, who two decades earlier had championed his pamphlet on the Constitution, reported that "prejudices against any American attempts to improve Dr. Johnson are very strong" in Charleston.

Though Webster was no longer surprised by all the hostility, he was still upset. To cope with his disappointment, he did what he often did—he put pen to paper. The result was a twenty-eight-page pamphlet, "A Letter to Dr. Ramsay . . . Respecting the Errors in Johnson's Dictionary," published that October, in which he attempted to justify the need for his complete dictionary. Comparing himself to Galileo, who was imprisoned for disseminating information about the Copernican revolution, the grandiose Webster argued that he, too, was being persecuted for uttering new scientific truths. Webster identified seven principal errors in Johnson's dictionary. While most were familiar objections which he had raised earlier such as Johnson's penchant for including vulgar words and his lack of attention to etymology, Webster did cover some new ground.

Webster vilified Johnson for his reliance on "authors who did not write the language with purity" as authorities on word usage. This charge, however, reflected little more than Webster's own prejudices. The authority Johnson most often cited was Shakespeare, and ever since his Yale days—when attending plays was frowned upon—Webster hadn't thought much of the Bard of Avon: "Shakespeare was a man of little learning; and altho, when he wrote the popular language of his day, his use of words was tolerably correct, yet whenever he attempted a style beyond that, he often fell into the grossest improprieties. . . . Whatever admiration the world may bestow on the Genius of Shakespeare, his language is full of errors, and ought not to be offered as a model for imitation."

Webster just didn't get it. Concerned only with putting the English language in order, he had no interest in literary elegance. In fact, he considered the "low language" of Shakespeare and his fellow playwrights toxic. "I . . . shall proceed," he wrote to Thomas Dawes in 1809, "as far as propriety requires in cleansing the Augean stable." And he was true to his word. As his copy of Johnson's 1799 dictionary, held in the New York Public Library, reveals, he put little black marks next to most Shakespeare quotations. And in his 1828 dictionary, Webster would rarely cite the immortal bard's actual words. Instead he would insert the occasional "Shak."—typically in definitions of derogatory terms such as "bastard," "bastardize," "characterless," "drunken," "drunkenly," "strumpet" (the rarely seen adjective defined as "false"), "stubborn," "unrightful" ("not just") and "whoreson" ("bastard").

But Webster's "Letter to Dr. Ramsay" wasn't just an angry rant. Buried within the contemptuous prose was a compelling reason to revise

Johnson. In a particularly perspicacious observation, Webster alluded to Johnson's "want of just discrimination in his definitions." To illustrate this objection, Webster complained about Johnson's characterization of "mutiny" as "insurrection, sedition," countering that "it is neither one nor the other, except among soldiers or mariners." This was Webster's brilliant analytic mind at its best, and here he was identifying a key contribution that he could make to English lexicography. His definitions would indeed possess a precision missing in Johnson. In the case of "mutiny," his 1828 dictionary would fix the problem by redefining the word as "an insurrection of soldiers or seamen against the authority of their commanders." If his pamphlet had focused solely on the added rigor he was bringing to the table, it might well have inspired his countrymen to rally around him. Instead, his sweeping denunciations—"not a single page of Johnson's Dictionary is correct—every page requires amendment or admits of material improvement"—alienated many potential supporters.

Webster's salvo against Johnson did little to help his cause. Calling Webster "a man of ordinary talents and attainments" who was trying to "palm himself on the public as a nonpareil . . . and destroy the well earned and long established celebrity of his predecessors," an anonymous reviewer in the *Norfolk Register* expressed the widely held sentiment, "There is a time to write and a time to cease from writing; and fortunate would it be for authors did they know when to terminate their labours."

Never one to doubt his ability or to back down from a fight, Webster decided that it was just the right time to begin.

A Lost Decade

FOLLY, n. 1.Weakness of intellect; imbecility of mind; want of understanding. . . . 2. A weak or absurd act not highly criminal; an act which is inconsistent with the dictates of reason, or with the ordinary rules of prudence.

When Webster turned forty-nine in October 1807, he had found his true calling. His one-track mind was obsessed with creating the mother of all dictionaries, which would do more than just cement the linguistic identity of the nation he loved. His interest in Anglo-Saxon having piqued his curiosity about etymology, he now planned to cover "the origin and history not only of the English, but also of the Greek, Latin and other European languages" in a supplement. Webster's estimate that he would need eight to ten years to finish this labor would undershoot the mark by more than a decade.

To complete his own daunting assignment, Webster was willing to pay any price, bear any burden. As he wrote at the end of the preface to his "compend":

> However arduous the task and however feeble my powers of body and mind, a thorough conviction of the necessity and importance of the undertaking, has overcome my fears and objections and determined me to make one effort to dissolve the charm of veneration for foreign authorities which fascinates the mind of men in this country

and holds them in the chains of illusion. In the investigation of this
subject, great labor is to be sustained, and numerous difficulties encountered; but with a humble dependence on divine favor, for the
preservation of my life and health, I shall prosecute the work with
diligence and execute it with a fidelity suited to its importance.

In contrast to Johnson, who once famously opined, "No man but a
blockhead ever wrote, except for money," Webster wasn't motivated by
financial gain. For Webster, the payoff was in the daily compiling and
arranging, which both mitigated his existential angst and gave him a
sense of purpose. Like Martin Luther, reaffirming his faith at the Diet
of Worms, he could do no other. Dictionary-making was now his raison
d'être.

Though Webster claimed in his "Letter to Dr. Ramsay" that his "her-
culean undertaking . . . is of far less consequence to me than to my
country," the opposite was true. Its completion was a matter of life and
death—but only to Webster. In contrast, few of his fellow citizens cared
about its progress. Initially, Webster was confident that the public—or
at least the literati—would soon come around. But as he moved ahead
with his defining, he received hardly any encouragement. Particularly
during the first few years, when he was also burdened with the responsibility of raising his brood of seven, he would be repeatedly immobilized
by despair. The prospect of not having the means to go on terrified him.
Webster would continue to face steep hurdles right up until the publication of the book's first edition in 1828.

IN CONTRAST TO WEBSTER'S "compend," the origin of *The American Dictionary* can be traced back to a precise moment in time.

The date was Tuesday, November 3, 1807. The Great Comet of
1807, that "illustrious stranger" which had intrigued Webster ever since
its first appearance on September 25, was still visible in the sky. That
morning, Webster walked up to his second floor study and put on the

spectacles, which he had recently begun wearing. Opening an 8½-by-11-inch notebook, he picked up his quill pen—he would continue to use this eighteenth-century implement long after the birth of the fountain pen. After putting the date in the top right-hand corner of the first page, he moved on to the task at hand—defining A.*

To compose his complete dictionary, Webster would follow a strict routine. He liked to get up half an hour before dawn to make the most of the sunlight. He would stop at four in the afternoon, as candlelight didn't appeal to him.

Webster worked at a large circular table, about two feet in diameter, upon which all his reference books were spread. Chief among them were Johnson's dictionary, the Latin-English dictionary compiled by British author Robert Ainsworth and the third edition of the *Encyclopædia Britannica*. Other key sources were contemporary scientific texts such as Thomas Martyn's *The Language of Botany: Being a Dictionary of the Terms Made Use of in that Science* and John Quincy's *Lexicon Physico-Medicum*.

For Webster, dictionary-making involved as much physical as mental exertion. He wrote standing up and paced back and forth as he consulted a particular volume. Sitting at a desk, he once wrote, is "an indolent habit . . . which always weakens and sometimes disfigures the body." The inveterate counter would keep track of his pulse. As he once noted, whenever he made an important philological discovery, it typically jumped up from its normal rate of sixty beats per minute to eighty or eighty-five. To make sure that he wouldn't be disturbed by the children, he packed the walls of his second-floor study with sand.

Though Webster would borrow heavily from Johnson, Ainsworth's Latin dictionary was his true starting point. By 1807, he aimed not just to update and Americanize Johnson, but also to do a more thorough job of connecting English to its roots than his predecessor. The Webster papers at the Morgan Library include cutout pages of Ainsworth pasted

---

* The first two pages of this notebook are reprinted on the frontispiece and the endpapers of this book.

onto blank sheets, upon which Webster added definitions. Webster saw himself not so much revising Johnson as starting a new English dictionary from scratch.

Webster's working definition of "adultery," also from a manuscript fragment housed at the Morgan, provides a window into his modus operandi. Carefully consulting Ainsworth and Johnson, Webster added a host of new meanings and distinctions absent in both. Johnson listed just one generic definition ("the act of violating the bed of a married person"), and Ainsworth, under the related Latin word "adulterium," listed three: "adultery," "whoredom" and "falsifying." In contrast, in his draft, Webster provided five, each of which carried his characteristic precision. In his first definition, "the incontinence of a married person," Webster was careful to add a qualifier, gathered from his legal training: "The commerce of a married person with an unmarried is adultery in the former and fornication in the latter." While Webster's next three definitions came from other sources such as the Bible and the *Encyclopedia Britannica*, his last definition, though attributed to Pliny ("Among ancient naturalists, the grafting of trees"), was actually lifted from Ainsworth, who cited this passage in the original Latin.

While Webster would mine Ainsworth's Latin dictionary for its wealth of definitions and allusions, he wasn't attempting to make the English language more Latinate. In fact, he was trying to do exactly the opposite. Ever the pragmatist, in his "Letter to Dr. Ramsay," Webster asserted that "Language consists of words uttered by the tongue; or written in books for the purpose of being read." He thus faulted Johnson for "inserting words that do not belong to the language" such as "adversable," "advestierate," "adjugate," "agriculation" and "abstrude." But Webster did add an occasional Latinate term when it described a new scientific development such as "adustion" ("the act of burning, scorching or heating to dryness").

In these early pages, Webster was interested in tracing English back to its roots in other European languages. Thus, for example, in his copy of Johnson's dictionary, next to "bread" he jotted down the French "pain,"

In his 1828 dictionary, Webster expanded on this working definition of "adultery." Realizing that many Americans didn't make the same fine distinctions he did, under the first sense Webster added: "In *common usage*, adultery means the unfaithfulness of any married person to the marriage bed."

the German "Brot," as well as the cognate in a half-dozen other European languages including Danish, Icelandic, Finnish and Norwegian. But after finishing the Bs, he also began exploring the relation between English and numerous non-European languages including Arabic, Hebrew and Ethiopian. Enthralled by his own findings, Webster now aimed to set forth a comprehensive theory of language in his etymological supplement. To attend to this massive undertaking, Webster would put all further definitions on hold. C would have to wait another decade.

This change in direction was tied to a "change of heart," which is how Webster would define "conversion" in his 1828 dictionary. In 1808, Webster became a devout Calvinist; from then on, all his literary efforts would be in the service of God.

THE NEW PASTOR of New Haven's First Congregational Church, Moses Stuart, was the complete package. The salutatorian of the Yale class of 1799, he was tall, lean and muscular. Stuart also had an amazing capacity for study— mastering the four conjugations of Latin verbs took him just one night. Dubbing the eloquent Stuart "the man of the short sentence," Connecticut's governor Roger Griswold rarely missed a sermon. A noted Hebrew scholar, Stuart would later earn the sobriquet "the father of biblical literature" for his pioneering contributions to American theology.

Soon after his ordination in March 1806, Stuart began electrifying the entire town. While his predecessor brought five new members into the church each year, Stuart brought fifty. Holding services by candlelight—a practice once considered scandalous—he helped usher in the period of religious revival later dubbed the Second Great Awakening.

Though twenty years Webster's junior, Stuart would also have a huge impact on the lexicographer's heart and mind.

But it was Webster's teenage daughters who were drawn to the pastor first. In the winter of 1807, under Stuart's tutelage, Emily and Julia discovered the hand of God. Rebecca soon followed.

Fearful of "being misled by the passions," Webster initially opposed this religious turn. Though a lifelong Congregationalist, Webster had never been particularly devout. In fact, upon settling in New Haven, he did not—in contrast to his wife—become a member of the Center Church. And in early 1808, he encouraged Rebecca and the girls to switch to Trinity Church, the local Episcopal church, where he applied for a pew. But the possibility of leading a separate religious existence from the rest of his family unnerved him. In deference to their fervor, he agreed to renew his study of the scriptures. Webster also had several conversations with Pastor Stuart about matters of faith. This soul-searching left him uncomfortable and barely able to concentrate: "I continued for some weeks, in this situation, unable to quiet my mind. . . . Instead of obtaining peace, my mind was more and more disturbed." His existential dilemma also affected his body. To a close friend, he described his health as "very indifferent."

But one morning that April, as he settled into his study, everything changed. He later recalled, "A sudden impulse upon my mind arrested me. . . . I instantly fell on my knees and confessed my sins to God, implored his pardon and made my vows to him that I would live in entire obedience to his commands."

The day after his personal encounter with God, Webster called a family meeting. Trembling, he spoke of his new religious convictions, adding, "While I have aimed for the faithful discharge of parental duty, there is one sign and token of headship, which I have neglected—family prayer." Bowing down, he then led his family in prayer—a practice he would engage in three times a day for the rest of his life.

While Webster's conversion was part of a broad social movement—it would be common among New England intellectuals during the first half of the nineteenth century—it also had roots in his personal circumstances. As the dictionary, his retirement project, began to heighten rather than reduce his inner turmoil, Webster lapsed into a midlife crisis. Weighed down by financial worries and the frosty reception to his "compend," he often felt confused about which way to turn. He was also shaken by the death of his infant son, Henry, in 1806. But whatever the underlying reasons behind his newfound religious faith, its calming effect on his nervous system was clear. "From that time," he later observed, "I have had perfect tranquility of mind." Webster also believed that his reconciliation to the "doctrines of scriptures" was responsible for permanently removing nagging bodily aches and pains.

Soon after his conversion, Webster ran for the U.S. House of Representatives. In the preliminary election in May, he received 212 votes, enough to emerge as a viable Federalist candidate. However, he lost in the fall. He would try again without success in 1810, 1812 and 1816. The highest political office this founding father would ever hold is state rep.

In the fall of 1808, Webster informed his extended family about his conversion. His older brother, Abraham, expressed support, remarking, "It has given me great joy to hear that God is carrying on a glorious work in New Haven." In contrast, his brother-in-law Thomas Dawes could barely digest the news. On October 25, 1808, the Boston lawyer wrote to him, asking "whether it be true that N.W. has lately received some impressions from above, not in the ordinary way of ratiocination." In response, Webster fired back a long missive explaining how he could be a man of both faith and reason, "I had for almost fifty years exercised my talents such as they are, to obtain knowledge and to abide by its dictates, but without arriving at the truth, or what now appears to me to be the truth of the gospel. . . . I now look, my dear friend, with regret on the largest portion of life of man, spent 'without hope, and without God in the world.'" Over the next year, Webster's remarks to Dawes, published both in the *Panoplist* and as a separate tract, *Peculiar Doctrines of the Gospel, Explained and Defended,* circulated widely.

Webster's pamphlet received plaudits from Trinitarian clergy, who urged him to turn his scholarly attention to theology—a suggestion which he declined. But his strict Calvinism, embracing both predestination and the inherent depravity of man, alienated leading Unitarians. At the time, New England was divided by a fierce religious rivalry that pitted the Trinitarians against the Unitarians, or Connecticut against

Massachusetts. Boston clerics such as Joseph Stevens Buckminster—the son of Webster's Yale tutor was then pastor at the Brattle Street Church—took a more optimistic view of human nature. The Bostonians ended up voicing their displeasure not in a direct critique of Webster's theological tract but in a belated assault upon his first dictionary. Webster became the favorite whipping boy of the Anthology Club, the Boston literary society located in the new subscription library called the Boston Athenaeum. As was noted in the society's proceedings on August 29, 1809, "The conversation of the evening was chiefly at the expense of Noah Webster, as long as the Secretary kept awake." A few months later, the group's periodical, *The Monthly Anthology and Boston Review,* published a scathing review of his "compend:" "We have marked with candour the most prominent faults in this work; and if it be asked why so little is said in commendation of it, we shall desire every one to compare it to Johnson . . . so many dangerous novelties are inserted, that no man can safely consult it without comparisons with others." As if that wasn't enough, the following year this journal devoted forty pages spread across three issues to further attacks. Attempting to comfort Webster, Moses Stuart noted, "The Anthology is outrageous against you. . . . Be assured, the object of their vengeance is more against your religion than against you."

Besides leading to more abuse for his "compend," Webster's conversion also brought about a permanent rift with Joel Barlow, who had been a steadfast champion of his work for more than thirty years. In 1803, after spending a decade and a half as a businessman and diplomat in Europe, Barlow returned to American soil. The former classmates then resumed a lively correspondence, sharing information about their respective literary projects. From his perch in the nation's capital, Barlow expanded his 1787 epic, *Visions of Columbus,* which he republished as the *Columbiad* in 1807. Though initially supportive, on October, 13, 1808, Webster stunned Barlow by announcing that he would abandon his promised review because of the poem's "atheistical principles." Referring to his correspondent in the third person, Webster added, "No man on earth not allied to me by nature or by marriage had so large a share in my affections as Joel Barlow until you renounced the religion which you once preached. But with my views of the principles you have introduced into the Columbiad, I apprehend my silence will be most agreeable to you and most expedient for your old friend and obedient servant." The self-righteous Webster had no idea of the emotional valence of this missive. Near the end of his life, on the back of his copy, he would note, "Mr. Barlow never wrote me a letter," indicating his sense that he—not Barlow—was the aggrieved party. Webster had succeeded in antagonizing his most enthusiastic supporter. In fact, on the same day that Webster excommunicated Barlow, this financial contributor to the dictionary wrote him a letter, passing along heartfelt encouragement: "I am anxious that your philological researches should be the best that have yet appeared in any age or nation."

As a born-again Christian, Webster felt a need to merge his scholarly pursuits with his religious beliefs. Convinced of the literal truth of the Book of Genesis, which declared that all human beings once spoke the same language, Webster began searching for the common "radical" words that linked all languages (a term he now used interchangeably with "dialects"). In 1809, he explained his new assumptions to Thomas Dawes: "That whatever differences of dialect might have been introduced at Babel, languages entirely different were not formed, as the radical words in the principal languages of Asia, Africa, and Europe are still the same." Webster was now focusing not just on English words and their sources but on the "origin and structure of language" per se. The completion of both his dictionary and his etymological supplement, he conceded to Dawes, would take longer than he had initially predicted: "The labor requisite to accomplish the work upon my plan is certainly double to that [the nine years] which Dr. Johnson bestowed upon his dictionary." With much work still to be done, Webster stepped up his fundraising efforts.

Today the best-known work of Joel Barlow (1754–1812) is the
mock-heroic poem "Hasty Pudding," written in 1793.

But once again, hampered by a lack of tact, he came up empty-
handed. Whatever networking skills he had formerly possessed were long
gone. In early 1809, Webster wrote to James Madison, requesting that
the president-elect send him to Europe on government business so that
he could procure rare books there. Remarkably, in that same missive, he
offered his damning opinion of Madison's idol, the outgoing president,
Thomas Jefferson: "If the next administration shall pursue," Webster
warned, "a system substantially the same, I must be opposed to it on
principle." Like his White House predecessor, Madison saw no reason
to maintain a correspondence with the emotionally tone-deaf Federalist

pedagogue. Observing Webster in a Salem lecture hall later that year, Simeon Colton, then a recent Yale graduate, also was taken aback by his arrogance: "I wish . . . he were not so confident in his own merit, but would be content to address the public as though there were some equal to himself."

The self-absorbed scholar was an easy target for satirists. In 1810, a North Carolina paper ran an article by "Tom Tinker Esq" which humbly proposed a new dictionary to none other than Noah Webster, Jr., himself. To remedy a "defect in English literature," Tinker claimed to have compiled his own glossary "intended as a supplement to a large and more solemn dictionary." The faux lexicographer observed, "It is easy to foresee that the idle and illiterate will complain that I have encreased [sic] their labours by endeavouring to diminish them." Among the entries included in his specimen were "tit for tat" ("adequate retaliation") and "shilly-shally" ("hesitation and irresolution"). Mocking Webster, "Tinker" also offered the prediction that "the whole . . . will appear sometime within the ensuing twenty years."

By 1811, Webster felt "cast upon the world," just as he had upon graduation from Yale in 1778. Once again, he was depressed and isolated and lacked the funds to continue his literary career. But on this occasion, the crisis was entirely of Webster's own making. Now a nationally recognized writer with the power to shape his own destiny, he had gone out of his way to alienate just about everyone he had ever known.

Surprisingly, Webster turned to Barlow as a confidant, as if nothing had ever come between them. On April 1, 1811, after a two-and-a-half-year hiatus, he wrote his Yale classmate, "My prospects depress my spirits and impair my health—while there is danger that some of my family who have less fortitude will sink under the pressure of anxiety. Still I have hope and while life and health remain, I shall prosecute my studies." Webster also complained about the "measures of government, which have deranged business," even though as he well knew, Barlow himself had just joined the Madison administration as the new ambassador to France. In another startling act of brazenness, Webster asked the departing Barlow to buy some reference works for him, for which he offered no compensation but copies of his dictionary. Summing up his predicament, he added in his last letter to Barlow, who would die suddenly a few months later in Europe, "I wish to have all the help that *books* can furnish—for I have no aid from *man.*"

Amidst his despair about running out of money, Webster also experienced moments of deep intellectual satisfaction. In a letter in early 1811 to Josiah Quincy—the future president of Harvard, who was then a Federalist congressman from Massachusetts—Webster captured the divided nature of his existence:

> I am engaged in a work which gives me great pleasure; & the tracing of language through more than twenty different dialects has opened a new and before unexplored field. I have within two years past, made discoveries which if ever published must interest the literati of all Europe, & render it necessary to revise all the lexicons, Hebrew, Greek and Latin, now used as classical books. But what can I do? My own resources are almost exhausted and in a few days I shall sell my house to get bread for my children. . . . Yours in low spirits.

Quincy, too, didn't respond to Webster's request for a handout. Unable to find donors, Webster formulated a new plan: He would downsize.

But selling the Arnold House was not easy. With the economy in freefall on account of the ongoing conflict with Britain, which would soon escalate into war, there were few takers. The waiting heightened his anxiety. On June 29, 1812, he wrote another Yale classmate, Oliver Wolcott, "If I can find persons to take my property here at anything resembling a reasonable price, I may yet proceed with my studies. At present, I am compelled to throw aside my pen—the agitations of my mind disqualifying me for business." A few days later, a resigned Webster agreed to settle for about a third less than he had paid fourteen years earlier. On July 13, he bought a half-finished double house in the Massachusetts wilderness. Though the price was steep—$2,700—and he had to take out a mortgage, the cost of living would be much less. "The principal motive of this change of residence," he later wrote, "was to enable me to subsist my family at less expense."

IN THE FIRST WEEK of the cold but dry September of 1812, Webster stepped into a carriage with his wife, seven children and all their belongings, including the all-important circular table upon which he would continue to toil on the dictionary.

Their destination was Amherst, Massachusetts, then a tiny farm town with two hundred houses and a population of just fifteen hundred, still more than a decade away from sporting its first piano. Webster was heading back to the land of his ancestors. In 1659, in response to a relaxing of church rules by the pastor at the First Congregational Church of Hartford, Connecticut's governor John Webster had made a similar trek up the Connecticut River Valley. Webster's great-grandfather was buried in nearby Hadley, the town he founded, which had originally included Amherst.

Webster had also learned about the inviting hills of western Massachusetts from Timothy Dwight, who often rhapsodized about his hometown, Northampton, just eight miles from Amherst. Of Hampshire County, whose county seat remains Northampton, Dwight once wrote, "No county in the state has uniformly discovered so firm an adherence to order and good government, or a higher regard to learning, morals and religion." Amherst would remind Webster of his native Hartford.

But despite Amherst's appeal, the move was still a sacrifice born out of economic necessity, which some family members resented. Just as his father had once forced him out of his boyhood home, Webster was now displacing his wife and children from the beloved Arnold House. Emily and Julia were particularly upset because they were also leaving behind their beaus. The twenty-two-year-old Emily was already betrothed to William Ellsworth, the son of jurist Oliver Ellsworth, at whose house Webster had boarded in 1779. Like Ellsworth, Chauncey Goodrich, whom Julia, then nineteen, would wed in 1816, was both a member of the Yale class of 1810 and connected to Webster's past; his grandfather, the Reverend Elizur Goodrich, had first suggested the idea of the dictionary three decades before. Rebecca was also sad to be moving. Webster's wife would miss her tight-knit circle of New Haven friends with whom she experienced "the pleasures of religious converse without restraint."

The first night, the Websters stopped at a small hotel in Hartford, the halfway point of the eighty-mile journey. Along with his two eldest daughters, Webster met with Nathan Strong, pastor of the same First Congregational Church that a century and a half earlier had driven away John Webster. The venerable clergyman gave his visitors a tour of its recently constructed building.

A couple of days later, as the stagecoach reached the woods of South Hadley, the heartsick Emily and Julia burst into tears. As Eliza, then just nine, later wrote, "They realized the great change coming." In contrast, Eliza and eleven-year-old William were excited by the rustic surroundings and eagerly grabbed the boughs that hovered above their heads as the horses sped along. Eliza also noted, "It was all new to us."

Amherst had just two streets, one running north-south and the other east-west, which intersected near the large common at its center. Webster's new residence was located at the northeast corner of this pasture where the town's cows grazed. Though not as sumptuous as the Arnold House, it contained eight large rooms in addition to the kitchen. (After they moved away in 1822, "the Mansion house" was converted into a hotel; in 1838, it was destroyed in a fire.) From his study window on the second floor, Webster could glimpse the stone steps of the First Congregational Church located on the hills to the south. Through a series of transactions, Webster soon amassed ten acres of adjacent farmland, where he built a barn and chaise house and planted an exquisite garden. The orchard, known as the "best in town," featured pear, peach and apple trees as well as a vine of large, sweet white grapes, imported from his father's farm.

The Websters soon formed close bonds with their neighbors, who

Rebecca Greenleaf Webster (1766–1847) was deeply religious, even
more so than her husband. During his trip to Washington in the
winter of 1831, Webster felt compelled to remind her, "I caution you
against venturing to evening meetings in this severe season. I
sincerely hope your zeal will be kept under the control of prudence."

included Samuel Fowler Dickinson, the town clerk dubbed "Esq. Fowler"
by the locals; Hezekiah Wright Strong, the owner of a general store; and
David Parsons, pastor of the First Congregational Church. (Dickinson's
house is now the site of the Emily Dickinson Museum; his granddaughter, the famous poet, was born there in 1830.) Parsons, who had served
as pastor since 1782, lived in a gambrel-roofed house on the other side
of the green, where he and his wife, Harriet, raised their eleven children.
To amuse themselves on cold winter evenings, the Webster girls would

team up with the Parsons' six daughters to perform the simple religious plays of the eighteenth-century British writer Hannah More. A Harvard man, Parsons had turned down a professorship in divinity at Yale to serve the community he loved. Like Webster, the pastor also had pedagogy in his bones; he would educate wayward Harvard students in his home. In 1812, Parsons donated the land for Amherst Academy, a new private school, which, thanks to the fund-raising efforts of his neighbors Webster, Dickinson and Strong, opened in 1814.

Upon settling in Amherst, Webster, in contrast to the rest of his family, felt neither sadness nor excitement but relief. From his perspective, the change in venue meant only one thing—that he could stay in business, the business of dictionary-making.

But Amherst would grow on him. Shortly after his arrival, Webster discovered that he couldn't just work nonstop on his dictionary. He became a gentleman farmer who baled his own hay and milked his cows, Gentle, Comfort and Crick. In a series of articles for the *Hampshire Gazette* on agriculture, which he called "the first, the best and the noblest temporal business of man," he freely dispensed various trade secrets, such as how to kill worms and how to increase the quantity of manure per acre. As in New Haven, Webster also took time out for civic affairs. In February 1814, he was appointed a justice of the peace. That same year, he was also elected to the first of three one-year terms in the Massachusetts House of Representatives. In April 1820, the pedagogue became chairman of the board of managers of the town's first Sunday school. And that summer, he helped to found Amherst College. Of his decade in Amherst, Webster would later write, "The interruption of his sedentary labors was probably favorable to his health." In the quiet of Amherst, where he immersed himself in both his dream job as well as his favorite avocations, Webster attained a level of well-being that he had never before enjoyed.

For Webster, purposeful activity was a cure-all for both mental and social ills. If he spotted boys loitering near his garden, he would ask, "Are you needed at home?" If the lad happened to be idling, Webster was likely to suggest, "Pick the stones up from the road in front of my house." For this temporary employment, he paid the generous wage of twelve and a half cents an hour.

BY THE TIME HE REINSTALLED his circular table in his roomy study in Amherst, Webster had already developed a systematic protocol for working on his etymology, entitled *Synopsis of Words in Twenty Languages*. Having put aside his manuscript of A and B, as well as most of the reference books that he had initially consulted back in 1807, Webster would spend his workdays perusing a couple dozen foreign language dictionaries, which he had arranged in an orderly fashion. Working from right to left, he would fix upon a word and trace it through each of the twenty languages.

While Webster had initially been inspired by his religious conversion, his interest in uniting all languages was also in synch with the intellectual ferment of the day; with the birth of modern linguistics came the uncovering of heretofore hidden links between languages. In 1786, the Welsh orientalist Sir William Jones had observed that the Hindu language, Sanskrit, bore an affinity to both Latin and Greek, which he characterized as "so strong . . . that no philologer could examine all three, without believing them to have sprung from some common source." This insight was the basis of the famous Indo-European hypothesis, which maintained that a common ancestor language was the origin of Latin, Greek, Persian, German, the Romance languages and Celtic. But Webster distanced himself from Jones, whom he disparaged: "it is obvious that Sir William Jones had given little attention to the subject [etymology], and that some of its most common and obvious principles had escaped his observation." He also flat out ignored his contemporaries, such as the Germans Friedrich Schlegel and Franz Bopp, who expanded on Jones' work in Sanskrit and comparative philology.

According to Webster's working hypothesis, until the construction of the Tower of Babel, human beings all spoke the same ur-language, which he labeled Chaldee. To trace all twenty languages back to this ur-language, he created classes of words based on "primary elements"— namely, consonant pairs such as "bn," "br," "dl" and "sd." For each class, he listed numerous words in all twenty languages. Thus, under "bn," for example, he included the English "bone," "bin" and "ebony"; the German *"Bein," "Bahn"* and *"eben"*; the French *"bon," "bien"* and *"abonne"*; and the Latin *"bene," "bini"* and *"ubinam."* (For the purposes of his etymological research, he considered vowels irrelevant.) Whenever he found words in the same class that meant the same thing, he would see this as "proof" that they were etymologically linked. While these connections were true in a few instances—the French *bon* is indeed related to the Latin *bene*—as a rule, similarities in consonant structure don't typically translate into similarities in meaning. But that didn't stop Webster from reaching his desired conclusion; he would just devise some far-fetched explanation. He would then "discover" links between these words in European languages—"bone," "ebony," *"bene," "bini"* and the like—and the Semitic words containing "bn," which he had numbered and placed at the beginning of the class.

Webster's methodology was riddled with a fatal flaw: He was attempting to back up one speculative hypothesis with nothing more than a string of additional speculative hypotheses. Of this glaring problem with the *Synopsis,* the *Oxford English Dictionary's* James Murray would later write, "Etymology is simply Word-history, and Word-history, like all other history, is a record of facts, which did happen, not a fabric of conjectures as to what may have happened." And even if Webster had relied solely on verifiable facts, he wouldn't have gotten very far. His governing assumption turned out to be a fiction, too. Since Webster's day, linguists have discovered that Semitic languages are not based on the same root words as European languages. The two language families bear no etymological relationship to each other.

Webster's grandiosity had gotten the better of him. The task that he had assigned himself—of grounding all words in the putative language of his biblical namesake—was impossible. He also lacked the tools to do anything more than grope in the dark. While he tried to convey the impression that he had mastered all twenty languages by 1813, that claim was a myth later spread by the family. He was thoroughly familiar with only a handful of languages—those he had learned as a college student: Latin, Greek, Hebrew and French. For the rest, as with Anglo-Saxon, he had only a dictionary knowledge—not a reading knowledge. In his last letter to Barlow, he described exactly how he learned Oriental languages such as Arabic, Chaldee, Persian and Ethiopian: "I . . . made myself acquainted with the characters and travelled through [them] . . . a labor of ten months or two years." Language acquisition gets harder as one gets older, and at the age of fifty, Webster wasn't able to gain much more than a cursory understanding of these additional languages.

In the final analysis, Webster's *Synopsis,* begun while he was in the throes of an existential crisis, reveals infinitely more about the mind of its creator than about the origin of language. Paradoxically, the search for truth would lead this brilliant polymath to build an alternative universe entirely out of gibberish. Though some scholars have minimized its wrongheadedness—one early biographer alluded to its "worthy results"—the candid assessment of a pair of University of Chicago English professors appears closer to the mark: "The basis of his etymologizing was simple fantasy." The *Synopsis* was indeed Webster's private dream world, one over which he exercised complete control. Within its dozens of thin notebooks, each of which contained about ten sheets of paper stitched down the middle and folded neatly in two, he was always right; no matter what bogus claim he came up with—say, that the Hebrew root meaning "pure, clean, shining" is related to the Latin, English and Anglo-Saxon words meaning "rub, scour, open"—no one could challenge him. The isolated scholar had created his desideratum—a monument to harmony, which united all human beings throughout history in a common tongue.

Webster finished the *Synopsis* in 1817. He envisioned it as a third quarto volume to his dictionary, but his publisher would pass. Today this musty text resides in the manuscript archives of the New York Public Library.

In direct contrast to the dictionary, this gargantuan labor that had also entailed hardships for the entire family never had any meaning or use for anyone except Webster; but to him, its value was considerable. This opportunity to let his imagination run wild had grounded the loner during a stressful decade when he faced the daunting challenge of raising seven children. And even though Webster couldn't get anyone else too interested in the book's contents, he still felt an enormous sense of accomplishment upon its completion, which would translate into renewed vigor. While a colossal failure as literature, the *Synopsis* succeeded as therapy, helping Webster to both control and exorcise some of his inner demons.

IN EARLY OCTOBER 1814, Webster jumped on his horse Rolla (a name given by his daughter Mary, who had been reading a play about the conquest of Mexico) and headed back to the Purchase Street mansion of Thomas Dawes, where he stayed during his visits to Boston. Webster hadn't expected to be back in the state capital so soon, as the two-month legislative session typically ended in late June. But these were no ordinary times. In September, Massachusetts Governor Caleb Strong had called a special session to address the havoc caused by "Mr. Madison's War" (the War of 1812).

New England's once-robust economy was in shambles. With the loss of its favorite trading partner, Great Britain, its manufacturers had difficulty shopping their wares. Even more alarming, British forces had recently wrested control of a town in Maine, then still part of Massachusetts. To add insult to injury, the president refused to foot the $1 million tab for the Bay State's militia unless its soldiers would submit to the authority of the U.S. Army rather than their own commanding officers.

With Webster leading the charge, Massachusetts residents had been clamoring for peace since the beginning of the year. After attending a meeting of civic leaders in Northampton on January 19, Webster helped draft a circular letter to the Massachusetts General Court, calling for a convention among northern states to consider various measures to contest "the multiplied evils . . . of the late and present Administration." That spring, Webster turned anger against the federal government into the centerpiece of his successful campaign for a House seat. And in his Independence Day oration in Amherst, he again vented his frustration with a decade and a half of Virginians in the White House: "The union of all the states, it was once supposed, would repress the ambition, or restrain the power of the large states and preserve the just rights of each. A few years experience has shown the fallacy of this opinion." The patriot who had fervently preached American unity for the past thirty years had completed an abrupt about-face. Webster now openly talked about dividing America into three parts—North, South and West.

As the legislators convened, outrage against the Madison administration was widespread. On the first day of this extra session, October 5, a Mr. Low of Lyman suggested that a committee from the New England states personally inform the president "that he must either resign his office or remove those of his ministers . . . who have by their nefarious plans ruined the nation." Though Mr. Low withdrew his impetuous proposal the following day, legislators were itching to take some definitive action soon.

On October 13, Webster got his chance to stake out his position in a speech at the Massachusetts State House. "Mr. Speaker," he began, as he looked over at Timothy Bigelow, the House speaker, "The resolution under consideration proposes an extraordinary measure to meet an extraordinary crisis."

Webster stood in front of about three hundred of his fellow delegates, who sat transfixed in rows of tiered seats in the House chamber (where the state Senate meets today). Webster was staring into the midafternoon sun streaming in from the windows overlooking Beacon Street and the Boston Common. Painted on the wall behind him was the state's motto, *"Ense petit placidam sub libertate quietem"* [By the sword we seek peace but only under liberty]. And above him was architect Charles Bullfinch's celebrated dome.

Sounding just like the western Massachusetts farmers whom he had excoriated a generation earlier for lining up behind Daniel Shays, the new delegate insisted that the Commonwealth had to do whatever was necessary to protect its interests. The solution, he believed, required nothing less than a radical shake-up of the national political landscape. Arguing that America's founding document was no longer working, Webster was making the case for a new constitutional convention in Hartford.

Turning his eyes away from the House Speaker and toward his fellow delegates, Webster defined the crisis:

> The Constitution expressly declares that the United States shall guarantee to each state a republican government; and shall protect each of them from invasion. . . . Vast bodies of militia are summoned from their farms and their shops to defend our shores from a foe that threatens to destroy every town within his reach—a frightful mass of debt is daily accumulating—all confidence in the administration of the national government is at an end—we are surrounded by danger without and weakened by dissolution within.

According to Webster, just as the Philadelphia Convention of 1787 was needed to strengthen the federal government, the Hartford Convention was needed to weaken it. He thus exhorted his colleagues, "And our necessities are even more urgent than in 1785; the present constitution has failed to produce the effects intended; it neither protects us, nor promotes the common welfare—indeed for some years past, it has produced nothing but calamity." Despite—or perhaps because of—its hyperbolic rhetoric, Webster's speech, soon reprinted in its entirety in numerous papers across New England, swayed his colleagues. On October 16, by a vote of 260 yeas to 90 nays, the Massachusetts House voted to authorize the Hartford Convention.

In the months leading up to the convention, Webster's pique at the president continued to mount. On November 23, he reported to friends that he had come up with a new definition for the Madison administration—"the madmen of the south." "I say *madmen* for on *political* and *commercial* subjects," he emphasized, "I can not give them a better name. . . . the men in power for years past . . . usually have produced effects contrary to what was proposed—an infallible mark of the want of wisdom."

On December 15, twenty-six delegates from five New England states met in Hartford in closed-door sessions. The convention, which ultimately rejected secession from the Union, lasted three weeks. Webster was not present because Massachusetts required all twelve of its delegates to be native sons. He did, however, help draft its eleven proposed constitutional amendments, such as the one which would have precluded electing a president from the same state two times in a row. And when the Massachusetts legislature reconvened that May, Webster headed the committee charged with distributing five thousand copies of the convention's resolutions.

Despite all the fanfare, the convention would have little impact. A key reason was that the war with Britain ended before it did. As New Englanders debated among themselves, U.S. and British officials were putting the finishing touches on the Treaty of Ghent, which was signed on December 24, 1814. Though news of this diplomatic settlement didn't reach American shores until February, on January 8, 1815, General Andrew Jackson effectively ended the war with his stunning victory at the Battle of New Orleans. With peace now a certainty, the sense of urgency that had galvanized New Englanders was gone.

In the run-up to the Hartford Convention, New Englanders of all stripes had championed secession. Thomas Dawes wrote Webster in February 1814, "By the tyrant I mean, not merely Madison, but the

Southern Policy. . . . As to a separation, I think of it as old Sam Adams thought of *independence*. . . . said he, 'the time has come when we ought to part, for we can live together no longer.'" But in hindsight, this position seemed extreme. The convention would deal a body blow to Federalism, which became tainted by charges of disloyalty and treason. The party officially disintegrated in 1816, after the failed presidential run of Webster's old friend, the former New York senator, Rufus King. In a curious turnaround, Southerners, who were the original targets of the Hartford Convention, picked up its threads a couple of decades later when they began championing states' rights. In response, Massachusetts Senator Daniel Webster repeatedly denounced the convention in the halls of Congress, referring to it as "pollution."

In 1834, Noah Webster wrote to his cousin Daniel to protest the latter's critical assessment. "I knew most of the members of the Convention . . . and I can affirm with confidence," he observed to the unmoved senator, "that no body of men . . . ever convened in this country have combined more talents, purer integrity, sounder patriotism, and republican principles or more firm attachment to the Constitution of the United States."

Webster would forever carry a torch for the Hartford Convention. A month before he died, he published an essay on its origins, in which he declared, "All the reports which have been circulated respecting the evil designs of that convention, I know to be the foulest misrepresentations."

> *Literary labor well rewarded*—It is stated in the *New-Haven Journal*, that Noah Webster junr. Esq. has sold to George Goodwin and Sons, of Hartford, the copy right of his spelling book for forty thousand dollars.

THUS READ A NOTICE which ran in *The New York Evening Post* and numerous other newspapers across the country in June 1817. Though the press got some of the details wrong, Webster was about to become a rich man. He had indeed landed the first blockbuster book deal in the history of American publishing. Forty thousand dollars then was the equivalent of more than a million dollars today.

The facts were these: In April 1816, Noah Webster—after his father's death in 1813, he insisted that "Junior" be stricken from his name—signed an agreement with Hudson and Company, not Goodwin and Sons. Under its terms, he would receive forty-two thousand dollars for granting his new publisher the sole right to print his speller for fourteen years, beginning in March 1818. Webster was pleased to find a national distributor; he now would be relieved of the burdensome task of keeping track of the various state editions, which had sold some 286,000 copies the previous year. As part of the contract, Hudson and Company also agreed to hire his son, William. The teenager was to work as an apprentice in the firm's Hartford office until age twenty-one, at which time he would become a partner.

Both sides later agreed to revise the terms of the deal. In July 1817, a financially strapped Webster received a three-thousand-dollar advance from Hudson and Company. The following April, he accepted a lump-sum payment of twenty thousand dollars (in lieu of thirteen additional three-thousand-dollar annual payments), meaning that his speller brought in a total of twenty-three thousand dollars.

Buoyed by his new financial security, Webster burrowed into his dictionary.

As he was finishing up the *Synopsis,* a surprisingly even-tempered Webster dashed off a sixty-four-page manifesto on the American language. Nearing sixty, he now vowed to debate rather than demolish his opponents: "In controversy with my fellow citizens, on any subject, I will not be engaged. The following remarks . . . are not intended to provoke one; it is my sincere desire that my observations and statements may be marked by . . . candor and moderation." Though the lexicographer wouldn't keep this promise for long, the "Letter to the Honorable John Pickering," published in 1817, lacked his characteristic polemical fury.

Webster was responding to Pickering's 1816 treatise, *A Vocabulary, or Collection of Words and Phrases Which Have Been Supposed to Be Peculiar to the United States of America*. A prominent philologist, Pickering had learned how to read from Webster's speller, which had delighted his father, the former secretary of state Timothy Pickering; however, John Pickering now felt betrayed by America's foremost pedagogue, whose first dictionary, while not a best seller, was still making its mark. Many of Webster's ideas about word use and orthography were starting to catch on. For example, about a decade after the publication of his "compend," an anonymous writer for the *Wilmington Watchman* observed in an article, "To the Last of the Vowels": "I have not heard from U lately so often as I used to, before U was dismissed from many of your employments by Noah Webster. Though u are not in favor at present, with your superiors or your neighbors, yet u are always in security, and have still a respectable share in the public purse, without any thing to do with labor—by which it would seem that u must be concerned in a sinecure." Scholars such as Pickering had taken notice. For him, Webster embodied the new direction in American lexicography, which he wanted to stop in its tracks.

Pickering was reviving the old argument that Webster was an innovator guilty of corrupting the King's English. As he charged, Webster was attempting to "unsettle the whole of our admirable language." Pickering's three-hundred-page volume contained a long list of American words, each of which was followed by his objections. For "Americanize," after citing Webster's definition, "to render American," Pickering, a well-respected lawyer who lived in Salem, countered, "I have never met with this verb in any American work, nor in conversation." Likewise, he protested against "boating" because he did not find the term in the reigning English dictionaries. According to Pickering, who had served as a European diplomat in the Adams administration, Americans should use the same words as their brethren across the ocean.

In his pamphlet, Webster laid out a compelling case for his complete American dictionary. Though his politics kept waxing more and more reactionary, his approach to lexicography remained firmly democratic.

In the realm of words, the autocratic and judgmental Webster, who found evidence of human folly nearly everywhere, continued to place his trust in the good sense of the American people. He argued that he was just trying to keep pace with the innovation that was characteristic of his country:

> In most instances, the use of new terms is dictated by necessity or utility; sometimes to express shades of difference, in signification, for which the language did not supply a suitable term; sometimes to express an idea with more force; and sometimes to express a combination of ideas, by a single word, which otherwise would require a circumlocution. These benefits, which are often perceived as it were instinctively by a nation, recommend such words in common use. . . . New words will be formed, if found necessary or convenient, without a license from Englishmen.

While the Webster of the *Synopsis* was muddled, here he was making fine distinctions in clear, persuasive and even witty prose. While Webster chose not to "animadvert upon" all the words in Pickering's collection, he provided ingenious defenses for a select few: "For Americanize I can cite no authority—but it seems to be as necessary as *Latinize* and *Anglicize*. Every nation must have its *isms* and its *izes,* to express what is peculiar to it." Webster closed by repeating a sentiment that he had first used to market the speller a generation earlier: "But I trust the time will come, when the English will be convinced . . . that we can contend with them in LETTERS, with as much success, as upon the OCEAN."

Having regained his stride after a lost decade, Webster was now poised to make his indelible markup upon the English language.

The Walking Dictionary

ACHIEVEMENT, n. 1. The performance of an action.
2. A great or heroic deed; something accomplished by valor, or
boldness. 3. An obtaining by exertion. 4. An escutcheon or
ensigns armorial, granted for the performance of a great or
honorable action. *Encyc.*

A s the fifty-eight-year-old Webster returned to daily defining in
1817, he no longer felt weighed down by the exigencies of life.
Not only were his financial woes behind him, so, too, were the
bulk of his parental responsibilities; by the end of that year, only Eliza
and Louisa were still living at home. And once his daughters, whom he
dubbed his "angels," got married and moved away, he began enjoying
their company more than ever. He relished traveling around New England with his wife to spend time with them. As he remarked to his third
daughter, Harriet, then living in Portland, Maine, with her new husband,
Edward Cobb, "I wish we had wings occasionally that we might fly to
our dear children." However, these visits tended to be much more satisfying to him than to his offspring, whom he never learned how to treat
as separate people with their own feelings and aspirations. Shortly after
Harriet's 1816 marriage to Cobb, whose father, Matthew, was a wealthy
merchant from Portsmouth, New Hampshire, he wrote to his daughter,
then close to twenty, "I present my respects to the elder Mr. Cobb and
his lady—tell them that if you are not a *good girl*, they must write to me."
While Webster was writing a generation before Seneca Falls and the

birth of modern feminism, such obtuse remarks had more to do with him than with his times.

But as Webster made his way across the alphabet, he was leveled by a few family tragedies. In early 1818, Harriet and her husband traveled to the West Indies, where they both contracted yellow fever. Harriet would survive, but her husband did not. And upon her return to New England, Harriet discovered that her infant daughter, who had remained at home, had also died. In a letter dated February 25, 1818, Webster had trouble empathizing with his daughter's grief: "Often, my dear Harriet, have I found in the course of my life, that frustrated hopes have been beneficial to me." At Webster's suggestion, Harriet would move back to Amherst. About a year later, Webster's fourth daughter, Mary, who had met her husband, the widower Horatio Southgate, while visiting Harriet in Portland, died in childbirth. Webster was devastated. A poetry lover, Mary had been his favorite; as a teenager, she had helped him edit his essays and Fourth of July orations. The alluring fair-skinned Mary had blue eyes and light brown hair (in contrast to his other daughters, who were all brunettes). Though he prided himself on his emotional control, Webster couldn't stop crying. On March 8, 1819, he wrote his daughter Emily and her husband, William Ellsworth: "Submit we must and I hope we shall all submit with the patience and humility of Christians. In *theory,* I indulge no desire to have my own condition regulated by my own wishes or supposed interests or pleasure. Yet the dissolution of the most tender ties in nature touches all the sensibilities of my heart. I must weep—it is a pleasure to weep. O what would I give for a portrait of my dear Mary!"

To cope with his despair, Webster took recourse in words: he published a long obituary in the *Panoplist.* While he had not been able to travel to Mary's deathbed, he provided a detailed account of her final moments, surrounded by family and friends, "she fell asleep in Jesus without a struggle or a groan. . . . It seemed as if her soul drank at the fountain of bliss in that dark hour." Mary's infant daughter—also named Mary—survived, and Webster would raise her as his own. He didn't trust

Southgate, because the country lawyer was reported to be having an affair with a housekeeper.

IT RESEMBLED AN EPISODE out of the Old Testament. Like the Israelites, the townsfolk of Amherst were uniting to build a shrine to the Lord: a new institution of higher learning for seminary students.

At two in the afternoon on Wednesday, August 9, 1820, Amherst Academy's board of trustees gathered at the three-story white-brick schoolhouse on Amity Street. Just a few minutes later, the fifteen-member board, of which Pastor Parsons was president and Webster vice president, voted to "proceed immediately to lay the corner-stone of the edifice for the charitable institution." Descending back into the street, the board then joined a huge procession, which included academy students and preceptors, financial backers and workmen. Marching along the west side of the common, the throng headed to a hillside across from the First Church, where Webster was to make the ceremonial address.

Though Webster was eager to move ahead with the dictionary as fast as possible, he couldn't help but embrace this "common cause." Like his forefather Governor Webster, he would be bringing Connecticut Congregationalism to the Commonwealth. Equally important, this Yale man was also taking a stand against his enemies—namely, Harvard and Unitarianism. For Webster, these forces of darkness posed a threat not only to his dictionary-making—the harsh reviews of a decade earlier still stung—but to the moral fiber of New England. Amherst College, he observed, was needed "to check the progress of errors which are propagated from Cambridge. The influence of the University of Cambridge [Harvard], supported by great wealth and talents, seems to call on all the friends of truth to unite in circumscribing it."

Two years earlier, when Webster first joined the board, Amherst Academy was already thriving. It had 152 students, evenly divided between masters and misses, which included his children Eliza and William (who would be "fitted for college" after he ran afoul of his Hartford employer). About half were locals, but a few came from as far away as Virginia and Canada. Its rigorous curriculum featured chemistry, astronomy, natural philosophy, Latin and French, all taught by top-notch instructors. Eager to promote this bastion of Christian education, Webster was a frequent presence, attending the declamations held on Wednesday afternoons and opening his house for school receptions.

In the wake of the private school's meteoric rise, by 1818 its board had also set its sights on a new goal—a college. The prime mover was Colonel Rufus Graves, a devout chemistry instructor who had formerly taught at the Dartmouth Medical School. In establishing this institution, Graves turned the federal blueprint upside down; first came the constitution and then came the convention. In May 1818, Graves finished the fourteen-article founding document, which he showed to Webster's cousin Daniel to make sure that it was legally sound. Convinced that "the education of pious young men of the first talents in community, is the most sure method of . . . civilizing and evangelizing the world," Graves sought to raise fifty thousand dollars. A few months later, he organized a convention of sixty-nine clergymen from Hampshire and three surrounding counties, at which Noah Webster presented the new constitution. Webster was also appointed to head a committee to persuade Williams College, then languishing in desolate Williamstown, to merge with the new college and move to Amherst. By July 1819, enough subscribers had been found to meet the fund-raising goal, but the corporation of Williams College refused to go along with the plan. Undaunted, in May 1820, Graves, Webster and the other trustees secured a site in Amherst and began designing the first building, which was to be exactly one hundred feet in length and called South College.

As the crowd walked up the hill to hear Webster's speech that August afternoon, pride was the predominating emotion. With the charitable fund of fifty thousand dollars earmarked solely for students and faculty, the building committee had asked area residents to donate materials and labor. And the response from Amherst as well as from neighboring towns such as Hadley and Pelham—then best known as the birthplace of the rebel leader Daniel Shays—had been nothing short of miraculous. In just three months, thanks to contributions from a bevy of volunteers, a remarkable transformation had taken place. Working nonstop, those camping out at the site had finished preparing the ground and had dug the trenches. The Virginia fence—so-called because it was crooked—and the horse shed were gone. In their stead now stood a bounty of evidence testifying to the community's generosity—granite, lime, sand and lumber, flanked by pickaxes, hoes and shovels. The new temple was ready to be constructed.

All eyes were suddenly on Webster, who, stepping onto the ceremonial cornerstone laid down by Pastor Parsons, launched into his prepared remarks: "The object of this institution, that of educating for the gospel ministry young men in indigent circumstances, but of hopeful piety and promising talents, is one of the noblest which can occupy the attention and claim the contributions of the Christian public." Thinking of the new college as an extension of Yale, Webster harked back to the 1776 valedictory speech of Timothy Dwight. Webster applied Dwight's words—"The period, in which your lot is cast, is possibly the happiest in the roll of time"—to the conditions Americans faced a half century later: "Blessed be our lot! We live to see a new era in the history of man—an era when reason and religion begin to resume their sway, and to impress the heavenly truth, that the appropriate business of men is to imitate the Savior; to serve their God; and bless their fellow men." After Webster finished, he made a call for contributions. One man came forward whom no one recognized; he put down a silver dollar and declared, "Here is my beam, God bless it."

At the trustees' meeting the next day, Pastor Parsons resigned as president and Webster was elected to replace him. His charge was to step up fund-raising. But just as his repeated efforts to gain more subscribers for his dictionary flopped, so, too, did his outreach to potential donors. But once again, the fierce community spirit saved the day. Volunteers continued to make unexpected contributions. Esq. Fowler, for example, both lent his own horses and provided laborers, whom he boarded in his home. Webster later recalled, "And such were the exertions of the Board, the committee and the friends of the Institution that on the ninetieth day from the laying of the corner-stone, the roof timbers were erected on the building." In the words of Heman Humphrey, a future president of the college, "It seemed more like magic than the work of the craftsmen." After a year, the building was completed, with Webster, as board president, racking up only thirteen hundred dollars in unpaid bills.

On Sunday, September 18, 1821, at the parish church, Webster presided over the induction ceremony of the college's first president, Zephaniah S. Moore, whom he had recruited from Williams, and its first two professors. "So it is peculiarly proper," Webster declared, "that at an undertaking having for its special object the promotion of the religion of Christ should be commended to the favor and protection of the great Head of the Church."

The following day, the college was up and running. A total of forty-seven students enrolled, fifteen of whom, like the president, were Williams transplants; they would all reside in the four-story South College, which also contained the seven-hundred-volume library, the dining hall and the classrooms. That same day, Dr. Moore replaced Webster as president of the board. "The business of founding this Institution," Webster later wrote in his diary, "has been very laborious and perplexing. . . . As soon as I was satisfied the Institution was well established by the Induction of Officers, I resigned my seat in the Board of Trustees."

Noah Webster remains a formidable presence on the Amherst College campus. Today, a massive bronze and granite statue of a likeness—sporting a toga and sandals like a Roman statesman—sits behind the main library. A gift from alumnus Richard Billings, it was erected about a century after Webster's famous speech at South College. Webster's combination of moral and intellectual rigor reminded Billings of his father, the industrialist Fredric Billings. A forgotten founder of the University of California, the elder Billings had first suggested that the northern Californian school be named after the Irish philosopher, Bishop

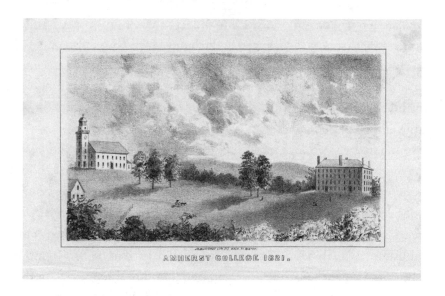

AMHERST COLLEGE 1821.

In his memoir, Webster wrote, "The principal event which took place while NW resided in Amherst, and in which he was concerned as an actor, was the establishment of a college in that town."

Berkeley. Said Richard Billings, "The thing I had always wished some one would do for my father, I determined to do for Noah Webster."

ON NOVEMBER 7, 1821, just as Webster was turning his attention from the college's financial future back to his own, he heard from his onetime Federalist Party colleague John Jay. In a brief letter, Jay, who had retired to his Westchester farm after stepping down as governor of New York two decades earlier, asked about the progress of the "great work." He also enclosed a hundred-dollar donation for two additional subscriptions for his two sons; the former chief justice had ordered one for himself back in 1813.

Webster was very moved that Jay had offered to help "without solicitation." He wrote back right away and supplied a brief overview of his *Synopsis,* of which he boasted, "the discoveries, proceeding from this investigation will be quite important and as *new* in Europe as in America." Noting that he was "engaged in the letter H," Webster also updated Jay on the new financial obstacles to completing the dictionary: "I cannot revise and complete the work without the help of men and books, which I cannot have in *the country,* and my income will not maintain my family in one of our large towns."

Amherst was no longer suiting Webster's purposes. Fifteen years into his magnum opus, he lacked access both to rare books and to fellow scholars to examine his manuscript. In addition, under a new state law, the stock that he owned in the Hartford Bank, upon which he was already paying Connecticut taxes, was now also subject to taxes in Massachusetts. By early 1822, Webster was convinced that he had to move to "give the work the correctness and perfection desired." And for the Webster family, the needs of the dictionary would continue to reign supreme.

That summer, the Websters headed back to New Haven. With the waterfront now a business district, Webster chose to live near the Yale campus. Temporarily renting a small house at the corner of Wall and College streets, he commissioned the well-known Connecticut architect David Hoadley to build a permanent home on Temple Street. Webster himself supervised the building of this commodious neoclassical structure. (In 1938, Henry Ford had this slice of Americana transported to his museum in Dearborn, Michigan, where it still stands.) The downstairs featured a formal drawing room and a parlor, for Rebecca to do her needlework and the children to play the piano. To prevent distractions, Webster had double walls installed in his second-floor study, where he would both conduct his literary activity and sleep on a narrow mattress. Just a few houses down on Temple Street lived his daughter Julia and her husband, Chauncey Goodrich, then a professor of rhetoric at Yale. In 1822, the Webster household included fourteen-year-old Louisa and three-year-old Mary Southgate (who would call Webster and his wife "father" and "mother") as well as eighteen-year-old Eliza and twenty-five-year-old Harriet, who were both about to start families of their own.

In 1825, Eliza would move to New Britain with her new husband, Henry Jones, a pastor. That same year, the widowed Harriet married William Fowler, who would soon land a teaching job at Middlebury College. Prone to drinking bouts, William Webster continued to flounder. In the fall of 1820, he enrolled at Yale, but he never graduated. Though William was an able classicist and a talented flutist, he lacked the very quality that defined his father—perseverance. Webster would repeatedly strategize about how to set up his son in a profession.

By the end of 1823, when Webster had reached R, the end of the dictionary was in sight. On December 12, he wrote his longtime friend Dr. Samuel Latham Mitchill, "In order to give my work all the completeness of which it is susceptible, I purpose to go to England the next summer, if life and health permit, and there finish and publish it. I want some aid in books and knowledge, which I cannot obtain in this country." To cover his travel expenses, Webster hoped to raise two thousand dollars from a few wealthy donors. But he was unwilling to promise to repay the advance. After a decade of rejection, Webster had lost his characteristic self-confidence. As he also told Mitchill, "I am apprehensive that any applications I might make for this object would be unsuccessful . . . and if I fail, I shall be left in reduced circumstances." The benefactors never materialized. Webster instead relied on a thousand-dollar loan from his daughter Harriet (which he wouldn't be able to pay back for six years) and the sale of some books in his private library. The following spring, he added Paris to his itinerary; he also planned to visit the acclaimed Royal Library, then the world's largest with some one million books and eighty thousand manuscripts.

As Webster prepared to set sail for Europe, he was a celebrity in his home country, but not a celebrated lexicographer. While his speller was about to reach the unheard-of five million mark in total sales, his proposed complete dictionary was still an object of ridicule. On April 14, 1824, *The New London Gazette* carried this brief item: "It is said that Noah Webster is about to proceed to England to publish *there* his large Dictionary, promised to the public eighteen years ago in the preface to

his small one. If he executes this plan, (says the statesman) he will succeed in one sense at least, in making an English Dictionary." In fact, as
papers across New England reported two months later, Webster himself had already reversed course. He no longer intended to publish an
expanded version of his small American dictionary. Instead of trying to
unite Americans through a distinct American language, he now planned
to unite Americans with their English brethren through a new international form of English. Retitled *The Universal Dictionary,* his book
would, like Johnson's dictionary, now emanate from London and shape
language use on both sides of the Atlantic.

The sixty-six-year-old wordsmith now felt less connected to America
than to Europe, which as a young man he had derided as "grown old in
folly, corruption and tyranny."

AT ELEVEN O'CLOCK on the morning of Tuesday, June 15, 1824, the *Edward Quesnel,* buoyed by a fair northwest wind, set off from New York.
The spanking new ship was bound for Le Havre.

On board were twenty-one passengers, hailing mostly from Europe,
attended to by a crew of twenty. In addition to the ten French travelers
were an English couple with their son and female servant, plus a German, a Swede and a Canadian. Webster and his son, William, whom he
brought along as his transcriber, were among the four Americans. The
company, Webster wrote to Rebecca, was actually a mix of bipeds and
quadrupeds, as it also included geese, fowl, turkeys, pigs and sheep.
However, the animals were less of a presence the closer the ship got
to Europe; most were consumed during the sumptuous three o'clock
dinners.

Just three days into the trip, a severe gale rattled the passengers.
With the howling winds causing the ocean to foam and roar, few ven-
tured on deck. That first Friday aboard the ship, William stepped out of
his berth just once. Observing all the tossing and tumbling, he blurted
out, "I had no idea of this," before rushing back below. William was

particularly apprehensive because the *Edward Quesnel* was on its maiden voyage and "unused to the perils of the deep." The one notable exception was Webster, whose stomach "was not in the least disturbed." Struck by the stark contrast between his constitution and his father's, William observed in his diary, "It is rather singular that while poor I am suffering what would at once have released the Israelites from captivity had the curse of seasickness been Pharaoh's first plague, my father remains perfectly well. During the most tremendous swell of the sea, he is not in the least possible degree affected. A fact that astonishes even himself." Webster's nervous system didn't work quite the same way as anybody else's. While everyday social encounters could make him anxious, the prospect of imminent danger didn't faze him at all.

Throughout the monthlong journey, Webster was in an uncharacteristically placid state of mind. While even the slightest noise from the children would upset him at home, on the high seas he was unflappable. To Rebecca, he wrote, "Indeed we have a great variety of music & discords. The squealing of the pigs, the bleating of the sheep and goats, the crowing of the cocks, and the squalling of the Englishman's child, alternately or jointly salute our ears. These with the jabbering of the Frenchmen and with their humming and whistling give us no little amusement." However, Webster was annoyed that there was "no appearance of religion among the passengers," who failed to distinguish between Sundays and other days, playing whist on both.

At Webster's insistence, those aboard the ship celebrated Independence Day on Monday, July 5, rather than on the Sabbath. As the Americans were a distinct minority, the morning was ushered in without the firing of a single gun or the ringing of a solitary bell—just the animating cry, "Ho heave yoe," of the seamen. At three, a splendid repast was served. Afterward, the accomplished July Fourth orator requested to give a brief address. With Webster now intending to erase the divisions between American and British English, his remarks had a surprising new twist; he dwelled chiefly on the advantages that had accrued to both England and France since America's separation from the old country.

He then led his fellow passengers in nine toasts. While the first four covered familiar ground—saluting the day, the United States, its Constitution and its president—number six was one this veteran of the American Revolution had never before uttered: "Great Britain, Great and free in herself, may her power be exerted to defend the freedom of other nations."

A second round of thirteen additional toasts would follow, each one given by a different member of the dining party. Captain Hawkins hailed "the ladies and gentlemen on board the Edward Quesnel." Going around the table, a Monsieur Sournalet of France added, "The sage of Monticello," leading Webster to grimace. When it came William's turn, he exclaimed, "Washington and Lafayette, strangers in birth, but brothers by affection." (Upon their arrival in Le Havre a week later, Webster and his son, who had his boots cleaned for the occasion, were supposed to spend an evening with the Marquis, but they just missed "Washington's brother," who had already set off on his voyage back to America.) Webster himself raised a glass for the thirteenth and final toast, "Our families and the friends we love."

"So tanned that I look like a Spaniard," wrote Webster, still in good spirits as the ship arrived in Le Havre on Saturday, July 10. The following Saturday at ten in the evening, father and son reached Paris. The tall, slender Webster, wearing his typical outfit of black trousers, a black coat and black silk stockings, stood out. Spotting him in a hotel lobby the following week, a fellow New Englander, Samuel Goodrich, who later achieved fame as an author of children's books, described the lexicographer as "a curious quaint, Connecticut looking apparition strangely in contrast to the prevailing forms and aspects in this gay metropolis." While Webster complained about the seventy dollars a month that he had to pay for the rooms at Madame Rivière's at No. 19 Rue Bergère, the Royal Library left him nearly speechless. He reported to Rebecca, "I cannot give you a description of my feelings. To have an adequate idea of this collection of books, you must imagine rows of shelves 30 feet high from the corner of my house to the Green, or public square." But the rhythms of Parisian life alienated him. After two weeks, his calm had turned to agitation: "Little regard is had to the Sabbath. . . . The theaters are open every night, & one of the greatest inconveniences I experience is the noise of carriages at the breaking up of plays, about 12 at night. I must submit to be thus annoyed at present in every way imaginable, but I think these things may shorten my stay in France." Indeed, he would be gone by mid-September, a month earlier than originally planned.

Not particularly eager to explore the city—"I came here not for the gratification of curiosity"—Webster buried himself in his work. He got up at six, and wrote for a couple of hours before breakfast. He spent two days a week at the library, where he pored over the first edition of *The Dictionary of the French Academy,* published in 1694. In contrast to England, continental Europe had always seen dictionary-making as a group enterprise—Florence's Accademia della Crusca produced the first modern dictionary in 1612—and Webster sought to familiarize himself with this tradition. To hunt for scientific terms missing in Johnson, Webster also consulted the work of the French encyclopedists as well as the recent *Dictionary of Natural History* by Georges Cuvier. In his occasional outings around town, Webster tended to be unimpressed by what he saw. "But the Palais Royal," he wrote to his daughter Emily, "and the palace of the Tuilleries where the King now resides, are so tarnished by time & weather that they are the color of an old barn." Unlike his father, William, who studied French with the help of a native tutor and would do some sightseeing on his own, he took a liking to what he called "the land of the frogs." On September 13, their final day in Paris, Webster's son wrote, "If man were not an accountable being, I know of no spot under Heaven where one could pass an earthly existence with more delight."

Sailing from Dieppe, the Websters made brief stopovers in Brighton and London before heading to Cambridge. On September 22, they settled into a suite of rooms at the university, courtesy of Dr. Samuel Lee, a professor of Arabic. With his letter of introduction to Lee, Webster also gained access to the books at Trinity College's Wren Library.

Webster was eager to turn his attention to "business." On September 24, he wrote Rebecca, "I want certainly the comfort & happiness of the presence of my dear consort & children. This thought sometimes chills me for a moment, but I am not distressed or unhappy. . . . And it is a pleasant thing to get among people that look & dress & eat & talk like our own people." A few months later, he tried to set in motion his grand scheme of uniting America and England in a common tongue. On December 20, he wrote to Dr. Lee, proposing a summit on the future of the English language. The three parties—members of the Oxford and Cambridge faculty, along with him representing American literati—would attempt to bring about agreement on "unsettled points in pronunciation and grammatical construction." The expert salesman clearly intended to turn the resolutions of these academics into publicity for his new book. However, in his letter to Lee, Webster claimed that his motives were purely scholarly: "But the gentlemen would disavow any intention of imposing their opinions on the public as authoritative; they would offer simply their opinions, and the public would still be at liberty to receive or reject them." While Dr. Lee and his Cambridge colleagues were intrigued, Oxford never responded. But Webster continued defining, and in late January 1825, with his right thumb "almost exhausted" from overuse, he finished his manuscript. It was a moment Webster would never forget. He later recalled, "When I had come to the last word, I was seized with trembling which made it somewhat difficult to hold my pen steady for the writing. . . . But I summoned strength to finish the last word, and then walking about the room a few minutes I recovered." Webster attributed the intense anxiety to the thought that he might not live to finish the work. But he was perhaps more worried about what was to happen next. After all, for nearly thirty years, finishing the dictionary had been the organizing force of his life.

Though his proposed academic conference never got off the ground, Webster still pressed ahead with his plan to publish his dictionary of a unified English. Leaving Cambridge in February, he moved to London to shop the idea. He sent part of the manuscript to John Murray, but the distinguished publisher of Jane Austen and Lord Byron turned him down. In his memoir, Webster offered the following account of this episode: "The booksellers declined publishing *The American Dictionary*; the great publishers being engaged in a new edition of Todd's *Johnson,* and in the works of Richardson." While the competition posed by the lexicographers Henry John Todd, who was about to release a revised edition of Johnson's dictionary, and Charles Richardson, then composing his *New Dictionary of the English Language,* did drown out interest in Webster's complete dictionary, Webster's explanation did involve some revisionist history. That's because in 1825, Webster was not trying to sell *The American Dictionary*; distinguishing American English from British English was then the furthest thing from his mind. In fact, while in Cambridge, Webster wrote to his cousin Daniel, requesting that the Massachusetts representative push through Congress a bill enabling him to import his forthcoming British book, *A Dictionary of the English Language,* to America duty-free. But with the negotiations in London going nowhere, this legislation, which was passed on March 3, 1825, never did him any good. By April, a dejected Webster was eager to be reunited with his family. On April 14, "Weby"—as William was known to his peers—confided to his friend Artemas Thompson, then a student at Amherst College:

> My father feels that the state of his health makes it a duty for him to return immediately. His mind is a good deal broken down by the most intense application to study and the infirmities incident to advanced age make it desirable that he should relax himself and return to the bosom of his family. . . . He has given up the intention of publishing his work in England. The superintendence of the publication would require more exertion and confinement than would be prudent for him—indeed it might prove fatal. . . . What I have written respecting my father's health, I wish you not to mention, as it might give our friends in New Haven unnecessary anxiety and alarm, should it reach them.

As he sailed back to New York with William aboard the *Hudson* in May, Webster reverted to his original plan, which was to publish his *American Dictionary* in America. If Webster's year-long trip to Europe had ended successfully, Americans and Britons might today be speaking the same version of English.

GIVEN A HERO'S WELCOME in New Haven—both by the Yale faculty and Rebecca and the children—Webster soon regained his stamina. Several months later, he found an American publisher, Sherman Converse, then also the editor of the New Haven paper, *The Connecticut Journal*. Converse prepared a specimen of a few pages, which he circulated among prominent people in the hope of accumulating endorsements for the dictionary. One of the first came from Webster's old friend John Trumbull, who noted, "I do not hesitate to recommend it to all who wish to acquire a correct knowledge of the English language, as a valuable addition to the science of philology and an honor to the literature of our country." Converse also reached out to two former presidents. On February 20, 1826, Thomas Jefferson politely declined: "Sir, I have duly recieved [*sic*] your favor the 6th asking my examination and opinion of the plan of Mr. Webster's dictionary, of which you inclosed me a sample, but worn down with age, infirmity and pain, my mind is no longer in a tone for such services. I can only therefore express my respect and best wishes for its success." Jefferson may not have wanted to help his onetime Federalist critic; however, he was indeed frail and would die just a few months later. But James Madison, whom Webster had also once vilified, did come through. "The plan embraces so many commendable objects," wrote Jefferson's successor in the White House to Converse from his retirement home in Montpelier, Virginia, "beyond the ordinary scope of such works that its successful execution must be a substantial improvement on them." By May, Converse had racked up a total of fourteen recommendations, including one from Supreme Court Justice

Joseph Story and one from the philologist John Pickering, who had criticized the first dictionary so harshly a decade earlier.

While Converse worked out an arrangement with Hezekiah Howe of New Haven to print the book, Webster began preparing his manuscript for publication. This last round of editing would take two years. The conscientious Webster did whatever he could to remove errors from his definitions. On March 3, 1826, he wrote the French linguist Peter Du Ponceau, who worked as an attorney in Philadelphia, "I have inserted in my vocabulary the word phonology from some of your writings. I believe I understand it, but for fear I may not, I will thank you to give me your meaning in a brief definition." Webster asked the Yale professors Benjamin Silliman and Denison Olmsted to review the scientific terms. And in January 1827, he hired Dr. James Gates Percival, a Yale-educated physician and celebrated poet fluent in ten languages and able to write verse in thirteen, to proofread his entries. But Webster's temperamental employee, who had given up medicine after seeing his first patient, would abandon his assignment two months before the dictionary went to press.

While Percival had the ideal qualifications for the job, he was even more eccentric than Webster. The stubborn and volatile bachelor also preferred books to people; though condemned to a life of poverty, he would eventually amass a library of ten thousand volumes. The closest Percival ever came to embracing a woman was grazing the hand of a pupil whom he tutored in her home; this momentary contact filled him with so much emotion that he immediately left the room, never to return. The signature poem of the humorless Percival was "The Suicide," which featured dozens of chilling verses such as the following:

> He once could love, but Oh! That time was o'er,
> His heart was now the seat of hate alone,
> As peaceful—is the wintry tempest's roar
> As cheerful—torture's agonizing groan.

By 1821, when the twenty-six-year-old poet published his highly regarded first collection, he had already attempted suicide twice. The tall and blond Percival, neatly clad in the brown camlet coat which he wore day after day, had large blue eyes with dilated pupils that were fixed in a permanent stare. While Webster occasionally flirted with madness, Percival incarnated the thing in itself. Percival was the man Webster might have become had he not stumbled upon his reliable sources of comfort—his loving wife, his religious faith, his sealed-off second-story hideaways and his dictionary.

Percival was initially thrilled to be working with Webster. Sharing a passion for defining, he also loved tracing words back to their roots. In fact, he was a step ahead of his boss, as he kept abreast of the latest German scholarship on etymology. When once asked by a friend if his tasks were dry, Percival responded, "I took more pleasure in editing Webster's Dictionary than in anything else I have done." Percival was supposed to proof the printed pages, but the printing proceeded so slowly that he had to read the manuscript as well. He didn't get started until May 1827, and he soon felt oppressed by the grueling fourteen-hour workdays. On December 4, 1827, he confided to his friend Dr. George Hayward, "My situation is one of disgust and toil. . . . I regret that I have ever engaged in the thing. It will be one of the miseries of my life to think of it." Later that month, Webster left Percival a note about his alleged untidiness: "I have to request you not to write on the MSS, as many of your remarks are illegible and they injure the writing, which is already bad enough. You will oblige me to write all your re-marks, as Prof. Olmsted does, on a separate piece of paper." An enraged Percival shot back, "If you have confidence in me, my articles had better remain as they are. If you have not, it is idle for me to have any further connection with the dictionary." Though the two men soon reconciled, Percival then started challenging Webster's etymologies. When Webster insisted that his assistant focus solely on proofreading, Percival began sneaking in some changes on his own. To express his now unspeakable pique, Percival lapsed into Latin in his January 9, 1828, update to Hayward, *"Multa absurda removi"* [Many absurd things I have removed]. By September, Percival, whose name would not appear in the dictionary, had moved on.

In the months immediately preceding the publication of "his great book," Webster was highly agitated. Henry Howe, the son of his publisher, who at the age of eleven delivered page proofs from his father to Webster, later recalled, "I do not remember to have seen him smile. He was a too-much pre-occupied man for frivolity, bearing, as he did, the entire weight of the English tongue upon his shoulders." On September 15, Webster informed Harriet, "I remain troubled with head ache and can but little business. To write this letter is for me great effort." On Wednesday morning, November 26, 1828, the last pages of *An American Dictionary of the English Language* came off Howe's printing press. The following day, in honor of "the great event," Rebecca invited dozens of guests over to Temple Street for "a solid Thanksgiving supper."

Webster soon would have even more to celebrate. Having languished as a persona non grata in his own country for nearly a quarter of a century, he had staged a remarkable comeback. On January 31, 1829, *The Connecticut Mirror* compared Webster to the Roman poet Horace, who had famously created a literary "monument more lasting than steel," observing, "We are aware of no other publication in this country or in Europe, upon which equal research and labor has ever been expended by a single individual." A week later, Webster wrote to his son-in-law William Fowler: "My great book seems to command a good deal of attention. Mr. Quincy, now president of Harvard, spent an hour with me on Thursday. He assures me the book will be well reviewed. Chancellor Kent writes me that the best judges of New York speak of it with the highest respect, and he has no doubt it will supersede Johnson. It is considered as a national work." The timing was much better than for the "compend." Americans had gotten used to the idea that Johnson's day had come and gone. The public was also prepared to accept that Webster was not a wild innovator, as his critics had once charged. In April 1829, James L. Kingsley, a Yale Latin professor, wrote a fifty-page review in the *North American Review,* in which he concluded, "The proper effect of the author's labors in the cause of the language of his country will not fail, sooner or later to be produced. . . . it will be seen in the more correct use of words, in the check which will be put on useful innovations. . . . in the increased respect . . . with which the author will be viewed." However, this review by Kingsley—a Temple Street neighbor who had provided a blurb three years earlier—left a drained Webster, whose headaches still hadn't gone away, disappointed. Right after reading it, he complained to Fowler, "This will probably satisfy my friends, but there are some differences between us and in some points the reviewer is certainly wrong. I believe however that I shall let it pass unnoticed." As more positive feedback came in, Webster could afford to lie low. On May 29, 1829, he reported to Fowler from New York, "From the observations of many literary gentlemen and all I have seen, I find that public sentiment is pretty fully settled as to the substantial merits of my great book."

The comprehensiveness of Webster's *American Dictionary* was breathtaking. It contained seventy thousand words, some twelve thousand more than the 1818 version of Johnson edited by Henry John Todd. Webster succeeded in forever expanding the scope of the dictionary. After Webster, all English lexicographers felt duty-bound to capture the language not just of literature, but also of everyday life. According to Webster's estimate, he added at least four thousand new scientific terms, including, for example, "phosphorescent" and "planetarium." He also inserted hundreds of commonly used words—"savings-bank," "eulogist," "retaliatory," "dyspeptic," "electioneer" and "re-organize" all became official. However, his inclusiveness occasionally made readers squirm. Of "co-bishop," one reviewer wrote, "We consider such a word . . . too vilely formed ever to be tolerated." In perhaps his greatest contribution, Webster transformed definitions from little more than lists of synonymous terms to tightly knit mini-essays, which highlighted fine distinctions. Compare, for example, Webster and his predecessor on "ability":

Johnson: The power to do any thing, depending on skill, riches or strength; capacity, qualification and power.

Webster: Physical power, whether bodily or mental; natural or acquired; force of understanding; skill in arts or science. *Ability* is active power, or power to perform, as opposed to *capacity,* or power to receive.

Webster was also the first lexicographer to turn his own examples into a central component of definitions. To explain morality, he noted, "We often admire the politeness of men whose *morality* we question."

While Webster improved upon Johnson, he also borrowed liberally from his rival. Based upon an examination of both Webster's copy of Johnson's 1799 dictionary and the 1828 dictionary, scholar Joseph Reed concludes that about one-third of Webster's definitions demonstrate the influence of Johnson. This figure includes a few direct transcriptions—sometimes without attribution—as well as numerous cases where Webster made slight alterations. Citing Reed's research, critics have occasionally tried to downplay Webster's achievement. But such attacks, which tend to be mounted by Johnsonians, are unwarranted. After all, as Reed concedes, "Borrowing—even plagiarism—is no sin to lexicographers." Particularly in the days before committees assembled dictionaries, compilers often recycled the work of one another. Johnson, for example, borrowed heavily from his direct predecessor, Nathan Bailey, author of *An Universal Etymological Dictionary,* originally published in 1721. Moreover, Reed himself is also struck by the remarkable breadth and originality of Webster's work, adding, "Webster did more than perhaps any other lexicographer to initiate the encyclopedic dictionary."

Since his return from Europe, Webster had also reworked his dictionary to give it a purely American flavor. To broadcast his intentions, he slapped on a highly patriotic preface. While he still hoped to market the book in Britain—and was no longer the anti-English rebel of the speller—he wholeheartedly embraced the goal that had first motivated him nearly thirty years earlier: "It is not only important, but in a degree necessary, that the people of this country, should have an *American Dictionary* of the English Language; for although the body of the language is the same as in England, and it is desirable to perpetuate that sameness, yet some differences must exist. Language is the expression of ideas; and if the people of one country cannot preserve an identity of ideas, they cannot retain an identity of language."

Citing Johnson's famous phrase, "The chief glory of a nation arises from its authors," Webster sought to celebrate America's founders—Franklin, Washington, Adams, Jay, Madison, Hamilton and Marshall—as "pure models of genuine English." He also felt it necessary to clarify the key terms of American politics. "The judges of the supreme court of United States," read one of his examples, "have the power of determining the *constitutionality* of laws." As in his speller a half century earlier, he also stuck in countless references to American locales. In the entry for the verb "view," which he defined as "to survey," he alluded to a favorite spot in western Massachusetts: "We ascended Mount Holyoke and *viewed* the charming landscape below."

Webster's "great book," like that of his idol, was also part autobiography. Just as Samuel Johnson had expressed his feelings toward Lord Chesterfield by defining "patron" as "a wretch who supports with insolence, and is paid with flattery," Webster also repeatedly dragged in incidents from his own life. In the definition for "embalm," he alluded to his own devastating loss: "The memory of my beloved daughter is *embalmed* in my heart. N. W." And under "when," he recalled his near-meeting with Washington's adopted son: "We were present *when* General Lafayette embarked at Havre for New York." Likewise, to illustrate the familiar meaning of "absent"—"not at home"—Webster mentioned an excuse that he himself often resorted to: "The master of the house is *absent*. In other words, he does not wish to be disturbed by company." While Webster didn't prescribe the right way to use language, he did prescribe the right way to live. The definitions frequently had a didactic tone that reflected Webster's values, particularly his Christian faith.

Under "seducer," Webster opined, "The *seducer* of a female is a little less criminal than the murderer"; and under "seduction," he volunteered some homespun advice: "the best safeguard is principle, the love of purity and holiness, the fear of God and reverence for his commands."

While Webster's *Synopsis* was not appended to the dictionary as he had hoped, his dubious etymological ideas made an occasional appearance. As in his "compend," he insisted on some archaic Anglo-Saxon spellings, such as "bridegoom" for "bridegroom." Though the former term is closer to the Anglo-Saxon "brideguma," this entry struck most readers as ridiculous. Citing this example, Britain's *Westminster Review,* which considered Webster's work "one of a very important character," accused him of having "a few words in which he is very adventurous in his orthography." In a handful of entries, Webster also left in incomprehensible references to the unpublished *Synopsis.* Under the verb "heat," in a long paragraph of fanciful etymology which came before the definition, Webster noted, "See Class Gd. No 39, and others. It may be further added that in W[elsh] *cas* is hatred, a *castle,* from the sense of separating; *casau,* to hate; and if this is of the same family, it unites *castle* with the foregoing words." Such "choice sentences" led another British periodical, *The Quarterly Review,* to issue one of the few pans, "There is everywhere a great parade of erudition and a great lack of real knowledge." But most Americans were forgiving of the lexicographer's odd notions. In 1829, the *Norwich Courier* observed, "Noah Webster, thinking that molasses 'by any other name would taste as sweet,' has in his new Dictionary spelt it Melasses. Notwithstanding this high authority, it is extremely questionable whether any Yankee can be made to swallow such a word with hasty pudding."

Webster suddenly commanded respect from America's literati, who had long abused him. Both financial security and lionization were soon to follow. In a speech at Yale, his old friend James Kent, the former chief justice of the New York State Supreme Court, compared his dictionary to the Parthenon and the pyramids of Egypt. Webster will, Kent declared, "transmit his name to the latest posterity. It will dwell on the tongues of infants as soon as they have learned to lisp their earliest lessons. . . . This Dictionary and the language which it embodies, will also perish; but it will . . . only go with *the solemn temples and the great globe itself.*" In a letter to Harriet, Webster dismissed Kent's remarks on his "great book" as "flights of imagination," but he savored every drop of praise.

"More Fleshy Than Ever Before"

FLESHY, adj. 1. Full of flesh; plump; musculous. The sole of his foot is *fleshy. Ray.* 2. Fat; gross; corpulent; as a *fleshy* man.

O
n October 29, 1829, the seventy-one-year-old Webster and his wife celebrated their "great anniversary." "Forty years ago today," Rebecca wrote that afternoon to Eliza, then living in Greenfield, Massachusetts, "your father and I joined our hands in marriage, and I will venture to say, few have jogged on together more harmoniously." To mark the occasion, Rebecca prepared a roast turkey and a host of desserts, including Webster's favorite, custard. Harmony would continue to prevail in the Webster family, which eventually consisted of more than three dozen grandchildren, but it typically came at the expense of catering to the aging patriarch's wishes. Webster made sure that the entire family continued to revolve around him. While his two sons-in-law, William Fowler and Chauncey Goodrich, along with his son, William, helped him manage his vast publishing empire, he never gave them any real authority. "We are treated like boys and girls," Emily, his eldest, once complained to Harriet. And whenever someone in the family struck out on his own, Webster became uncomfortable. In April 1838, when it became clear that William Ellsworth was to be elected Connecticut's governor, Webster joked with Emily, "We shall treat you just as we used to do, and we shall often mistake and call your husband *Mr.* Ellsworth."

In 1837, Emily Webster (1790–1861) published a book of
short stories, *Wild Flowers*. That year, her father wrote to her,
"Only think. NW's eldest daughter commenced authoress. It
stands you in hand to write pretty well, because the public will
expect it."

Despite his phenomenal success, Webster was not a man at peace
with either himself or the world. Though he was now less "peevish" than
in middle age, he was often seething. He detested President Andrew
Jackson as the second coming of Jefferson. In the 1832 election, he supported the third-party candidate William Wirt, as he no longer wanted
anything to do with either of the major political parties. By 1836, as he
confided to Fowler, he also looked down on his fellow Americans: "I

would, if necessary, become a troglodyte, and live in a cave in winter rather than be under the tyranny of our degenerate rulers. But I have not long to witness the evils of the unchecked democracy, the worst of tyrannies. . . . We deserve all our public evils. We are a degenerate and wicked people."

While Webster's reactionary rants were now a source of embarrassment to his friends and family, he remained as forward-thinking as ever on matters of language. That same year, as the last of the twenty-five thousand copies of the first edition of his complete dictionary were sold, he began making plans to publish a revision. To Fowler, he explained, "I have improvements to make and these are necessary to sustain the reputation of the work, which must keep pace with the language." In contrast to the various abridgements, the complete dictionary was not a big money-maker but a labor of love. Much to the consternation of the rest of the family, in 1838, the octogenarian would mortgage his Temple Street home to finance a second edition. The inveterate definer could not stop. As he was finishing this revised dictionary in 1841, he declared, "[Though] I desire . . . to be relieved from the toil of study and business . . . I am so accustomed to action that I presume inaction would be tedious and perhaps not salutary."

Webster, who would never lose the spring in his step, remained remarkably fit. In April 1835, he proudly reported to Fowler that his physician's bill the previous year had totaled just a dollar. "Except for a few days of rheumatism," he added, "I have better health the winter past than I had from 20 years old to 65." He attributed his vigor to his regular habits. His diet, which steered clear of "French dressings," featured plenty of vegetables and just one small—defined as "about the size of three fingers"—piece of lean meat a day. Though he eventually had to give up gardening, he would continue to take brisk walks around New Haven to buy supplies for his family. In 1842, Webster, who still had a full head of silver hair, confided to his daughter Eliza, "I am more fleshy than ever before. Everybody is surprised to see me walk as straight as a flag-staff."

Webster characterized "old age" as "an aristocracy resulting
from God's appointment."

AS THE EXHAUSTED compiler recovered from the strain of finishing up his
"great book," the marketing genius sprang back into action. By the end
of 1829, Webster published two abridged editions of *The American Dictionary*, a thousand-page octavo for the home and a five-hundred-page
duodecimo—a small square book, like the "compend"—for schools and
offices. On account of the modest price—the octavo was six dollars, as
opposed to twenty dollars for the two-volume quarto—the abridgements
would fly off the shelves and be reprinted dozens of times. For the octavo, Webster hired an editor, Joseph Worcester, to do the legwork under

the supervision of his son-in-law and neighbor, Chauncey Goodrich. In 1829, Webster also came out with a new edition of his *American Spelling Book,* whose copyright wasn't due to expire until 1832. As amended by Daniel Barnes and Aaron Ely, Webster's *Elementary Spelling Book* used the same orthography as his three new dictionaries. Webster then branded these four volumes as "Noah Webster's Series of books for the instruction in the English language." While he publicly downplayed his own financial motives—"But the great object is *the permanent improvement of the language* and . . . the *literature* of this country"—securing his financial future was now a paramount concern. In 1829, Webster also finalized a deal with E. H. Barker of Norfolk, England, to reprint his quarto under the title *A Dictionary of the English Language* in Britain. Appreciating his precise definitions, the British snapped up all three thousand copies within a couple of years, but they never took to the idea of letting an American dictate the future of their brand of English.

Having published a flurry of new works, Webster turned his attention to protecting his valuable assets. After returning from England, he had begun enlisting the help of his cousin Daniel, who had jumped from the House to the Senate in 1827, in his campaign to extend the term of copyright from fourteen to twenty-eight years, as was already the case in Britain. He also sought a provision that would grant an author's widow and children copyright protection in the event of an author's death. While these political goals weren't unreasonable, Webster had trouble distinguishing between his own personal needs and those of his country. To Senator Webster he observed, "I have a great interest in this question, and I think the interest of science and literature in this question, are by no means, inconsiderable." When William Ellsworth was elected to Congress in 1829, Webster stepped up his lobbying. But with Ellsworth unable to bring a bill before the House in his first year on Capitol Hill, Webster decided to take the matter into his own hands.

His ten-week sojourn in Washington would succeed beyond his wildest expectations; he would be feted as a national treasure.

———

IN LATE 1830, right after spending Thanksgiving next door at the Goodriches, Webster accompanied his daughter Emily and Ellsworth, as they
headed south for the opening of the second session of the Twenty-first
Congress.

The trio first stopped off in Manhattan. Though his room measured
only ten feet by ten feet, the author of *The American Dictionary* felt at
home at the elegant American Hotel at 229 Broadway, on the corner of
Barclay Street, opposite City Hall Park (where the Woolworth building
stands today). Noting that his bed was just three feet from a warm fire
fueled by coal, he reported to Rebecca on November 30, "O how comfortable it is." But Webster was irked by what he perceived as Emily's
extravagant lifestyle. Reflecting on her large trunk, which included a
couple of French caps, he added, "It seems to be necessary in this vain
world to make a display."

On December 13, Webster and his traveling companions arrived in
Washington, where they settled into Noah Fletcher's three-story double-
brick home on 6th Street, a boarding house frequented by members of
Congress. Suffering from a nasty cold, Webster hardly went out for the
first ten days. With his eyes bothering him so much that he couldn't
read, he spent many hours daydreaming by the fire. "The catarrh in my
head," he complained to Rebecca on the seventeenth, "makes it feel like
a cooking turnip."

Webster spent Christmas at the home of his brother-in-law William
Cranch, the D.C. circuit court judge, "where we had a tribe of the
Greenleaf descendants and were very happy." Webster was reunited with
his onetime patron, James Greenleaf, who by then was back in the family fold. Since his release from prison a generation earlier, Greenleaf had
climbed back up the social ladder and settled in a mansion at First and
C streets with his second wife, the wealthy and beautiful Ann Penn,
daughter of James Allen, the founder of Allentown, Pennsylvania.

On December 28, thanks to Senator Felix Grundy of Tennessee, who was also staying at the Fletcher house, Webster received an invitation to dine at the White House. As an outsider at this event attended by thirty congressmen, Webster sat directly to the right of the man who was perhaps his least favorite person in America, President Andrew Jackson. With his military bearing, the tall and gaunt "Old Hickory" bore a close physical resemblance to Webster. (In fact, during the president's visit to New Haven two years later, some people waiting to see him accidentally took Webster by the hand, supposing him to be Jackson; this mix-up prompted several bystanders to exclaim that they had shaken the hand of a better man.) Sitting down to eat at about six, Webster soon became incensed with Jackson for preferring European cuisine. Spread out on the table were various French and Italian dishes, whose names Webster didn't know or care to learn. But the fierce patriot kept his pique to himself. "As to dining at the president's table," the lexicographer confided to Harriet the following day, "in the true sense of the word, there is no such thing."

The published version of that December 29, 1830, letter to Harriet, in which Webster described his White House visit, leaves out his update on his son: "William is here, but leaves us today. He has a comfortable living at Mr. Stuart's in Fairfax County, Virginia. He wishes to have a permanent living and is somewhat low-spirited. How his wishes are to be accomplished, I cannot see." Ever since his return from England, William's unsettled future had been a major source of family tension. He failed at one teaching job after another, and he accumulated many debts. While his children urged Webster to cut William loose, the aggrieved father kept trying to rescue his only son. In the latest plan, Webster had helped set up William as a private tutor at Chantilly, the Virginia estate of Charles Calvert Stuart, whose late mother Eleanor Calvert Custis had been Martha Washington's daughter-in-law. (Eleanor's first marriage to John Custis had produced "Wash" and "Nelly," the two boys George Washington had once asked Webster to tutor.)

During his brief stay in Washington, William had some big news to report: He had fallen in love with his employer's younger sister, Rosalie

Stuart, whom he planned to marry. Concerned about Webster's reaction, William mentioned his engagement only to his sister Emily, who eventually relayed it to her father. From Washington, a wary Webster confided his fears to Rebecca:

> How this connection is to affect William's future life can be known only to him who sees the future as well as the *present*. William has no property and has not a facility of planning for a subsistence. Rosalie had some lands, cultivated, I suppose, as all Virginia lands are, most miserably. In the hands of a New England [*sic*] industrious and experienced farmer, these lands would be productive; but William knows nothing of husbandry. She has now a small income from her lands, but not sufficient for family. The lady has been educated probably as all southern ladies are; having a slave to do everything for her.

The wedding took place on May 4, 1831, in Virginia. For the next decade, the couple would zigzag across the country, living in New Haven; Cincinnati; Lafayette, Indiana; New Haven (again); and Brooklyn. Though Webster would grow fond of Rosalie, the marriage would prove as rocky as William's career as a salesman and editor of his father's books. William would also wage a lifelong struggle against depression. As he later confided to Webster, "I am subject to protestation of spirits." And after the death of both their sons during the Civil War,* William and Rosalie would divorce.

At seven o'clock in the evening on Monday, January 3, 1831, Webster gave a speech on the floor of the House of Representatives on the origin, history and present state of the English language. Avoiding any direct mention of "his series of instructional books," Webster stressed the importance of passing the copyright bill. He also highlighted the

---

* William Eugene Webster, who fought in the Confederate Army, and Calvert Stuart Webster, who fought for the Union, both died in 1862. These two grandsons of Noah Webster were the last of his descendants to bear the Webster name.

After his father's death, William Webster
(1801–1869) helped edit various
editions of the dictionary. In 1864, he
obtained a divorce from Rosalie Stuart,
whom he called "unamiable and
rebellious" on account of her support
for the South during the Civil War. Two
years later, he married Sara Appleton.

need to standardize American English. His remarks went over well. A
Philadelphia paper reported, "the worthy lexicographer shows his wisdom in commencing the remedy at the very seat of disease" (thus alluding to the frequent abuse of language in the halls of Congress). A few
days later, the House passed the bill, which Daniel Webster then shep-
herded through the Senate; a month later, it became the law of the land.
But the seventy-two-year-old Webster wasn't done. He intended to give
another lecture, at the end of which he would call for a vote on a propo-
sition "to encourage the use of my books as standards of spelling." But

since the snowy weather made a second gathering difficult to arrange, he drew up a paper "recommending the American Dictionary as a standard, to prevent the formation of dialects in this extensive country." By mid-February, more than a hundred members of Congress signed on. Even more gratifying, he wrote Eliza, were the affectionate personal greetings:

> The most agreeable circumstance that attends me, wherever I go, is the expressions of kindness and respect I receive from gentlemen who have learned how to read in my books. I suppose four fifths of the members of Congress are of this number. Wherever these men meet me, they take me by the hand and express for me most cordial good feelings, whether they are from New England or from Georgia, Kentucky or Virginia. So warm and sincere are these good feelings that the gentlemen are disposed to do anything reasonable for me, to reward me for my labors in literature.

Though Webster was now being hailed by Americans from across the land, during his last few weeks in the capital, he still "avoided parties . . . except those which are given by N. England people."

Having personally lobbied the executive and legislative branches of government, Webster did not neglect the judiciary. He was hoping to get the Supreme Court to unite behind a certificate in support of his dictionary. Though Webster once remarked to Justice Story, who had blurbed his "great book" a few years earlier, that he "was not a friend of obtaining recommendations of books," he had been avidly gathering celebrity endorsements for nearly half a century. On January 14, Chief Justice John Marshall turned down his request, arguing that the justices could engage in such actions only as individuals—not as a group. But the letter, which the chief justice sent over to Webster's room at the Noah Fletcher house, did not fail to render a positive verdict: "There are few if any of us who do not possess your large dictionary and who do not entertain a just opinion of its merits."

———

AS AN IMPATIENT WEBSTER slowly made his way back to New England—the steamboats from Baltimore, where he lectured on February 25, were shut down by ice—chaos was breaking out at 58 Temple Street.

In early March, Rebecca's thoughts typically turned to the thorough reordering of the house that she conducted every spring. "Her purifications for the season," as she called them, involved "regulating" drawers and tidying up closets. But this year, on account of the family turmoil, she would get a late start.

On the afternoon of Tuesday, March 1, the nearly twenty-three-year-old Louisa was seated in the parlor near the bust of Washington. With an expression of horror on her face, she suddenly stood up. Walking over to Rebecca and looking directly into her black eyes, Louisa declared, "Mother, hell is a dreadful place!"

Dropping her needlework, Rebecca got up out of her sewing chair by the window and tried her best to stay calm.

Rebecca had noticed that ever since the recent conversion of Lucy Griffin, the family's black servant, Louisa had become extremely anxious. Lucy, whose jams and preserves placated Webster's sweet tooth, was an integral part of the family; and Louisa and Lucy, who sometimes slept in the same room, were particularly close. According to her mother, Louisa's status as the only nonbeliever in the household was wearing on her. Louisa's "serious impressions," Rebecca later wrote to her older sister Eliza, had begun on February 27 and had "increased to such a degree that her flesh trembled and the terrors of hell were never out of her mind."

Wracking her brain, Rebecca desperately sought a cure for what ailed Louisa. Reaching for her Bible, she found passages of scripture that she considered ideally suited to the matter at hand. But over the next few days, as she read numerous hymns out loud, Louisa hardly responded. Anxiety now gripped Rebecca, too, as she fretted over the state of her daughter's burdened soul.

But by March 7, when Rebecca sent off her update to Eliza, she felt more hopeful:

> She was in this distressing state til yesterday—her mind is now tranquil except when unbelieving fear comes over her and then she has lots of terror. Dr. T [Nathaniel Taylor, Stuart's successor at the First Church], Mr G. [Chauncey Goodrich] and Mr. Fowler have all visited her and have no doubt the Holy Spirit is operating again on her heart. . . . We must wait awhile before we can decide in a case so difficult . . . her situation has excited great interest among all our friends . . . many prayers have been offered up in her behalf.

Nine months later, on December 25, 1831, Webster and his wife arranged for Louisa to be admitted into the First Church of Christ along with the rest of the family. But Louisa's conversion would not mean the end of her mental suffering.

Ever since her infancy, something had been terribly wrong with the Websters' seventh child; her central characteristics, as Rebecca once put it, were "her queer speeches and simplicity." Webster and his wife never expected their last child to build a life of her own like her siblings. She wasn't able to attend school, nor was she able to maintain normal interactions with her peers. While Louisa has often been described as "mentally retarded," severe autism is a more likely diagnosis. Repetitive behaviors seemed to soothe her. In a letter to her sister, Eliza, composed two decades after her conversion, she alluded to "rocking back and forth in my chair [for] twenty-four hours at least." Though Louisa's thinking could be odd, even delusional, she was no simpleton. In that same January 8, 1854, letter to Eliza, written from the Goodrich house, where she lived after her parents' death, Louisa made a few subtle jokes at the expense of Chauncey Goodrich, who was then teaching theology—as opposed to classics—at Yale: "You will see at a glance from the formation of my sentences, that I dwell under the roof of a man once professor of rhetoric. Hearing so much criticism gives me great consternation and sometimes the ablative comes in most uproariously." Louisa signed off by sharing a grandiose fantasy with her sister, "your letters . . . will be printed with the rest of my correspondence when I die because . . . my letters would be very touching and prolific to the people, besides making money."

Louisa, who was then living off a small annuity contained in her father's will, would eventually lose her mind. In 1855, when Webster's last child was forty-seven, the Goodriches and the Ellsworths filed a petition with the probate court for the District of New Haven asking for the appointment of a conservator to intervene in her daily life. Dated May 14, 1855, the document began, "That Louisa Webster . . . of New Haven is by reason of mental incompetency incapable of taking care of herself or of managing her affairs and has been in this condition from her infancy to this time . . . that she . . . has personal estate which needs to be taken care of and managed." Exactly what specific incidents or developments prompted the family to take this drastic action remains unclear. However, Louisa's life didn't seem to change much afterward; she remained with the Goodriches and kept to her usual routine, rarely venturing out of the house except to attend church with the family.

LOUISA WASN'T WEBSTER'S only child to suffer from a disabling illness. In early 1836, not long after the birth of her fourth child, a son named Webster, Harriet suddenly became bedridden. The family feared the worst—tuberculosis. Her father arranged for Harriet to be examined by Dr. Eli Ives and Dr. Jonathan Knight, two professors at Yale's new medical school. On July 8, 1836, Webster reported to Harriet's husband, William Fowler, "Their opinion is that her case is a dangerous one, but not incurable. They think her lungs not ulcerated, but recommend riding & have prescribed two or three medicines. She is cheerful and seems to be better." However, she continued to suffer from an array of debilitating symptoms—pain, lethargy and stomachaches—for which she often took morphine. Two years later, the lexicographer wrote to Fowler,

"Your account of Harriet's illness gives us no little pain. It seems her complaint is what is called neuralgy; pain of the nerves, if we can judge its symptoms. It is movable from the stomach to the lungs." That diagnosis didn't quite fit either, and Harriet would never recover. After her death at the age of forty-six in 1844, Rebecca observed, "I have no doubt that her sufferings, the last eight years of her life, have been far more severe than we apprehended. Nervous affections rendered her irritable. And sometimes unreasonable and unjust."

Harriet's mysterious illness brought Webster closer to her first child, Emily Ellsworth Fowler, born in 1826. While Webster was often cold and judgmental with his children, he could be a doting grandparent, and Emily Fowler emerged as his unabashed favorite. "Little Em," he wrote her father in 1832, "is a book worm, it seems, and she is fairly entitled to be such by hereditary right. Tell her I love her very much, and hope to hear good things of her." In Emily's company, Webster's playful side came out. In June 1834, he mentioned to Harriet, "Emily shall examine my head to see whether I am a good lexicographer. I am no phrenologist myself. I learn what bumps people have by their own conduct." Webster kept pressing Harriet to have his granddaughter write to him in Latin, which for him was the language of love, and Emily obliged by the age of twelve. With her mother frail, Emily came to live in New Haven for a year, and Webster showered her with affection and caresses. His granddaughter later recalled, "I have never lived with anyone who entered so entirely into my wishes and necessities." On February 27, 1839, Webster reported to William Fowler, "Your hopping, dancing, waltzing, chattering daughter is quite well; she uses a knife and fork with great dexterity; and says that she has grown this winter an inch, I mean upward, not sidewise." Two months later, Webster noted, "She often animates us with her vivacity and music and we shall feel a want of her company to enliven the dullness of old age."

After leaving New Haven, Emily Fowler headed off to Amherst, where her father had just taken a position as a professor of rhetoric at Amherst College. Inspired by Webster's tutelage, Emily Fowler would grow up to become a significant figure in nineteenth-century American literature. In 1842, Webster's beloved Emily began studying classics with the eleven-year-old Emily Dickinson at Amherst Academy. The two Emilys participated in the school's Shakespeare club and discussed the poetry of New England notables such as Henry Wadsworth Longfellow. Dickinson looked up to Fowler, who was four years older, as a fountain of wisdom. In 1849, the shy Dickinson wrote to her friend, "I know I can't have you always. . . . some day a brave dragoon will be stealing you away and I will have farther to go to discover you at all." Four years later, when Emily Fowler married Gordon Lester Ford, a prominent New York businessman, Dickinson included a lock of her auburn hair in one of her missives. Emily Ford later became a well-known poet and writer in her own right, whose final project involved compiling her grandfather's personal papers. The literary line continued with her son, Paul Leicester Ford, who was both a leading Americanist—he edited the complete works of Jefferson—and a best-selling novelist. But Paul, like his grandmother Harriet, would suffer an untimely death. On May 8, 1902, his recently divorced older brother, Malcolm Webster Ford, a journalist who had fallen upon hard times, murdered the thirty-seven-year-old author in his Manhattan townhouse before shooting and killing himself.

"WITH THIS, I bring my literary labors to a close."

Noah Webster would write this sentence dozens of times over the last decade of his life, but he would never really mean it.

More disgusted than ever by the disorder in the world, Webster felt he still had much to accomplish. But by the early 1830s, America's preeminent pedagogue was less interested in gathering and disseminating new knowledge than in rectifying errors. In 1832, Webster took on the Bible, which he considered "the chief moral cause of all that is good, and the best corrector of all that is evil in human society." In his new version published the following year, Webster fixed what he saw as the flaws of the 1611 King James edition—namely, its use of obsolete and "indelicate words." Webster sought to eradicate all those Shakespearean locutions which he felt shouldn't be spoken in mixed company. As part of his cleanup, he also desexualized its terminology, changing "teats" to "breasts" and "fornication" to "lewdness." Despite Webster's active marketing campaign, which featured an endorsement from the Yale faculty, the book never caught on. "They don't want the word of Webster, but the word of God," commented one pastor about the reluctance of missionaries to purchase it. Four years later, Webster followed with a slender volume entitled simply *Mistakes and Corrections*. In addition to biblical translation, the six essays addressed various philological matters. One concerned Charles Richardson's recently published *New Dictionary of the English Language*. While the book was eccentric—it often supplied quotations rather than definitions—Webster's assault on the British lexicographer was merciless, "And now our country is furnished with a fresh supply of mistakes in Richardson's Dictionary, many of which are so enormous as to deserve nothing but derision."

Next up was what Webster called the "correction" of his own "great book." Though this would be the last dictionary authored by one man, Webster reached out to numerous experts for help. As he was getting started in 1835, he wrote to Benjamin Silliman, a professor of chemistry at Yale, "If you know of any corrections which will be proper, I will make them, if you will be good enough to give me a memorandum for my direction; and if there are any words of good authority in the sciences which you teach, which you wish to have added to my vocabulary, I will thank you to make notes of them as they occur to you." While he relied on others, Webster would have the final say. When Fowler suggested adding "alerity" and "otherness," he shot back, declaring that such "outrageous anomalies" had no place in the language. In the advertisement, he would thank only Dr. William Tully, Yale's professor of *materia medica*, for the "correction of definitions in several of the sciences." The second edition of *The American Dictionary*, a royal octavo, which contained fifteen thousand words more than the original quarto, began coming off the press on October 22, 1839. When the last page of the fifteen-dollar book was printed on January 30, 1841, Webster, who still was fond of tallying seemingly random facts and figures—the number of students enrolled in Yale every fall rarely escaped his notice—made a note to himself that publication had taken a total of "fifteen months and eight days."

THE DATE WAS TUESDAY, April 21, 1840. The place was the Center Church in Hartford, and the time, as Webster noticed on his gold watch, was eleven o'clock. The Connecticut Historical Society was celebrating the two hundredth anniversary of the state's first written constitution, and the eighty-one-year-old lexicographer was about to give its keynote address. Though Webster was supposed to provide a "historical discourse," he chose to focus on "the prevalent errors of our people."

Webster was staying at the Hartford home of his son-in-law William Ellsworth, then the state's governor, who that month would be reelected to a second two-year term. Webster skipped the festivities the night before, hosted by the society's head, Thomas Day (the brother of Webster's good friend, Jeremiah Day, who had succeeded Timothy Dwight as Yale's president in 1817). At this masquerade party, which Webster's former paper, *The New York Commercial Advertiser*, speculated was "perhaps the first ever in the land of steady habits," dozens of young men and women donned the Puritan garb of their great-grandparents.

Webster had been nervous about taking center stage. A few weeks earlier, he confided his fears to his daughter Emily: "And then only think how many people are expecting great things from your father! How can such an old man as I am gratify such an audience as will be present. But I must encounter the task." With his lower legs sore, it pained him to stand. And on account of his hoarseness, Webster had to shout out his words in order to be heard in every corner of the church.

Webster started by dipping into Hartford's history, but this part of his speech wasn't entirely flattering to his hometown. He talked of how his ancestor, John Webster, "wearied with dissension," set off for Amherst to seek a new settlement. From this preamble, he moved on to the degenerate state of America, the main subject of what turned out to be a ninety-minute speech. "Let us attend," the lexicographer stated, "to the public evils which may result from the use of indefinite words, and the errors, which may proceed from vague ideas." Webster was horrified by what he saw as a misreading of America's most hallowed text:

> In the Declaration of Independence, it is affirmed to be a self evident truth that all men are created equal. If the gentlemen who signed that instrument had been called on to define these words, they doubtless would have given to them a correct interpretation. . . . Nothing can be more obvious than that by the appointment of the Creator, in the constitution of man and of human society, the conditions of men must be different and unequal. . . .
>
> The rich depend on the poor for labor and services; the poor depend on the rich for employment and the means of subsistence. The parent depends upon the child for assistance in his business and for support in old age; the child depends on the parent for food and raiment; for protection and instruction. . . . The husband depends on his wife for the management of his domestic concerns, and the care of his young children; the wife depends on her husband for support and protection. . . .
>
> Remove these dependencies arising from different and unequal conditions, and we should wholly derange or wholly interrupt the employments and the order of society, and to a great degree, the very civilities of life. This inequality of conditions, which political dreamers stigmatize as injustice, is, in reality, the support of the social system; the basis of all subordination in families and in government.

Inequality, an embittered Webster had come to believe, was inherently good. While, as the papers reported, he still "retained the full power of his faculties," Webster had lost touch with the promise of America, which he himself had championed a half century earlier. It was the expert definer rather than his fellow countrymen who could no longer appreciate the true meaning of "liberty" and "equality."

ON THE AFTERNOON of Wednesday, May 24, 1843, Eliza Jones knocked on the door of her father's study. Upon entering, she saw something that she had never seen before. Wrapped in a cloak, Webster was lying down.

That spring, though bothered by a lame foot which had been crushed by his rocking chair, Webster had been carrying on as usual. In early April, while New Haven was overwhelmed by four feet of snow, he had finished a new book, *A Collection of Papers on Political, Literary and Moral Subjects,* which gathered together essays from the past fifty years. On April 11, he reported to Fowler, "We are all in pretty good health. . . . The state of our country, in point of government, is gloomy. . . . we have no remedy but in industry and economy."

On Monday, May 22, Webster had twice gone to the post office, as he continued to monitor his business activities through an active correspondence. That afternoon, he received a visit from Yale president Jeremiah Day, before retiring to his study. Suddenly feeling a chill, Webster asked Lucy to start a fire. Alarmed that he was gulping down large amounts of water—Webster never drank between meals—Lucy notified Rebecca, who called in both Julia and Dr. Ives. As the doctor soon determined, Webster was suffering from pleurisy (a lung inflammation) and needed to rest.

On Friday night, Eliza slept in the study with her father, giving him medicine every half hour to treat his constant coughing. The next morning at eight, Eliza sent a note to her husband, Henry Jones: "Our solicitude for dear father is very *great.* He is *very sick.* Dr. Ives tells us frankly his apprehensions. . . . It was the first time he had permitted any of the family to be with him at night—so accustomed is he to do every thing for himself."

On Sunday, May 28, the entire family gathered around Webster, with William and Emily Ellsworth arriving from Hartford and his son, William, returning from Manhattan where he had been away on business. Moses Stuart, Webster's spiritual father, who happened to be in New Haven from Andover, also paid a visit. To Stuart, Webster declared, "I have confidence in God. I know in whom I have trusted. I am wholly submissive."

At ten minutes before eight, Webster breathed a final sigh.

Two hours later, Eliza wrote another letter to her husband, "All is over. Father, dear father, has gone to rest. . . . He said his work was *done*, and he was *ready*."

A year after Webster's death, the Amherst publisher J. S. and C. Adams published his final work, *An American Dictionary of the English Language, containing the whole vocabulary of the quarto, with corrections.* (A copy of this lexicon soon made it into the hands of a teenage Emily Dickinson, who later called it her "only companion.") This update of the 1841 edition of his "great book," completed by William, featured fifteen pages of new addenda, including "aerodynamics," "agronomy" and "puritanically." Though the octogenarian had soured on American politics, he never lost his passion for defining with his characteristic precision American English. For this task, the cantankerous, driven and indomitable New Englander had always been ideally suited. And nobody, before or since, has ever done it any better.

Epilogue

Webster's after Webster:
The Director of Defining

SEQUEL, n. 1. That which follows; a succeeding part; as the *sequel* of a man's adventures or history. 2. Consequence; event. Let the sun or moon cease, fail or swerve, and the *sequel* would be ruin. *Hooker.*

A
t first, there's this moment of anxiety when you realize that you're actually writing the dictionary. It's very intimidating," says Stephen J. Perrault, the director of defining at Merriam-Webster, Inc. Despite three decades of experience and the authority conveyed by his own imposing title, the wiry and soft-spoken wordsmith admits, "You never quite get over it."

This modern-day Noah Webster supervises forty full-time lexicographers at the Springfield, Massachusetts–based company, which bought the rights to the Connecticut Yankee's words shortly after his death in 1843. Started by the brothers George and Charles Merriam in 1831, the G. & C. Merriam Company, as the firm was originally known, released its first *American Dictionary* in 1847. This revision of Webster's 1841 dictionary, compiled by his son-in-law Chauncey Goodrich, cost just six dollars. Sales were robust, and the Webster family would reap more than $250,000 in royalties. In 1859, under Goodrich's editorship, the firm published another edition, which featured pictorial illustrations and a section on synonyms.

That same year, Dr. C. A. Mahn was brought over from Berlin to clean up Webster's fanciful etymologies. Published in 1864, "the Webster-Mahn," as the first contemporary-looking *Webster's* was commonly called, was edited by Yale philosophy professor Noah Porter. This was the first edition to rely on a team of lexicographers; among the distinguished contributors was William C. Minor, then a New Havenite who had just finished his surgery training at Yale Medical School. In his preface, Porter praised Dr. Minor, who had worked primarily on terms pertaining to natural history and geology, for his "great ability and zeal." As readers familiar with Simon Winchester's compelling narrative, *The Professor and the Madman,* know, Dr. Minor would later send James Murray thousands of quotations from his cell in England's Broadmoor insane asylum. (Thus, as Winchester neglects to mention, the man who did so much to shape the *Oxford English Dictionary* actually received his training in lexicography from Porter.) Later a Yale president, Porter also edited the 1890 revision, *Webster's International Dictionary of the English Language*—the word "American" would no longer appear in the title of the unabridged—which contained 175,000 entries, one and a half times as many as in the previous edition.

When the Merriams' copyright ran out in 1889, other companies began slapping the name "Webster" on the cover of their dictionaries. Today, "Webster's" is a virtual synonym for a dictionary of American English. However, according to a district court ruling nearly a century ago, all publishers except Merriam-Webster—as the company has been called since 1982—must add the disclaimer, "This dictionary is not published by the original publishers of Webster's dictionary or their successors."

The headquarters of Merriam-Webster in downtown Springfield— just a stone's throw from the courthouse where Daniel Shays waged his rebellion a little more than two centuries ago—is a shrine to Noah Webster, Jr. When erecting the building shortly before World War II, its president selected its address—47 Federal Street—in order to pay homage to its first edition of *Webster's* a century earlier. The lobby is filled with glass cases containing original dictionary pages in Webster's hand, as well

William Chester Minor (1834–1920), the most famous of the thousands of volunteers who gathered the OED's illustrative quotations, was no amateur lexicographer, as historians have long assumed. In fact, two decades before he began working on the OED, Minor was paid $500 to define a wide range of scientific and medical terms for *Webster's*. While James Murray was greatly impressed by Minor's skills as a lexicographer—the editor would often ask the Broadmoor mental patient to review his complete notes for a given word—the eminent American naturalist and wordsmith Samuel Haldeman had grave doubts. In 1865, the professor complained to the publishers of *Webster's* that the natural history section was the weakest part of the book and that Dr. Minor was incompetent.

as early editions of his books, including his 1806 "compend." Sitting in a conference room, the only area where words are permitted to be uttered in the otherwise phoneless workplace, the shy Perrault opens up about his craft. Echoing the hypercritical Webster, Perrault defines a good definition by "the absence of error. It can't be too broad or too narrow. And it doesn't strike you as wrong or stupid." As an example of a clunker, he brings up the case of "fish stick," which *Webster's* once defined as "a stick of fish" before moving on to the current "small, elongated, breaded filet of fish." That entry broke a cardinal rule, which forbids using a related word in a definition. "Clarity is my obsession," Perrault adds, citing the credo of philosopher Ludwig Wittgenstein, "Everything that can be said can be said clearly." The lexicographer is rarely entirely satisfied with his own work: "The perfect definition is hard to come by. There are almost always shortcomings. But every once in a while, I jump up on my desk because I sense that I got it exactly right."

Like his recent predecessors in Springfield, Perrault adheres to Noah Webster's firm conviction that lexicographers should codify the language that people actually use. While this position is no longer hotly contested, that was not the case a generation ago. Upon its release in 1961, *Webster's Third New International Dictionary, Unabridged,* edited by Philip Gove, met with fierce opposition. In sharp contrast to Webster's *Second International Edition* of 1934, "W3," as it is known in the trade, assumed that correctness rests upon usage. Just as Noah Webster once faced a barrage of assaults for his purported attempt to destabilize the cosmic order with his "innovations," so, too, did Gove. In a review scattered over twenty-five pages in the March 10, 1962 edition of *The New Yorker,* Dwight Macdonald could hardly contain his outrage:

> The most important difference between Webster's Second . . . and Webster's Third . . . is that 3 has accepted as standard English a great many words and expressions to which 2 attached warning labels: *slang, colloquial, erroneous, incorrect, illiterate.* . . . Dr. Johnson, a dictionary-maker of the old school, defined *lexicographer* as "a

harmless drudge." Things have changed. Lexicographers may still be drudges, but they are certainly not harmless. They have untuned the string, made a sop of the solid structure of English, and encouraged the language to eat up himself.

In a cartoon that appeared a couple of weeks later, the magazine summed up the hullabaloo in five words. "Sorry. Dr. Gove ain't in," says a G. C. Merriam secretary to a surprised visitor. Dr. Gove didn't just list "ain't" in his treasure trove of 450,000 entries; he also gave this slang term his imprimatur, noting that it is "used orally in most parts of the U.S. by cultivated speakers." The harsh attacks were widespread. In a review entitled, "Dig Those Words," *The New York Times* went after Gove for citing actor Jimmy Durante's quip, "What I don't *dig* over there is the British money," as an authoritative quotation. But in "Webster's Way Out Dictionary," *BusinessWeek* conceded that Merriam's bold new direction might eventually turn out to be a canny business move, observing that "a one-product company . . . has just stuck its neck out with a version that could easily prove 20 years ahead of its market." In fact, once the furor died down, the thirteen-and-a-half-pound volume was widely considered a trailblazer. As one of America's preeminent lexicographers put it in 1997, *"Webster's Third* . . . attempted to apply the best standards of mid-twentieth century linguistics to dictionary-making. . . . No dictionary provides a fuller or more reliable picture of the American vocabulary at mid-century. . . . [it] remains the greatest dictionary of current American English."

While "W3" has been revised about every five years since 1961, it has not yet been replaced. Nor is there even a murmur about a "W4" over in Springfield. A major reason is that the digital revolution has turned the dictionary business, like all other branches of publishing, upside down. "W3" is already primarily a Web-based publication, as annual subscriptions for online access, which cost thirty dollars, now sell better than copies of the printed book. In contrast, the Collegiate edition, which can now be viewed for free on the Web, continues to do well at bookstores.

"Sorry. Dr. Gove ain't in."

Merriam-Webster still plans to publish a new edition of the Collegiate, which has sold 56 million copies since 1898, every decade. The next edition, the twelfth, is slated for 2013. And, true to the spirit of Noah Webster, the company continues to track every new word in the language so that it can release an updated version of its flagship dictionary every year. Recent changes include the additions of "chick flick," "blogosphere" and "LOL" as well as the elimination of "hodad" (a nonsurfer, who pretends to be a surfer), a term that the *Gidget* movies of the early 1960s popularized. Despite the challenge of adjusting to technological change, John M. Morse, the current publisher, remains bullish about the future. He isn't afraid that the wiki-model will ever replace the work of professional lexicographers. Sounding like Noah Webster, Jr., Morse observes, "Writing accurate definitions is not fun. It's hard work."

Acknowledgments

GRATITUDE, n. An emotion of the heart, excited by a favor or benefit received; a sentiment of kindness or good will toward a benefactor; thankfulness.

A Yale degree may well be a prerequisite for writing about this quintessential "Yale man"—the vast majority of Webster biographers have had one—and a delightful by-product of this project was the chance to renew the ties with my alma mater. I thank Lauralee Field of the Office of the Vice President and Secretary at Yale for inviting me to speak at the conference, "Noah Webster 250: Shaping a Language, Defining a Nation," held in New Haven on October 16 and 17, 2008. I was the lunchtime speaker on the seventeenth—I shared the bill with complimentary bowls of chowder (a word first defined by Webster). Portions of this lecture, "Noah Webster's Obsession and the Creation of America's First Dictionary," which argued that Webster's personality disorder was instrumental to his literary success, worked their way into the prologue.

The previous day, October 16, 2008, Noah Webster's 250th birthday, I had the distinct pleasure of dining with the roughly ten other presenters at Silliman College on the corner of Temple and Grove streets—the site of Webster's second New Haven residence. Throughout the conference, I enjoyed extended conversations with this All-Star Team of Webster scholars and aficionados, which included Harvard professor Jill Lepore, the keynote speaker; Yale professors emeriti Howard Lamar and Fred Robinson; Judith Schiff, Chief Research Archivist at the Yale University Library; and Peter Sokolowski, a lexicographer at Merriam-Webster. I also met Michael Magruder, a direct descendant of Noah Webster—his grandmother, Rosalie Eugenia Stuart Webster was the daughter of William Webster's son Eugene.

Given our shared obsession with all things Noah Webster, it isn't surprising that I would develop lasting friendships with these colleagues from the conference. I am particularly grateful to Howard Lamar for taking the time to read and comment on the entire manuscript. I am also indebted to Fred Robinson for his careful examination of chapters on the dictionary and for fielding all my questions about Anglo-Saxon (and Noah Webster's dubious knowledge thereof). Likewise, Judith Schiff was kind enough to review the parts of the manuscript related to Webster's life in New Haven. And I appreciate Peter Sokolowski's willingness to host me for a day at his office in Springfield and for helping to set up the interviews with Stephen J. Perrault, Merriam-Webster's director of defining, and John Morse, the company's CEO. (This dictionary publisher is also a dictionary sleuth, and his assistance proved critical in determining W. C. Minor's precise affiliation with *Webster's*.) And I thank Jill Lepore for both grounding me in current Webster scholarship and sharing her considerable insight into Noah Webster's troubled inner world. And thanks to Michael Magruder for filling me in on the family's history over a series of lunches in Cambridge.

I also reconnected with my undergraduate home, Trumbull College, where I stayed during the October 2008 conference. I was pleased to accept Master Janet Henrich's invitation to come back and give a Master's Tea on November 6, 2008. That second Yale talk given before Trumbull undergraduates and assorted guests, "The Yale College of Three Run-Down Buildings, Three Thousand Books and 'Injun Pudding' that Launched the Literary Career of America's Greatest Lexicographer" featured some of the material covered in chapter one.

One can't write about Webster without wrestling with the legacy of his idol and predecessor, Samuel Johnson, and I am grateful for the input of several Samuel Johnson/James Boswell scholars, including Jack

Lynch, Robert DeMaria, James Basker, Helen Deutsch, Gordon Turnbull, Allen Reddick, Anne McDermott and Peter Martin. Fortunately, I was able to track all of them down in the same place—the thoroughly engaging conference commemorating Dr. Johnson's three hundredth birthday hosted by Harvard's Houghton Library in August 2009.

I would also like to acknowledge other scholars who graciously responded to my queries, including Bob Arnebeck, Philip Barnard, Richard Buel, Carolyn Cooper, Simon Finger, Earle Havens, Jane Kamensky, Kate Keller and Brooks Swett.

Spending time in museums and archive libraries is one of the highlights of my day job. While numerous museum directors, curators and archivists provided valuable assistance, a few deserve special mention: Chris Dobbs, the director of the Noah Webster House; Willis Bridgeam, the librarian emeritus of Amherst College's Frost Library; James Rees, the executive director of George Washington's Mount Vernon Estate and Garden; Brian Lemay, the executive director of the Bostonian Society; and Thomas G. Lannon, assistant curator of Manuscripts and Archives at the New York Public Library.

At Putnam, I would like to thank Kathryn Davis, my editor, as well as Ivan Held for their steadfast dedication to this project. I'm also grateful to Marilyn Ducksworth, Stephanie Sorensen and Matthew Venzon in publicity and to Kate Stark and Chris Nelson in marketing.

My agent, Lane Zachary, provided insightful comments on the manuscript. And Rachel Youdelman conducted her impeccably thorough photo research, which unearthed several buried treasures.

I also thank the Virginia Center for the Creative Arts for a fellowship that funded a two-week residency in January 2009.

A Note on Sources

RESEARCH, n. Diligent inquiry or examination in seeking
facts or principles; laborious or continued search after truth.

A few years after Webster's death, his son-in-law Chauncey
Goodrich wrote the first detailed sketch of the lexicographer's
life, which was inserted into the 1847 edition of *The American
Dictionary*. A generation later, journalist Horace Scudder, who would go
on to become the editor of *The Atlantic Monthly*, published the first biography, *Noah Webster* (Boston, 1882). More interpretive essay than
scholarly treatment, Scudder's work focused on Webster's major achievements—the speller, the political writings and the dictionary. Scudder's
occasional allusions to the Connecticut Yankee's "idiosyncrasies" irked
the family. Of Scudder's slender volume, Webster's granddaughter Emily
Ford noted in 1892, "[it] seems to me to discolor his character, to belittle
his work as well as his aims and to make him out an egotist of persistent
self-conceit in his career." In response, Ford began compiling Webster's
personal papers. After Ford's death in 1902, her daughter, Emily Skeel,
finished the two-volume biography, *Notes on a Life of Noah Webster* (New
York, 1912). This privately printed work, which is available only at major
research libraries, features a wealth of valuable primary-source materials, including the complete text of Webster's diary, which he kept from
1784 to 1820, and extended excerpts from dozens of letters by and to
Webster.

Working closely with William Chauncey Fowler (Webster's great-grandson), Harry Warfel, a professor of history at the University of Maryland, published the first modern biography, *Noah Webster: Schoolmaster to America* (New York, 1936), as well as *The Letters of Noah Webster* (New York, 1953). John Morgan's *Noah Webster* (New York, 1975) leans heavily on Warfel's work. While Harlow Unger's *Noah Webster: The Life and Times of an American Patriot* (New York, 1998) is the most comprehensive biography to date, his account adheres to the idealized portrait painted by both Ford/Skeel and Warfel. Webster has also been the subject of two published doctoral dissertations. K. Alan Snyder's *Defining Noah Webster: A Spiritual Biography* (Washington, 2002) highlights the lexicographer's Christian faith. In contrast, Richard Rollins' *The Long Journey of Noah Webster* (Philadelphia, 1989) emphasizes Webster's turn toward reactionary politics in his old age. Rollins also edited *The Autobiographies of Noah Webster* (Columbia, S.C., 1989), which contains both Webster's diary as well as his previously unpublished sixty-three-page memoir written in 1832.

Besides the biographies, a few books cover specific aspects of Webster's legacy. In *Noah Webster: Pioneer of Learning* (New York, 1966), Erwin Shoemaker explores the impact of the speller, the reader and the dictionary on American education. Likewise, in *A Common Heritage: Noah Webster's Blue-Back Speller* (Hamden, Conn., 1983), Jennifer Monaghan delves deeply into his most commercially successful book, dissecting all the complicated publishing deals. David Micklethwait conducts a thorough scholarly investigation of the origins of Webster's magnum opus in *Noah Webster and the American Dictionary* (Jefferson, N.C., 2000).

I aimed not to write the definitive academic biography but to introduce Noah Webster to the broad reading public, who know him largely as a name pasted onto a reference book. Intrigued by the psychological turmoil which fueled his literary activity, particularly the dictionary, I was interested in bringing the full-bodied human being to life. To tackle this assignment, I deemed it necessary to peruse as many primary source materials as possible, especially since Webster's descendants had done so much to sculpt his public image. I examined the Websteriana at the following institutions:

> American Antiquarian Society
> American Philosophical Society
> Amherst College
> Boston Athenaeum
> Connecticut Historical Society
> Connecticut State Library
> Dickinson College
> Harvard University (Houghton Library and Countway Library)
> Historical Society of Pennsylvania
> Historical Society of Washington, D.C.
> Indiana University (Lilly Library)
> The Jones Library in Amherst, Mass.
> The Library of Congress
> Massachusetts Historical Society
> Massachusetts State House Library
> The Morgan Library
> New Haven Museum
> The New-York Historical Society
> The New York Public Library
> The Noah Webster House
> Trinity College
> University of Virginia
> Yale University (Beinecke Library and Sterling Library)

Among my major finds were the first pages of the 1828 dictionary in the New Haven Museum as well as Webster's marked-up pages of Robert Ainsworth's Latin-English dictionary at the Morgan Library, which illustrate his extensive reliance on that book. At Yale, I located several dozen letters by Webster to his daughter Harriet Fowler and her husband, William Fowler, which the Beinecke Library purchased a few years ago from the family. Warfel was the only previous writer to have had access to these documents, which deepen our understanding of Webster's complicated relationships with his children—but he was under the watchful eye of Webster's heirs. In 2007, Yale's Sterling Library acquired Webster's commonplace book, a term defined in his 1828 dictionary as "a book in which are registered such facts, opinions or observations as are deemed worthy of remembrance, so disposed as any one may be easily found." This hundred-page manuscript of his favorite literary passages extends our knowledge of his intellectual formation. At the Historical Society of Washington, D.C., I located letters addressed to his brother-in-law Daniel Greenleaf, in which Webster revealed his sense of being betrayed by James Greenleaf, the speculator who helped build our nation's capital. Previous biographers have downplayed the scandalous behavior of this brother-in-law, with whom Webster was once extremely close. At Amherst College, I found some letters by Webster's wife, Rebecca, concerning the couple's disabled daughter, Louisa, which helped to clarify what ailed her.

I also immersed myself in Webster's own published words. As the first Webster biographer of the digital age, I could do much of this reading on my own laptop. The online resource The Archive of Americana, now features scanned copies of most American newspapers between 1690 and 1922. By searching Webster's name, I was able to find countless newspaper articles by and about this prolific journalist, including some not mentioned in the six-hundred-page tome *A Bibliography of the Writings of Noah Webster,* edited by Edwin H. Carpenter (New York, 1958). Likewise, the early American imprints section of this database includes the full text of many of Webster's books and speeches, such as his various Independence Day orations and his 1806 "compend." (I was also able to download other key works of the era, such as the dictionaries of America's first lexicographer, Samuel Johnson, Jr.) While this digital archive does not contain the first edition of *The American Dictionary,* that book is now available both in a free online version (http://1828

.mshaffer.com) as well as in an inexpensive facsimile edition (Chesa-peake, Virginia, 1967). All the chapter epigraphs are culled from Webster's "great book."

I list below some additional sources—along with a few explanatory notes—by chapter:

Prologue: George Washington's Cultural Attaché

Donald Jackson and Dorothy Twohig, eds., *The Diaries of George Washington,* vol. 4, 1784–June 1786 (Charlottesville, Va., 1978).

Howard Lamar, "Revolutionary Patriot, Outspoken Federalist, Connecticut and Yale Loyalist, Abolitionist, Epidemiologist, Public School Reformer and Intellectual Nationalist" (lecture, Noah Webster's 250th Birthday Celebration, New Haven, October 16, 2008).

Joseph Ellis, *After the Revolution: Profiles in Early American Culture* (New York, 1979), pp. 161–212.

Jill Lepore, "Historians Who Love Too Much: Reflections on Microhistory and Biography," *Journal of American History* (June 2001), pp. 129–44.

Jill Lepore, *A Is for American* (New York, 2002), pp. 3–42.

Jill Lepore's *New Yorker* article on the two hundredth anniversary of Webster's "compend" is reprinted as the introduction to a recent sampling from the 1828 dictionary, Arthur Schulman, ed., *Webster-isms* (New York, 2008).

Peter Martin, *Samuel Johnson: A Biography* (Cambridge, Mass., 2008).

Joshua Kendall, "Field Guide to the Obsessive-Compulsive," *Psychology Today* (March/April 2008), pp. 43-44. This piece describes the benefits of obsessive-compulsive personality disorder for people in various professions, including home design and lexicography.

Chapter 1: Hartford Childhood and Yale Manhood

William Love, *Colonial History of Hartford* (Hartford, 1914).

The multivolume reference book *Annals of the American Pulpit* (New York, 1857–1869), edited by William Sprague, provides useful biographical sketches of influential pastors such as Nathan Perkins, Joseph Buckminster, Timothy Dwight and Ezra Stiles.

The Massachusetts Historical Society holds the unpublished manuscripts of a few of Joseph Buckminster's fast-day sermons.

Elizabeth Whitman's doomed relationship with Joseph Buckminster was the raw material for the 1797 best-selling novel *The Coquette,* by Hannah Foster.

Brooks Kelly, *Yale: A History* (New Haven, 1974).

The Laws of Yale-College in New-Haven in Connecticut, Enacted by the President and Fellows (New Haven, 1774).

Rollin G. Osterweis, *Three Centuries of New Haven, 1638–1939* (New Haven, 1953).

Theodore Zunder, *The Early Days of Joel Barlow* (New Haven, 1934).

Theodore Zunder, "Noah Webster as a Student Orator," *Yale Alumni Weekly* (November 19, 1926), p. 225.

Earle Havens, *Commonplace Books: A History of Manuscripts and Printed Books from Antiquity to the Twentieth Century* (New Haven, 2001).

Moses Coit Taylor, *Three Men of Letters: George Berkeley, Timothy Dwight and Joel Barlow* (New York, 1895).

Franklin Dexter, ed., *The Literary Diary of Ezra Stiles,* vols. 2 and 3 (New York, 1901).

Chapter 2: Spelling the New Nation

Alain C. White, *The History of the Town of Litchfield, Connecticut, 1720–1920* (Litchfield, 1920).

William Brown, *The Life of Oliver Ellsworth* (New York, 1902).

The Noah Webster House has recently published a facsimile edition—a tiny 120-page paperback with a blue cover—of Webster's speller, *A Grammatical Institute of the English Language, Part I* (West Hartford, Conn., no date). This is a reprint of the original version released by the Hartford firm Hudson and Goodwin in 1783.

Helen Everston Smith, *Colonial Days and Ways as Gathered from Family Papers* (New York, 1900).

Joel Benton, "An Unpublished Chapter in Noah Webster's Life. Love and the Spelling Book," *Magazine of American History* (July 1883), pp. 52–56.

Chapter 3: Traveling Salesman

James Hammond Trumbull, *The Memorial History of Hartford County, 1663–1884* (Hartford, 1886).

Allen Walker Read, "The Spelling Bee: A Linguistic Institution of the American Folk," *PMLA* (June 1941), pp. 495–512.

The June 25, 1788, letter to publisher Isaiah Thomas is held at the American Antiquarian Society, the repository of Americana founded by Thomas.

Kate Keller, *Dance and Its Music in America 1528–1789* (Hillsdale, N.Y., 2007).

Chapter 4: Counting His Way across America

I read George Washington's personal copy of Webster's *American Magazine* at the Boston Athenaeum. Washington wasn't an underliner, and the only marks on the volume are his printed signature, "G. Washington." Washington also stuck in a bookplate containing the family's coat of arms and the quotation "Exitus acta probat" [The outcome justifies the deeds], a line from the Roman poet Ovid.

Webster's words in his Baltimore speech are taken from the notes of M. I. Warren, which are held at the Historical Society of Pennsylvania.

Raphael Semmes, *Baltimore as Seen by Visitors, 1783–1860* (Baltimore, 1953).

David Franks, *The New York Directory for 1786, Illustrated with a Plan for the City, Also Changes in the Names of the Streets, Prefaced by a General Description by Noah Webster* (New York, 1905 facsimile edition).

Chapter 5: Courtship at the Constitutional Convention

Frank D. Prager, ed. *The Autobiography of John Fitch* (Philadelphia, 1976).

Massachusetts Historical Society. Collections. *The Jeremy Belknap Papers; Correspondence between Jeremy Belknap and Ebenezer Hazard, Fifth Series,* vol. 3 (Boston, 1877).

Chapter 6: Marriage and a Turn Away from Words

Allen Walker Read, "The Philological Society of New York, 1788," *American Speech* (April 1934), pp. 131–36.

Regarding the family's spin on Webster's floundering legal career in the early 1790s, Chauncey Goodrich wrote in his memoir, "Mr. Webster found his business profitable and continually increasing, during his residence . . . in Hartford." Likewise, in her biography, Emily Ford noted, "his profession . . . was interesting and fairly remunerative to him."

Chapter 7: Editor of New York City's First Daily

On September 26, 1793, Webster summed up his dinner with Genet in an affidavit, which he sent to Oliver Wolcott. This document is now housed at the Connecticut Historical Society.

Bryan Waterman, *Republic of Intellect: The Friendly Club of New York City and the Making of American Literature* (Baltimore, 2007).

James Cronin, ed., *The Diary of Elihu Hubbard Smith (1771–1798)* (Philadelphia, 1973).

Allen Clark, *Greenleaf and Law in the Federal City* (Washington, D.C., 1901).

Gary Coll, "Noah Webster Journalist, 1783–1803" (dissertation, Southern Illinois University, 1971).

Marcus Daniel, *Scandal and Civility: Journalism and the Birth of American Democracy* (New York, 2009).

John Blake, "Yellow Fever in 18th Century America," *Bulletin of the New York Academy of Medicine* (June 1968), pp. 673–86.

John Duffy, "Yellow Fever in the Continental United States During the Nineteenth Century," *Bulletin of the New York Academy of Medicine* (June 1968), pp. 687–701.

Robert Lawson Peebles, *Language and Written Expression in Revolutionary America* (Cambridge, Eng., 1998). Chapter 2, "A Republic of Dreams," has an illuminating discussion of Webster and his two fellow architects of "republican culture," Benjamin Rush and Jedidiah Morse.

Chapter 8: Setting His Sights on Johnson and Johnson Jr.

Allen Walker Read, "Noah Webster's Project in 1801 for a History of American Newspapers," *Journalism Quarterly* (September 1934), pp. 258–75.

Christopher Bickford, Carolyn Cooper and Sandra Rux, eds., *Voices of the New Republic: Connecticut Towns, 1800–1832* (New Haven, 2003), vol. 1, *What They Said.*

Aldred Scott Laird, "Noah Webster as Epidemiologist," *Journal of the American Medical Association* (March 17, 1923), pp. 755–64.

Martha Gibson, "America's First Lexicographer: Samuel Johnson, Jr.," *American Speech* (December 1936) pp. 283–92.

Martha Gibson, "Identifying Samuel Johnson, Jr.," *New England Quarterly* (December 1936), pp. 688–89.

Charles Brockden Brown, "On the Scheme of an American Language," *Monthly Magazine and American Review* (July 1800), pp. 1–4. Though Brown doesn't mention Webster by name, he is clearly referring to his particular plan, which received wide press coverage a month earlier.

Chapter 9: Paterfamilias

Kenneth Thompson, "The question of climate stability in America before 1900," *Climatic Change* (September 1981), pp. 227–41.

Charlton Laird, "Etymology, Anglo-Saxon and Noah Webster," *American Speech* (February 1946), pp. 3–15.

Chapter 10: A Lost Decade

Fred Robinson, "Noah Webster's 'Synopsis of Words in Twenty Languages'" (unpublished manuscript, 2008). Dr. Robinson, a professor emeritus of English at Yale, has deposited this useful overview of Webster's etymology in the Webster papers at the New York Public Library to assist researchers combing through this nearly incomprehensible work. Dr. Robinson has reworked this manuscript into the article "Noah Webster as Etymologist," *Neuphilologische Mitteilungen* (April 2010), 167–74.

James Murray, *The Evolution of English Lexicography* (Oxford, 1900).

Jonathon Green, *Chasing the Sun: Dictionary Makers and the Dictionaries They Made* (New York, 1996).

Everett Thompson, "Noah Webster and Amherst College," *Amherst Graduates Quarterly* (August 1933), pp. 289–99.

W. S. Tyler, *History of Amherst College During Its First Half Century, 1821–1871* (Springfield, Mass., 1873).

Edward Carpenter, *The History of the Town of Amherst, Massachusetts* (Amherst, 1896).

Noah Webster, "Origin of Amherst College," *A Collection of Papers on Political, Literary and Moral Subjects* (New York, 1843), pp. 222–54.

Chapter 11: The Walking Dictionary

William Webster's European diary is held at the New York Public Library.

Julius Ward, *The Life and Letters of James Gates Percival* (Boston, 1866).

Harry R. Warfel, ed., *Uncollected Letters of James Gates Percival, Poet and Geologist, 1795–1856* (Gainesville, 1959).

Joseph Reed, "Noah Webster's Debt to Samuel Johnson," *American Speech* (May 1962), pp. 95–105.

According to the Samuel Johnson scholar, Jack Lynch of Rutgers University, charges of plagiarism have dogged nearly all one-man lexicographers. Even Robert Cawdrey, the author of the first English-language dictionary, *Table Alphabeticall*, published in 1604, was not immune. Critics were furious that Cawdrey lifted half of the head words directly from the 1596 textbook, *English Schoole-Maister*, written by Edmund Coote. (Jack Lynch, "Disgraced by Miscarriage: Four and a Half Centuries of Lexicographical Belligerence" (lecture, opening the exhibition "Everything from A to Z: The Edward J. Bloustein Dictionary Collection," Alexander Library, New Brunswick, N.J., February 6, 2007).

Chapter 12: "More Fleshy Than Ever Before"

Brooks Swett, "A Portrait of the Webster Family During the Civil War" (unpublished manuscript, 2008).

The 1855 petition filed by the family concerning Louisa Webster's mental competence is located at the Connecticut State Library.

The author of the 1936 biography contests the scholarly consensus on Webster's translation of the Bible, arguing that it was his "crowning achievement." Harry Warfel, "The Centenary of Noah Webster's Bible," *New England Quarterly* (September 1934), pp. 578–82.

Webster intended to publish his 1840 speech commemorating the two hundredth anniversary of Connecticut's constitution, but never did. I read a typed version of the manuscript at the Connecticut Historical Society.

Epilogue: *Webster's* after Webster

Herbert Morton, *The Story of Webster's Third: Philip Gove's Controversial Dictionary and Its Critics* (New York, 1994).

James Sledd and Wilma Ebbitt, *Dictionaries and That Dictionary: Casebook on the Aims of Lexicographers* (Chicago, 1962).

Illustration Credits

First page of American Dictionary, 1807 (frontispiece and endpapers). Courtesy The Whitney Library of the New Haven Museum.

Webster birthplace. Woodcut "Noah Webster's Boyhood Home," in J. W. Barber, *Connecticut Historical Collections.* Courtesy The Connecticut Historical Society, Hartford, Connecticut.

Portrait of John Trumbull by his cousin, John Trumbull, 1793. Courtesy Images of Yale Individuals, Manuscripts and Archives, Yale University Library.

1786 Yale campus. Woodcut by Daniel Bowen. Courtesy Yale University Buildings and Grounds Photographs, Manuscripts and Archives, Yale University Library.

Young Noah Webster. Courtesy Images of Yale Individuals, Manuscripts and Archives, Yale University Library.

American Spelling Book *title page.* Courtesy Beinecke Rare Book and Manuscript Library, Yale University.

Handwritten list of houses and cities, 1785. Courtesy Noah Webster Papers, Manuscripts and Archives Division, The New York Public Library, Astor, Lenox and Tilden Foundations.

John McComb's 1789 "Plan of the City of New York." Courtesy Library of Congress.

James Greenleaf. Oil on canvas by Gilbert Stuart, 1795 (29 x 24 in.). Deposited by J. Rush Ritter on behalf of the Livingston Family. Courtesy The Pennsylvania Academy of Fine Arts, Philadelphia.

American Minerva *page.* Courtesy Beinecke Rare Book and Manuscript Library, Yale University.

Noah Webster, ca. 1795. Attributed to James Sharples, but possibly by Ellen Wallace Sharples. Pastel on light gray wove paper, lined with canvas (9 ¾ x 7 ³⁄₁₆ in.). Bequest of Charles Allen. Image copyright © The Metropolitan Museum of Art/Art Resource, NY.

Benedict Arnold House. Courtesy Dana Collection, The Whitney Library of the New Haven Museum.

Compendious Dictionary *title page.* Courtesy Beinecke Rare Book and Manuscript Library, Yale University.

Handwritten definition of "adultery" in American Dictionary of the English Language: *autograph manuscript [n.d.].* Courtesy The Pierpont Morgan Library, New York. MA 301. Photography: Graham Haber, 2010.

Joel Barlow. Courtesy Library of Congress.

Rebecca Greenleaf Webster. Oil on canvas (33 ¼ x 27 ⅞ in.). Courtesy Fruitlands Museum, Harvard, MA.

Amherst College. Lithograph, 1821. Courtesy Amherst College Archives and Special Collections.

Emily Webster Ellsworth. Oval ivory miniature painted by Anson Dickinson (2 ⅞ x 2 ⅜ in.), 1812. Courtesy Collection of the Litchfield Historical Society, Litchfield, Connecticut.

Elderly Noah Webster. Courtesy Images of Yale Individuals, Manuscripts and Archives, Yale University Library.

William Webster. Courtesy Dana Collection, The Whitney Library of the New Haven Museum.

Contract of William C. Minor. Courtesy G. & C. Merriam Company Archive. General Collection, Beinecke Rare Book and Manuscript Library, Yale University.

New Yorker *cartoon.* © Alan Dunn/Condé Nast Publications/www.cartoonbank.com.

Index

Page numbers in italics indicate illustrations.

About the Author

Joshua Kendall is the author of *The Man Who Made Lists: Love, Death, Madness, and the Creation of* Roget's Thesaurus, a biography of the Victorian physician and wordsmith Peter Mark Roget. Kendall's award–winning journalism, which has focused on health care and psychiatry as well as biography, has appeared in numerous publications, including *The Boston Globe, BusinessWeek, The Los Angeles Times, Psychology Today, The Wall Street Journal* and *The Washington Post*. He received his B.A. in comparative literature summa cum laude from Yale College. He also did graduate work in comparative literature at Johns Hopkins. Kendall, who lives in Boston, is currently an Associate Fellow at Yale's Trumbull College.

A

A is the first letter of the Alph...
ges of the earth; in the Ethiopic
Munie the ~~alphabet~~ tenth. It is ~~natu~~
represents the first ~~absolute~~ vocal
human organs; being the so...
a ~~mere~~ opening of the ~~lips~~ mouth with
to alter the natural position or ...
letter is found in ~~a~~ many words
are the names of the objects with
as the breast, & the parents. Hence
ⴃ⅄ ab, is Father. In Chaldee & Sy...
in Ethiopic, abi; in Malayan & Ber...
we retain dady; in old Greeks & in Go...
acta; in Lapponie, atmi; in Abyssin...
nie & Melinda ne, African dialects,
many nations. Hence the Latin ma...
use, the name of mother; in hardihs...
be greatly extended; but these example...
round, & entitled to the first place in ...
letter, aleph, signifies, a leader.

A has, in English, three sounds,
broad, ~~which is thought~~ as in ...